Political Theory and Animal Rights

EDITED BY PAUL A.B. CLARKE AND
ANDREW LINZEY

PLUTO  PRESS
London • Winchester, Mass

First published 1990 by Pluto Press
345 Archway Road, London N6 5AA
and 8 Winchester Place, Winchester, MA 01890, USA

British Library Cataloguing in Publication Data
Political theory and animal rights.
    1. Animals. Relations with man. Ethical aspects
    I. Clarke, Paul A. B. *1946–*   II. Linzey, Andrew
    1952–
    179'.3

    ISBN 0–7453–0386–2 hb
    ISBN 0–7453–0391–9 pb

US Library of Congress Cataloging-in-Publication Data
Political theory and animal rights / edited by Paul A.B. Clarke and
Andrew Linzey.
        p.   cm.
ISBN 0–7453–0386–2. – ISBN 0–7543–0391–9
1. Animals, Treatment of–Political aspects.   I. Clarke, Paul A.
B., 1946–   .   II. Linzey, Andrew.
HV4711.P65   1990
179'.3–dc20

                                                           89-23087
                                                              CIP

Typeset by Ponting–Green Publishing Services, London
Printed in Great Britain by Billing and Sons Ltd, Worcester

Contents

Acknowledgements

We would like to thank Ildi Clarke for her work in the research and preparation of this reader. We would also like to thank the Centre for the Study of Theology at the University of Essex for the congenial environment in which we have been able to pursue our study and for their warm encouragement of multi-disciplinary ventures of this kind. We are indebted to Professor Tom Regan, who has already established himself as a leading authority in this field, for honouring us with a foreword to the book. Our thanks also go to Ian Lee for his copyediting and to Anne Beech of Pluto Press for her kind co-operation and support for this project.

Our thanks are also due to the following copyright-holders for permission to use some of the extracts: Oxford University Press (Plato in Part I, Aristotle in Part III, Rawls); Richard Pegis (Aquinas in Part I); Harvester-Wheatsheaf (Hobbes in Part I, Birke); Cambridge University Press (Herder, Hegel, Locke in Part II); Lawrence and Wishart (Marx); Methuen & Co. (Midgley, Kant in Part III); Burns & Oates/ Search Press (Aquinas in Part II); Oceana Publications (Pufendorf); Thomas Nelson (Pope); Macmillan Publishing (Kant in Part III); International Thomson Publishing Services (Fichte); Unwin Hyman (Russell, Schweitzer); Crossroad/Continuum Publishing Group (Horkheimer); William Collins, Sons & Co. (Coward); New American Library (Madison); International Thomson Publishing Services, University of Toronto Press, and Routledge & Kegan Paul (Mill); International Society for Animal Rights (Salt, Regan); Brigid Brophy (Brophy); Peter Singer (Singer); Basic Books, Inc. (Nozick).

Foreword

TOM REGAN

Revolutions have been a favourite topic of political theorists. And not just political revolutions. Intellectual revolutions – revolutions of ideas – have commanded equal time. Indeed, the ideas of political theorists often have laid the foundations of real-world revolutions. One need only mention Rousseau and Marx to confirm the point. Without bread, the human body perishes. But without ideas, the human spirit withers. It is not for bread alone that political theorists have laboured.

It is odd, then, that most contemporary political theorists have been conspicuous by their absence in the revolutionary times in which we find ourselves. For there is a revolution of ideas afoot, one which, whether well- or ill-conceived, and whether successful or not, already is having effects that are trickling down to the realm of political action. Taking their cue from philosophers of science, some partisans refer to the change as the emergence of a 'new paradigm', a concept which, at this point in time, may be more aspirational than descriptive. The plain fact is that there is no single 'new paradigm' that has taken hold. Rather, there is a variety of contenders each at war with the others, each vying for widespread acceptance, each having to face the hard fact that theirs is but one voice among many – and that a voice which more often than not speaks to (and is heard by) 'the converted'. Deep ecology. Feminism. Animal rights. These are among the voices in the insistent choir of dissent, and the message of one is seldom the same as that of the others.

Usually, that is. But not always. Dissonant though their demands often are, one main theme is the same: traditional moral anthropocentrism is dead. This is the faith shared by deep ecologists, feminists, proponents of animal rights, and other critics of the intellectual status quo. Their common task is to bury Protagoras once and for all. Humans are *not* the measure of all things. And while it is true that the death of the 'old paradigm' by itself does not give birth to a new one, ideas may be like forests. Sometimes the stands of old trees must be destroyed by fire before the new growth can flourish. In the present case it is Protagoras and his descendants that find themselves in the furnace.

One part of this conflagration is being fuelled by those thinkers and political activists who constitute the animal rights movement. Among our contemporaries it was moral philosophers who struck the first match. *Animals, Men and Morals*, published in 1972, marks the beginning, followed by Peter Singer's 1975 landmark book *Animal Liberation*, and then, in 1977, by Stephen Clark's *The Moral Status of Animals*. Since then there has been a steady stream of work by moral philosophers, some opposed to, but most in favour of, enfranchising non-human animals in the moral community. Andrew Rowan, Dean of Special Programs at Tufts University's School of Veterinary Medicine in the USA, and himself a notable critic of traditional moral anthropocentrism, does not overstate the case when he observes that within the past 20 years contemporary moral philosophers have written more on the topic of human responsibility to other animals than their predecessors had written in the previous two thousand years.

This monumental change in moral scholarship has occasioned a no less monumental change in the teaching of moral philosophy. Whereas only 20 years ago there was not a single student discussing animal rights in moral philosophy's classrooms, today there are upwards of 100,000 students a year who encounter this idea – just in America. Although the number predictably would be smaller, comparable changes likely have taken place throughout the English-speaking world and, judging from the evidence at hand, are well under way throughout Europe.

Theologians, too, have added their voice, and none more forcefully or influentially than Andrew Linzey, one of this volume's editors. If his most recent book, *Christianity and the Rights of Animals* (1988), is generally recognized as the most thorough attempt to ground the rights of nonhuman animals in Christian doctrine, his earlier book *Animal Rights: A Christian Assessment* (1976) retains its historical significance. For it was that earlier book that heralded the beginning, in earnest, of the growing theological assault on traditional moral anthropocentrism. And it is the fruits of these labours that we are now beginning to see in religion's classrooms, where normative questions about our responsibilities to other animals increasingly are being asked and debated.

Contemporary political theorists, by contrast, have had comparatively little to say on the issue of animal rights. The revolution of ideas, it seems, has caught them napping. Even among those influential theorists who have broached the topic, the views we find are familiar descendants of the moral anthropocentrism currently under siege from other quarters. In Robert Nozick's libertarian theory, for example, nonhuman animals have no moral rights. And the same is true of John Rawls' very different contractarian theory. Why this exclusion from full membership in the moral community should continue to characterize the most widely discussed alternatives in contemporary political theory, while many secular and religious moral theorists are united in their opposition to what they regard as this prejudicial tradition (which they refer to as 'speciesism'), is a question that perhaps only future generations of scholars can be in a position to answer.

If this turns out to be true – if a later generation of political theorists explains this apparent anomaly – then the more enlightened vantage point from which this insight is commanded will be in no small measure due to this important, timely anthology. For it is in these pages that, for the first time, the most influential political theorists in the Western tradition speak to one of the issues that informs part of the contemporary revolution of ideas – the issue of animal rights. But not to this issue only. The selections compiled here touch on much else besides – in particular, the more general issue of the place of humans in nature. In this way all the thinkers represented here speak to the larger issue of moral anthropocentrism. In this way, therefore, those contemporary political theorists who use this book, whether in their research or in their classrooms, will become involved in the debate about the adequacy of this tradition and play the vital role they should in deciding whether, and, if so, how, the revolt against this tradition succeeds. Or fails.

Introduction

The main purpose of this book is to show a long and continuing relation between political theory and concerns about the status of animals. In exhibiting those concerns, issues are raised which not only have bearings on the particular question of animal rights but also upon the grounds on which justice, both for humans and for animals, has been based and challenged. To some the relation between political theory and animal rights may appear tenuous. Surely, it may be questioned, the notion that the non-human world has rights is a modern, almost contemporary, idea, quite separate from political theory with its roots in ancient traditions of thought. In one sense this objection has force. The giants of political theory, Aristotle, Hobbes, Locke – to take only three examples – were certainly not concerned with the issue of animal rights as we understand it today. But neither, of course, were these thinkers concerned with the issue of human rights in the contemporary sense. In another sense, however, the objection is profoundly mistaken for it falsely assumes that ideas come from nowhere.

For almost every significant idea there is a history, indeed we might even say that every idea contains a history. This is as true, perhaps even more so, of our ideas of rights and justice as it is of any of those ideas which compose our intellectual heritage. We are reminded of the view expressed by a celebrated physicist to the effect that if he saw further than others it was due in no small measure to his ability to stand on the shoulders of others. This does not mean, of course, that every aspect of intellectual development is necessarily superior to what preceded it. There can be regress as well as progress, and at least some of what we take to be progress today may well be judged by our successors to be the former. But if talk of rights and obligations retains a continuing appeal then we need to appreciate the predecessor notions of justice of which they are, at least in some way, developments.

Differences between Humans and Animals

The way in which ideas encounter each other within a tradition, or even challenge that tradition, is seen clearly in the first section on the 'Differences between Humans and Animals'. At first sight the range of extracts selected from Plato to Nietzsche might suggest a wide variety of views largely at odds with each other. It is indeed correct that there is a wide range of views expressed in this section, as one might expect from theorists as different in outlook as Aquinas, Marx, and Nietzsche, for example. On the other hand what is significant is the way in which the Aristotelian–Thomist tradition provides a core of ideas within which intellectual encounters take place. To some extent this is unsurprising. To develop a tradition is to work within its general parameters, expanding those parameters where that seems appropriate. Significant social change, for example, would provide a need for intellectual change. Occasionally there are protests against an entire range of thought. But it is only a thinker as radical as Nietzsche who, in attempting to espouse all tradition, refuses to engage with most of his predecessors.

It may be surprising, to some, how much the Aristotelian–Thomist core supplies unity to the way in which ideas encounter each other. It provides the base on which that encounter takes place. Aristotle's classic definition of 'man as a political animal' provides a foundation upon which subsequent discussion about the relation between the human and the non-human animal takes place. 'It is the peculiarity of man in comparison with the rest of the animal world, that he alone, possesses a perception of good and evil, of the just and the unjust, and of other similar qualities; and it is association in (a common perception of) these things which makes a family and a polis.' From this fundamental perception of difference, Aristotle draws the logical conclusion that only those beings – who he classes as beasts or gods – are unable to share the benefits of political association. It is St Thomas Aquinas who, drawing heavily upon Aristotelian philosophy, emphasises the rationality of humanity as the key distinguishing mark in separating the human and non-human worlds. Drawing upon a concept of divine providence, Aquinas asserts that humans are governed for their own sake, whereas animals are appointed for human use. 'Hereby is refuted the error of those who said it was sinful for a man to kill brute animals,' he writes, '[for] by divine providence they are intended for man's use according to the order of nature.' The conclusion of both pieces is clear: the political (and moral) worlds cannot include animals. In short: animals have no rationality, no freedom of will, no ability to enter into political agreements and, of course, no immortal souls.

It is this presentation of the difference between humans and animals which provides the foundations of subsequent discussion. This is not to suppose that the Aristotelian–Thomist view is unthinkingly repeated throughout what is, after all, a living and not unchallenged tradition. Hume, for example, in an encounter with the Aristotelian tradition, takes a clearly contrary view. He argues that,

Next to the ridicule of denying an evident truth, is that of taking much pains to defend it; and no truth appears to me more
evident, than that beasts are endow'd with thought and reason as
well as men.

To the Thomist view that animals act naturally or by instinct, Hume
argues that 'reason is nothing but a wonderful and unintelligible
instinct in our souls.'

As the tradition, with all its subtleties and challenges, unfolds so
distinctions and counter-distinctions emerge. Leibniz, for example,
appears to take issue with Descartes on the question of animal souls.
Descartes, we may recall, took the Aristotelian–Thomist view to its
limits and denied that animals, in view of their lack of a rational soul,
could be thinking, self-conscious beings at all. For Descartes animals
were simply intricate mechanisms. However, Leibniz, while differ-
entiating between animal soul and rational spirits is in no doubt that
animals do have souls. As he puts it, '[It] may be said that not only the
soul [the mirror of an indestructible universe] is indestructible, but
also the animal itself is indestructible, though its mechanism may often
perish in part and take off or put on an organic slough.'

A related question of self-consciousness in animals is also, and
variously, examined. Hegel, for example, is certain that while humans
possess the capacity for self-awareness animals do not have reflective
capacities. They are not, therefore, reflectively self-aware, as humans
are. Animals lack a fundamental inner coherence of will and spirit.
Because of this an individual animal 'can only respond to those
external stimuli to which it is already inwardly susceptible.' In short
'[the] animal is divided from itself and within itself.' This idea of the
lack of a reflective capacity in animals is developed further by Marx in
his claim that humans alone may be conscious of themselves as a
'species–being'. Thus it is the ability of humans to mentally distance
themselves from themselves, and to reflect upon their condition, which
makes them unique. In contrast to them, the 'animal is immediately
one with his life activity. It is not distinct from that activity; it *is* that
activity.' For Marx, if humans are alienated from their species being
(and other aspects of their life) then their existence will be little more
than animal.

Nietzsche emphasises the role of communication in consciousness.
He anticipates what is now taken to be a central feature of some
contemporary philosophy. '[It] seems to me as if the subtlety and
strength of consciousness always were proportionate to a man's (or
animal's) *capacity for communication*.' For Hobbes, however, while

animals have voice and communication only humans have true language and speech. This distinguishes humans from animals. It also has a political significance. That 'we can command and understand commands is a benefit of speech, and truly the greatest ... Without this there would be no society among men, no peace, and consequently no disciplines; but first savagery, then solitude, and for dwellings, caves.' In this way, we return to the Aristotelian dictum that only humans are *zoon politikon*, political animals. For, as Hobbes observes '... though among certain animals there are *seeming polities*, these are not of sufficiently great moment for living well.'

The views expressed within this section may, at first sight, appear rather distant from the contemporary issue of animal rights. An observation of *mere* difference between humans and animals does not provide, in itself, any moral or political imperatives. Non-moral difference is not a sufficient reason for treating one group of beings as morally less worthy than another group of beings. On the other hand, if one group of beings is to be treated as morally less worthy than another group of beings, then some (relevant) difference is a necessary condition of such moral differentiation. Certainly there are differences between humans and animals, but whether or not the differences are morally relevant and should exclude animals from the domain of justice is one of the issues raised in the second and third sections.

Dominion and the Limits to Power

In this second part of the book the selections show that an important set of issues arise out of the various conceptions of the place of humans in the universe. Just as many of the great political theorists have considered the differences between humans and animals, so they have also considered the place of humans in the cosmos, and the care, dominion and power that they may rightfully exercise over the world that they inhabit. In one sense the notion of 'dominion' is wholly descriptive. It simply denotes the powerful position which humans have in relation to the natural world. In other senses, it has an inevitably prescriptive element, for it can be taken not merely as a description of power over the world but also as justifying the exercise of it. The concept of dominion comes from the opening chapter of Genesis where God is pictured as imparting a divine image to humans and also giving them a divine commission to rule over creation. It is perhaps worth pointing out that in the original concept there is no suggestion of despotism as such. The authority given to humans is a dependent authority, one that had to be exercised with restraint and always in conformity with God's moral rule.

Although it is undoubtedly true that political theory was influenced by what is often referred to as the Judaeo-Christian tradition, and its conception of 'dominion', it is worth noting that the idea of human power over creation predates that tradition. As the first extract in this section shows, the Platonic view in *The Statesman* records a time when all life lived in harmony. Similar also to the Genesis saga is the depiction of God as sharing his power over the world through the appointment of 'tutelary deities'. Even more striking perhaps is the description of the advent of a 'cosmic fall' of creation when violence afflicts the earth and beasts turn savage.

Interestingly enough, it is Aquinas who rejects the Platonic, and some might say Biblical, view of the cosmic fall. In so doing, he opposes the view that human mastery belongs to the state of corrupted nature – on the contrary God, according to Aquinas, destined humans to rule over creation – even in their state of innocence – unencumbered by any moral restraints. It is in this sense that we should understand the passage from St Augustine. Killing is viewed as part of the right of dominion. Because 'animals have no rational association' with humans it follows that there can be no moral relationship between them.

Against this view, we should note the protest of Montaigne in particular. Warning against drawing moral conclusions from the mere fact of difference, he argues that humans 'are neither superior nor inferior to the rest'. Neither our difference from animals nor our power over them justifies the abuse to which we subject them. Indeed: 'if we would claim any superiority from the fact that we have it in our power to seize them, employ them in our service and use them at our pleasure, it is but the same advantage we have over one another. On these terms we have our slaves.'

A midway position may, perhaps, be glimpsed in the passage from John Locke. In a well-known section of the *Second Treatise*, Locke appears to argue that no person has the liberty 'to destroy himself, or so much as any creature in his possession', except when 'some nobler use, than its bare preservation, calls for it.' In other words, humans have no right to destroy even the least creature except when some higher use demands it. Arguably in the same vein, and written at about the same time, is Pope's appeal for a responsible stewardship over animals. 'I cannot think it extravagant to imagine', he begins, 'that mankind are no less, in proportion, accountable for the ill use of their dominion over creatures of the lower rank of beings, than for the exercise of tyranny over their own species.' Pope concludes with an appeal for a qualified dominion over animals. '[As] for such as are mortal or noxious, we have a right to destroy them', but for the rest 'that are neither of advantage or prejudice to us, the common enjoyment of life is what I cannot think we ought to deprive them of.'

In contrast, both Fichte and Sidgwick return us to a basic implication of Thomist thought, namely that animals belong to humans and have no independent status. Fichte insists that it is right for humans to possess animals as property. As with any other resource or utility, animals can be taken over and made subservient to human needs. Duties to them only arise in so far as some human interest is at stake. Sidgwick's reasoning is similar. While wild animals must first be tamed and subdued before complete possession can take place, 'tame' animals are classed as utilities. To Sidgwick, '[It] is obvious that the exclusive use of such animals may be appropriated to individuals without much more difficulty than that of inanimate things.' We may observe how it is with these two thinkers in particular that the notion of dominion has been translated into the modern conception of property.

Two of the last extracts in this section suggest, in different ways, that domination and dominion rest on an unjustified exercise of mere power. Bertrand Russell is adamant that there is 'no impersonal reason for regarding the interests of human beings as more important than animals.' It would seem that there is no dominion only mere power. 'We can destroy animals more easily than they can destroy us; that is the only solid basis of our claim to superiority ... All ethical systems, in the last analysis, depend upon weapons of war.' Horkheimer recoils from a 'pragmatic' view which sees animals simply as utilities or 'obstructors of traffic.' He criticises the western Christian tradition for failing to recognise the independent worth of nature, and animals in particular. The principle of copying nature, he argues, involves regression 'to primitive urges.' Not only do animals suffer because of this, but also 'such expedients lead from historically reasonable to utterly barbaric forms of social domination.'

Justice, Rights and Obligations

Whereas the first two sections provide a theoretical base for historical and contemporary debates, the third and final section builds on this background to address, in a variety of ways, a question of practical philosophy, namely: 'What, if anything, is owed by humans to animals?'

The material exhibits four major, overlapping debates: one is whether justice requires friendship with animals, and whether it is rational to exclude animals from such a relationship. Aristotle in a short but influential argument develops a view already noted in Sections 1 and 2, that humans have nothing politically relevant in common with animals. 'For where there is nothing common to ruler and ruled, there is not friendship either, since there is not justice ... neither is there friendship towards a horse or an ox, nor to a slave *qua* slave.' Unsurprisingly the thought of Aquinas follows the same pattern. Irrational creatures in themselves do not merit friendship and because of this we have no duties of charity towards them. Montaigne, however, emphatically rejects this view. He argues that animals do indeed reflect some of our notions of justice, and also distribute their goods equally. From observation of animals, he concludes that 'it is not upon any true ground of reason, but from a foolish arrogance and stubbornness, that we put ourselves before the other animals, and remove ourselves from their condition and fellowship.'

To bring the issue up to date, John Rawls discusses whether animals are outside the scope of a proper theory of justice. He concludes, in only a mild departure from the Aristotelian–Thomist tradition, that only human persons are entitled to equal justice. Rawls is clear that 'it is wrong to be cruel to animals and [that] the destruction of a whole species can be a great evil,' but 'it does not seem possible to extend the contract doctrine so as to include them in a natural way.' Some readers may see some correspondence here between this view and that advanced by Madison, centuries earlier, that animals must be distinguished from slaves on the grounds that the latter are, in some respects at least, constitutional persons and the former are not.

A second overlapping debate concerns the issue of equal treatment. Hume expresses views similar to those found in Aristotle and Aquinas. He argues that since there is no society with animals, there can be no possibility of an equal claim to justice. According to Hume, our 'intercourse with [animals] could not be called society, which supposes a degree of equality, but absolute command on one side, and servile obedience on the other.' By contrast, Humphry Primatt argues for a basic equality in the treatment of humans and animals in respect of a common capacity to experience pain and endure suffering. While there are significant differences between humans and animals, these cannot by themselves justify unequal treatment. '[If] the difference of complexion or stature does not convey to one man a right to despise and abuse another man, the difference of shape between a man and a brute, cannot give to a man any right to abuse and torment a brute.' Peter Singer develops the argument for equal treatment still further. For Singer, it is not only the act of making an animal suffer (all other circumstances being equal) which is unjust, so too is the act of killing;

again all circumstances being equal. To discriminate against any being, on the grounds of race, sex, or species alone, is to engage in racism, sexism, or 'speciesism'.

A third major issue concerns the precise nature of human duties or obligations towards animals. Thomas Hobbes is clear that because there can be no social contract with animals, so humans can have no clear duties towards them. Kant, too, holds that there are no direct duties towards animals, such duties as exist are indirect and derived from our duties towards humankind. Schopenhauer accepts that there are some fundamental limits to our right over animals, but, in his view, 'the pain that the animal suffers through death or work is still not so great as that which man would suffer through merely being deprived of the animal's flesh or strength.' William Godwin, in turn, stresses the ineradicability of suffering in the world as we now experience it, detailing its horrors and general injustice, and warning us against any easy optimism about moral improvement.

However, some writers do stress both particular and general duties. Locke indicates his abhorrence of cruelty, which he thinks unnatural, arguing that children who are cruel to animals may well end up being cruel to humans. For Bentham, the duty to minimise suffering should involve us in an utilitarian calculation which includes the suffering of animals. While opposed to the doctrine of natural rights, he does advocate positive, or legal, rights. In a well-known line, he foresees a time when there may be positive animal rights: 'The day *may* come, when the rest of the animal creation may acquire those rights which never could have been witholden from them but by the hand of tyranny.'

Mill, in support of Bentham, maintains that obligations to animals are direct. For both Mill and Bentham 'it is as much a moral duty to regard the pleasures and pains of other animals as those of human beings.' Whether any utilitarian view is satisfactory is a question addressed by Nozick. His conclusion leaves the question open: 'Even for animals, utilitarianism won't do as the whole story, but the thicket of questions daunts us.'

Avoiding a utilitarian defence of animals, both Schweitzer and Nietzsche find other reasons to make a strong plea for increased sensitivity to animal life and suffering. 'The sight of blind suffering is the spring of the deepest emotion,' argues Nietzsche. Schweitzer in a similar vein argues that '[a] man is truly ethical only when he obeys the compulsion to help all life ... and shrinks from injuring anything that lives.'

A fourth debate addresses the question of animal rights itself.

Pufendorf, in a significant discussion based on natural law as well as divine providence, argues strongly against the intrinsic rights of animals. He maintains that it is possible to conclude 'from the fact that the Creator established no common right between man and brutes, that no injury is done to brutes if they are hurt by man, since God himself made such a state to exist between man and brutes.' Herman Daggett takes the contrary view. In the earliest known American treatise on animal rights, he argues that such rights are, like human rights, inalienable. 'I know of nothing in nature, in reason, or in revelation which obliges us to suppose that the unalienated rights of a beast, are not as sacred, and inviolable, as those of a man.'

This point is reinforced by Henry Salt. While he views theories of 'natural' (as opposed to positive or legal) rights, as unsatisfactory, he argues that *if* rights can be justified at all then the principle of animal rights is as sound as the principle of human rights. He sees no good ground for denying non-human beings the same rights we claim for our own species. Tom Regan, too, develops a theory of animal rights, one that frees us from the limitations of 'contractualism' or utilitarianism, and enables us to view animals as subjects of 'inherent value' in their own right. From this he develops a biting critique of existing practices: 'The fundamental wrong is the system that allows us to view animals as *our resources*, here for *us* – to be eaten, or surgically manipulated, or exploited for sport or money. Once we accept this view of animals – as our resources – the rest is as predictable as it is regrettable.'

The issues presented in this introduction are not, of course, exhaustive. No single book could, nor should, pretend to be complete in itself. However, the literature presented here should speak for itself and the reader may well find issues beyond that discussed here. The intention of the introduction and the extracts is to provide a guide to the literature, and to stimulate thought about the status of animals in the history of our political ideas. A careful reading of the extracts, however, will reveal that the issues raised go beyond questions of animal rights; they go right to the heart of the matter of justice.

There is no single criterion for justice; as a practical question justice depends on the different views of practical reason which each generation and each period works out within its own circumstances. It would be unreasonable to expect otherwise. Nevertheless, the boundaries have been fairly tightly drawn as to who should and who should not be included within the domain of justice. From Aristotle to the present there is a view that justice can be properly applied only to those who belong to a particular group; whether the criteria for belonging are friendship or personhood seems, over that period of time at least, to be a relatively minor change.

But in spite of such tightly drawn boundaries, and in spite of a surprising degree of continuity, those boundaries are not entirely fixed; it does appear that they are mutable. As the boundaries have shifted, so, to take two examples, slavery has been abolished, and women, at least formally, have been included in the domain of justice. It is not inconceivable that the boundaries could shift yet again. Nor is it inconceivable that the boundaries, in shifting, might yet include some part of the non-human world. Whether such a view is either cogent, or morally acceptable, is a choice for the reader to make. Here we attempt to exhibit some important arguments about the status of animals that have taken place within a central tradition in political theory.

In doing this it may be that some insight can be obtained, not merely into the influence of our intellectual past, or even into the issue of animal rights, but also into what is involved in the challenge of obtaining justice for all.

P.A.B. Clarke
Department of Government
University of Essex

Andrew Linzey
Centre for the Study of Theology
University of Essex

March 1990

Part I
Differences Between
Humans and Animals

1. Creation of the Universe

Plato   427–347 B.C.

Timaeus: Let me tell you then why the creator made this world of generation. He was good, and the good can never have any jealousy of anything. And being free from jealousy, he desired that all things should be as like himself as they could be. This is in the truest sense the origin of creation and of the world, as we shall do well in believing on the testimony of wise men. God desired that all things should be good and nothing bad, so far as this was attainable. Wherefore also finding the whole visible sphere not at rest, but moving in an irregular and disorderly fashion, out of disorder he brought order, considering that this was in every way better than the other. Now the deeds of the best could never be or have been other than the fairest, and the creator, reflecting on the things which are by nature visible, found that no unintelligent creature taken as a whole could ever be fairer than the intelligent taken as a whole, and again that intelligence could not be present in anything which was devoid of soul. For which reason, when he was framing the universe, he put intelligence in soul, and soul in body, that he might be the creator of a work which was by nature fairest and best. On this wise, using the language of probability, we may say that the world came into being – a living creature truly endowed with soul and intelligence by the providence of God.

This being supposed, let us proceed to the next stage. In the likeness of what animal did the creator make the world? It would be an unworthy thing to liken it to any nature which exists as a part only, for nothing can be beautiful which is like any imperfect thing. But let us suppose the world to be the very image of that whole of which all other animals both individually and in their tribes are portions. For the original of the universe contains in itself all intelligible beings, just as this world comprehends us and all other visible creatures. For the deity, intending to make this world like the fairest and most perfect of intelligible beings, framed one visible animal comprehending within itself all other animals of a kindred nature. Are we right in saying that there is one world, or that they are many and infinite? There must be one only if the created copy is to accord with the original. For that which includes all other intelligible creatures cannot have a second or companion; in that case there would be need of another living being which would include both, and of which they would be parts, and the likeness would be more truly said to resemble not them, but that other

3

which included them. In order then that the world might be solitary, like the perfect animal, the creator made not two worlds or an infinite number of them, but there is and ever will be one only-begotten and created heaven ...

Now the creation took up the whole of each of the four elements, for the creator compounded the world out of all the fire and all the water and all the air and all the earth, leaving no part of any of them nor any power of them outside. His intention was, in the first place, that the animal should be as far as possible a perfect whole and of perfect parts, secondly, that it should be one, leaving no remnants out of which another such world might be created, and also that it should be free from old age and unaffected by disease. Considering that if heat and cold and other powerful forces surround composite bodies and attack them from without, they decompose them before their time, and by bringing diseases and old age upon them make them waste away – for this cause and on these grounds he made the world one whole, having every part entire, and being therefore perfect and not liable to old age and disease. And he gave to the world the figure which was suitable and also natural. Now to the animal which was to comprehend all animals, that figure would be suitable which comprehends within itself all other figures. Wherefore he made the world in the form of a globe, round as from a lathe, having its extremes in every direction equidistant from the center, the most perfect and the most like itself of all figures, for he considered that the like is infinitely fairer than the unlike. This he finished off, making the surface smooth all around for many reasons – in the first place, because the living being had no need of eyes when there was nothing remaining outside him to be seen, nor of ears when there was nothing to be heard, and there was no surrounding atmosphere to be breathed, nor would there have been any use of organs by the help of which he might receive his food or get rid of what he had already digested, since there was nothing which went from him or came into him, for there was nothing besides him. Of design he was created thus – his own waste providing his own food, and all that he did or suffered taking place in and by himself. For the creator conceived that a being which was self-sufficient would be far more excellent than one which lacked anything, and, as he had no need to take anything or defend himself against anyone, the creator did not think it necessary to bestow upon him hands, nor had he any need of feet, nor of the whole apparatus of walking. But the movement suited to his spherical form was assigned to him, being of all the seven that which is most appropriate to mind and intelligence, and he was made to move in the same manner and on the same spot, within his own limits revolving in a circle. All the other six motions were taken away from him, and he was made not to partake of their deviations. And as this circular movement required no feet, the universe was created without legs and without feet ...

Thus far and until the birth of time the created universe was made in the likeness of the original, but inasmuch as all animals were not yet comprehended therein, it was still unlike. Therefore, the creator proceeded to fashion it after the nature of the pattern in this remaining point. Now as in the ideal animal the mind perceives ideas or species of a certain nature and number, he thought that this created animal ought to have species of a like nature and number. There are four such. One of them is the heavenly race of the gods; another, the race of birds whose way is in the air; the third, the watery species; and the fourth, the pedestrian and land creatures. Of the heavenly and divine, he created the greater part out of fire, that they might be the brightest of all things and fairest to behold, and he fashioned them after the likeness of the universe in the figure of a circle, and made them follow the intelligent motion of the supreme, distributing them over the whole circumference of heaven, which was to be a true cosmos or glorious world spangled with them all over. And he gave to each of them two movements – the first, a movement on the same spot after the same manner, whereby they ever continue to think consistently the same thoughts about the same things, in the same respect; the second, a forward movement, in which they are controlled by the revolution of the same and the like – but by the other five motions they were unaffected, in order that each of them might attain the highest perfection. And for this reason the fixed stars were created, to be divine and eternal animals, ever abiding and revolving after the same manner and on the same spot, and the other stars which reverse their motion and are subject to deviations of this kind were created in the manner already described. The earth, which is our nurse, clinging around the pole which is extended through the universe, he framed to be the guardian and artificer of night and day, first and eldest of gods that are in the interior of heaven. Vain would be the attempt to tell all the figures of them circling as in dance, and their juxtapositions, and the return of them in their revolutions upon themselves, and their approximations, and to say which of these deities in their conjunctions meet, and which of them are in opposition, and in what order they get behind and before one another, and when they are severally eclipsed to our sight and again reappear, sending terrors and intimations of the future to those who cannot calculate their movements – to attempt to tell of all this without a visible representation of the heavenly system would be labor in vain. Enough on this head, and now let what we have said about the nature of the created and visible gods have an end.

Plato, 'Timaeus' in Benjamin Jowett (tr) *Plato's Timaeus*, 4th edn (Oxford University Press, 1953) 1162–9.

2. Animals are not Political

Aristotle   384–322 B.C.

When many villages so entirely join themselves together as in every respect to form but one society, that society is a city, and contains in itself, if I may so speak, the end and perfection of government: first founded that we might live, but continued that we may live happily. For which reason every city must be allowed to be the work of nature, if we admit that the original society between male and female is; for to this as their end all subordinate societies tend, and the end of everything is the nature of it. For what every being is in its most perfect state, that certainly is the nature of that being, whether it be a man, a horse, or a house: besides, whatsoever produces the final cause and the end which we desire, must be best; but a government complete in itself is that final cause and what is best. Hence it is evident that a city is a natural production, and that man is naturally a political animal, and that whosoever is naturally and not accidentally unfit for society, must be either inferior or superior to man: thus the man in Homer, who is reviled for being 'without society, without law, without family'. Such a one must naturally be of a quarrelsome disposition, and as solitary as the birds. The gift of speech also evidently proves that man is a more social animal than the bees, or any of the herding cattle: for nature, as we say, does nothing in vain, and man is the only animal who enjoys it. Voice indeed, as being the token of pleasure and pain, is imparted to others also, and thus much their nature is capable of, to perceive pleasure and pain, and to impart these sensations to others; but it is by speech that we are enabled to express what is useful for us, and what is hurtful, and of course what is just and what is unjust: for in this particular man differs from other animals, that he alone has a perception of good and evil, of just and unjust, and it is a participation of these common sentiments which forms a family and a city. Besides, the notion of a city naturally precedes that of a family or an individual, for the whole must necessarily be prior to the parts; for if you take away the whole man, you cannot say a foot or a hand remains, unless by equivocation, as supposing a hand of stone to be made, but that would only be a dead one; but everything is understood to be this or that by its energic qualities and powers, so that when these no longer remain, neither can that be said to be the same, but something of the same name. That a city then precedes an individual is plain, for if an individual is not in himself sufficient to compose a perfect government, he is to a city as other parts are to a whole; but he that is incapable of society, or so complete in himself as not to want it, makes no part of a city, as a beast or a god. There is then in all persons a natural impetus to associate with each other in this manner, and he who first founded civil society was the cause of the greatest good; for as by the completion of it man is the most excellent of all living beings, so without law and justice he would be the worst of all, for nothing is so difficult to subdue as injustice in arms: but these arms man is born with, namely, prudence and valour, which he may apply to the most opposite purposes, for he who abuses them will be the most wicked, the most cruel, the most lustful, and most gluttonous being imaginable; for justice is a political virtue, by the rules of it the state is regulated, and these rules are the criterion of what is right.

Aristotle, 'Politics' in William Ellis (tr) *The Politics of Aristotle*, Everyman edn (London: Dent, 1912) 1252b–3b.

3. Animals are not Rational Creatures

St Thomas Aquinas   1225–74

That Rational Creatures are Governed for Their Own Sake, and Other Creatures as Directed to Them

In the first place, then, the very condition of the rational creature, as having dominion over its actions, requires that the care of providence should be bestowed on it for its own sake; whereas the condition of other things, that have no dominion over their actions, shows that they are cared for, not for their own sake, but as being directed to other things. For that which acts only when moved by another is like an instrument, whereas that which acts by itself is like a principal agent. Now an instrument is required, not for its own sake, but that the principal agent may use it. Hence, whatever is done for the care of instruments must be referred to the principal agent as its end; whereas any action directed to the principal agent as such, either by the agent itself or by another, is for the sake of the same principal agent. Accordingly, intellectual creatures are ruled by God as though He cared for them for their own sake, while other creatures are ruled as being directed to rational creatures.

Again. That which has dominion over its own act is free in its action, because 'he is free who is his own master,' whereas that which by some kind of necessity is moved by another to act is subject to slavery. Therefore every other creature is naturally under slavery; the intellectual nature alone is free. Now, in every government provision is made for the free for their own sake; but for slaves that they may be useful to the free. Accordingly, the divine providence makes provision for the intellectual creature for its own sake, but for other creatures for the sake of the intellectual creature.

Moreover. Whenever things are directed to a certain end, if any of them are unable of themselves to attain to the end, they must needs be directed to those that attain to the end, which are directed to the end for their own sake. Thus the end of the army is victory, which the soldiers obtain by their own action in fighting, and they alone in the army are required for their own sake; whereas all others, to whom other duties are assigned, such as the care of horses, the preparing of arms, are requisite for the sake of the soldiers of the army. Now it is clear from what has been said that God is the last end of the universe, Whom the intellectual nature alone obtains in Himself, namely, by knowing and loving Him, as was proved above. Therefore the intellectual nature alone is requisite for its own sake in the universe, and all others for its sake.

Further. In every whole, the principal parts are requisite on their own account for the establishment of the whole, while the others are required for the preservation or betterment of the former. Now, of all the parts of the universe, intellectual creatures hold the highest place, because they approach nearest to the divine likeness. Therefore, the divine providence provides for the intellectual nature for its own sake, and for all others for its sake.

Besides. It is clear that all the parts are directed to the perfection of the whole, since the whole is not for the sake of the parts, but the parts for the sake of the whole. Now intellectual natures are more akin to the whole than other natures; because, in a sense, the intellectual substance is all things, inasmuch as by its intellect it is able to comprehend all things, whereas every other substance has only a particular participation of being. Consequently, God fittingly cares for other things for the sake of intellectual substances.

Besides. Whatever happens to a thing in the course of nature happens to it naturally. Now we see that in the course of nature the intellectual substance uses all others for its own sake: either for the perfection of the intellect, which sees the truth in them as in a mirror; or for the execution of its power and the development of its knowledge, in the same way as a craftsman develops the conception of his art in corporeal matter; or, again, to sustain the body that is united to the intellectual soul, as is the case in man. It is clear, therefore, that God cares for all things for the sake of intellectual substances.

Moreover. If a man seeks something for its own sake, he seeks it always, because 'what is per se, is always'; whereas if he seek a thing for the sake of something else, he does not of necessity seek it always but only in reference to that for the sake of which he seeks it. Now, as we proved above, things derive their being from the divine will. Therefore whatever is always is willed by God for its own sake; and what is not always is willed by God, not for its own sake, but for another's. Now intellectual substances approach nearest to being always, since they are incorruptible. They are, moreover, unchangeable, except in their choice. Therefore, intellectual substances are governed as it were for their own sake, while others for the sake of intellectual substances.

The fact that all the parts of the universe are directed to the perfection of the whole is not in contradiction with the foregoing conclusion, since all the parts are directed to the perfection of the whole, in so far as one part serves another. Thus in the human body, it is clear that the lungs belong to the body's perfection, in that they serve the heart; and hence there is no contradiction in the lungs being for the sake of the heart, and for the sake of the whole animal. In like manner, that other natures are for the sake of the intellectual is not contrary to their being for the perfection of the universe; for without the things required for the perfection of the intellectual substance, the universe would not be complete.

Nor again does the fact that individuals are for the sake of the species argue against what has been said. Because, through being directed to their species, they are directed also to the intellectual nature. For a corruptible thing is directed to man, not for the sake of only one individual man, but for the sake of the whole human species. Yet a corruptible thing could not serve the whole human species, except in terms of its own entire species. Hence the order whereby corruptible things are directed to man requires that individuals be directed to the species.

When we assert that intellectual substances are directed by the divine providence for their own sake, we do not mean that they are not also referred to God and to the perfection of the universe.

Accordingly, they are said to be provided for for their own sake, and others for them, because the goods bestowed on them by the divine providence are not given them for another's profit. Whereas those bestowed on others are in the divine plan intended for the use of intellectual substances.

Hence it is said (Deuteronomy iv, 19): 'Lest thou see the sun and the moon and the other stars, and being deceived by error, thou adore and serve them, which the Lord thy God created for the service of all the nations that are under heaven;' and (Psalms viii, 8): 'Thou hast subjected all things under his feet, all sheep and oxen; moreover, the beasts also of the field;' again (Wisdom of Solomon xii, 18): 'Thou being master of power, judgest with tranquillity, and with great favour disposest of us.'

Hereby is refuted the error of those who said it is sinful for a man to kill brute animals; for by the divine providence they are intended for man's use according to the order of nature. Hence it is not wrong for man to make use of them, either by killing or in any other way whatever. For this reason the Lord said to Noah (Genesis ix, 3): 'As the green herbs I have delivered all flesh to you.'

And if any passages of Holy Scripture seem to forbid us to be cruel to brute animals, for instance to kill a bird with its young (Deuteronomy xxii, 6), this is either to remove man's thoughts from being cruel to other men, lest through being cruel to animals one become cruel to human beings; or because injury to an animal leads to the temporal hurt of man, either of the doer of the deed, or of another; or because of some signification, as the Apostle expounds (I Corinthians ix, 9) the prohibition against 'muzzling the ox that treadeth the corn' (Deuteronomy xxv, 4).

That the Rational Creature is Directed to its Actions by God not only in What Befits the Species, but also in What Befits the Individual

Hence it is clear that the rational creature alone is directed to its actions by God, not only in what befits the species, but also in what befits the individual. For everything is for the sake of its operation, since operation is the ultimate perfection of a thing. Therefore each thing is directed to its action by God, according as it is subject to the divine providence. Now the rational creature is subject to the divine providence as being for its own sake governed and cared for, and not, as other corruptible creatures, for the sake of the species only. For the individual that is governed only for the sake of the species is not governed for its own sake, whereas the rational creature is governed for its own sake, as we have made clear. Accordingly, rational creatures alone are directed by God to their actions for the sake, not only of the species, but also of the individual.

Besides. Things that are directed in their actions only so far as these refer to the species, have not the power to act or not to act; since whatever results from the species is common and natural to all the individuals contained in the species, and we have no choice about what is natural. Hence, if man were directed in his actions only in reference to what befits the species, he would not have the power to act or not to act, but he would have to follow the natural inclination common to the whole species, as is the case with all irrational creatures. It is therefore clear that rational creatures are directed in their actions, not only in accord with what befits the species, but also in accord with what befits the individual.

Moreover. As we have proved above, the divine providence extends to every single thing, even the least. Therefore whatever things have actions outside the inclination of the species, must in such actions receive from the divine providence a direction beyond that which pertains to the species. But many actions are found in the rational creature, for which the inclination of the species is not sufficient; and a sign of this is that they are not the same in all, but differ in different subjects. Therefore the rational creature must be directed to its actions by God, not only in accord with what befits the species, but also in accord with what befits the individual.

Again. God provides for every nature according to its capacity. For he made each creature such that He knew it to be adapted to obtain its end through His government. Now the rational creature alone is capable of being directed to its actions, not only in accord with what befits the species, but also in accord with what befits the individual. For it has intellect and reason, and hence is able to perceive the different ways in which a certain thing is good or evil in relation to various persons, times and places. Therefore the rational creature alone is directed by God to its actions, not only in accord with what befits the species, but also in accord with what befits the individual.

Besides. The rational creature is subject to the divine providence in such a way, that not only is it governed thereby, but is able to know something of the nature of providence; so that it is capable of exercising providence and government in relation to others. This is not the case with other creatures, for they participate in providence only by being subject to it. Now through being capable of providence, a man can direct and govern his own actions also. Therefore the rational creature participates in the divine providence not only in being governed, but also in governing; for it governs itself in its own actions, and also other things. Now every lower providence is subject to the divine providence as to the highest providence. Therefore the government of a rational creature's acts, as personal acts, belongs to the divine providence.

Again. The personal acts of a rational creature are properly those that proceed from the rational soul. Now the rational soul is capable of perpetuity, not only in respect of the species, like other creatures, but also in respect of the individual. Therefore the acts of a rational creature are directed by the divine providence, not only in so far as they belong to the species, but also inasmuch as they are personal.

Hence it is that, though all things are subject to the divine providence, yet Holy Scripture ascribes the care of men to it in a special manner, according to Psalms viii, 5: 'What is man that thou art mindful of him?' and I Corinthians ix, 9: 'Doth God take care of oxen?' These things are said because God watches over man's actions not only as belonging to the species, but also as personal acts.

St Thomas Aquinas, 'Summa Contra Gentiles' in Anton C. Pegis (tr) *Basic Writings of Saint Thomas Aquinas* (New York: Random House, 1945) vol. II, pp. 220–4.

4. The Human and the Beast

Niccolò Machiavelli   1469–1527

It is unquestionably very praiseworthy in princes to be faithful to their engagements; but among those of the present day who have been distinguished for great exploits few indeed have been remarkable for this virtue or have scrupled to deceive others who may have relied on their good faith.

It should therefore be known that there are two ways of deciding any contest: the one by laws, the other by force. The first is peculiar to men, the second to beasts: but when laws are not sufficiently powerful, it is necessary to recur to force: a prince ought therefore to understand how to use both these descriptions of arms. This doctrine is admirably illustrated to us by the ancient poets in the allegorical history of the education of Achilles, and many other princes of antiquity, by the centaur Chiron, who, under the double form of man and beast, taught those who were destined to govern that it was their duty to use by turns the arms adapted to both these natures, seeing that one without the other cannot be of any durable advantage. Now, as a prince must learn how to act the part of a beast sometimes, he should make the fox and the lion his patterns. The first can but feebly defend himself against the wolf and the latter readily falls into such snares as are laid for him. From the fox, therefore, a prince will learn dexterity in avoiding snares; and from the lion, how to employ his strength to keep the wolves in awe. But they who entirely rely on the lion's strength will not always meet with success: in other words, a prudent prince cannot and ought not to keep his word except when he can do it without injury to himself or when the circumstances under which he contracted the engagement still exist.

I should be cautious in indicating such a precept if all men were good: but as the generality of mankind are wicked and ever ready to break their words, a prince should not pique himself in keeping his more scrupulously, especially as it is always easy to justify a breach of faith on his part. I could give numerous proofs of this and show numberless engagements and treaties which have been violated by the treachery of princes, and that those who enacted the part of the fox have always succeeded best in their affairs. It is necessary, however, to disguise the appearance of craft and thoroughly to understand the art of feigning and dissembling: for men are generally so simple and so weak that he who wishes to deceive easily finds dupes.

One example, taken from the history of our own times, will be sufficient. During his whole life Pope Alexander VI played a game of deception; and notwithstanding his faithless conduct was extremely well known, his artifices always proved successful. Oaths and protestations cost him nothing; never did a prince so often break his word or pay less regard to his engagements. This was because he so well understood this chapter in the art of government.

It is not necessary, however, for a prince to possess all the good qualities I have enumerated, but it is indispensable that he should appear to have them. I will even venture to affirm that it is sometimes dangerous to use them though it is always useful to seem to possess them. A prince should earnestly endeavour to gain the reputation of kindness, clemency, piety, justice, and fidelity to his engagements. He ought to possess all these good qualities but still retain such power over himself as to display their opposites whenever it may be expedient. I maintain that a prince, and especially a new prince, cannot with impunity exercise all the virtues, because his own self-preservation will often compel him to violate the laws of charity, religion, and humanity. He should habituate himself to bend easily to the various circumstances which may from time to time surround him. In a word, it will be as useful to him to persevere in the path of rectitude, while he feels no inconvenience in doing so, as to know how to deviate from it when circumstances dictate such a course. He should make it a rule above all things never to utter anything which does not breathe of kindness, justice, good faith, and piety: this last quality it is most important for him to appear to possess, as men in general judge more from appearances than from reality. All men have eyes, but few have the gift of penetration. Every one sees your exterior, but few can discern what you have in your heart; and those few dare not oppose the voice of the multitude, who have the majesty of their prince on their side. Now, in forming a judgement of the minds of men, and more especially of princes, as we cannot recur to any tribunal we must attend only to results. Let it then be the prince's chief care to maintain his authority; the means he employs, be what they may, will, for this purpose, always appear honourable and meet with applause; for the vulgar are ever caught by appearances and judge only by the event. And as the world is chiefly composed of such as are called the vulgar, the voice of the few is seldom or never heard or regarded.

There is a prince now alive (whose name it may not be proper to mention) who ever preaches the doctrines of peace and good faith: but if he had observed either the one or the other, he would long ago have lost both his reputation and dominions.

Niccolò di Bernardo dei Machiavelli, *The Prince* [c.1652] (London: Philip Allan, 1925) pp. 107–11.

5. Animals as Automata

René Descartes   1596–1650

I had expounded all these matters with sufficient minuteness in the treatise which I formerly thought of publishing. And after these, I had shown what must be the fabric of the nerves and muscles of the human body to give the animal spirits contained in it the power to move the members, as when we see heads shortly after they have been struck off still move and bite the earth, although no longer animated; what changes must take place in the brain to produce walking, sleep, and dreams; how light, sounds, odours, tastes, heat, and all the other qualities of external objects impress it with different ideas by means of the senses; how hunger, thirst, and the other internal affections can likewise impress upon it divers ideas; what must be understood by the common sense (*sensus communis*) in which these ideas are received, by the memory which retains them, by the fantasy which can change them in various ways, and out of them compose new ideas, and which, by the same means, distributing the animal spirits through the muscles, can cause the members of such a body to move in as many different ways, and in a manner as suited, whether to the objects that are presented to its senses or to its internal affections, as can take place in our own case apart from the guidance of the will. Nor will this appear at all strange to those who are acquainted with the variety of movements performed by the different automata, or moving machines fabricated by human industry, and that with help of but few pieces compared with the great multitude of bones, muscles, nerves, arteries, veins, and other parts that are found in the body of each animal. Such persons will look upon this body as a machine made by the hands of God, which is incomparably better arranged, and adequate to movements more admirable than is any machine of human invention. And here I specially stayed to show that, were there such machines exactly resembling in organs and outward form an ape or any other irrational animal, we could have no means of knowing that they were in any respect of a different nature from these animals; but if there were machines bearing the image of our bodies, and capable of imitating our actions as far as it is morally possible, there would still remain two most certain tests whereby to know that they were not therefore really men. Of these the first is that they could never use words or other signs arranged in such a manner as is competent to us in order to declare our thoughts to others: for we may easily conceive a machine to be so constructed that it emits vocables, and even that it emits some correspondent to the action upon it of external objects which cause a change in its organs; for example, if touched in a particular place it may demand what we wish to say to it; if in another it may cry out that it is hurt, and such like; but not that it should arrange them variously so as appositely to reply to what is said in its presence, as men of the lowest grade of intellect can do. The second test is, that although such machines might execute many things with equal or perhaps greater perfection than any of us, they would, without doubt, fail in certain others from which it could be discovered that they did not act from knowledge, but solely from the disposition of their organs: for while reason is an universal instrument that is alike available on every occasion, these organs, on the contrary, need a particular arrangement for each particular action; whence it must be morally impossible that there should exist in any machine a diversity of organs sufficient to enable it to act in all the occurrences of life, in the way in which our reason enables us to act. Again, by means of these two tests we may likewise know the difference between men and brutes. For it is highly deserving of remark, that there are no men so dull and stupid, not even idiots, as to be incapable of joining together different words, and thereby constructing a declaration by which to make their thoughts understood; and that on the other hand, there is no other animal, however perfect or happily circumstanced, which can do the like. Nor does this inability arise from want of organs: for we observe that magpies and parrots can utter words like ourselves, and are yet unable to speak as we do, that is, so as to show that they understand what they say; in place of which men born deaf and dumb, and thus not less, but rather more than the brutes, destitute of the organs which others use in speaking, are in the habit of spontaneously inventing certain signs by which they discover their thoughts to those who, being usually in their company, have leisure to learn their language. And this proves not only that the brutes have less reason than man, but that they have none at all: for we see that very little is required to enable a person to speak; and since a certain inequality of capacity is observable among animals of the same species, as well as among men, and since some are more capable of being instructed than others, it is incredible that the most perfect ape or parrot of its species, should not in this be equal to the most stupid infant of its kind, or at least to one that was crack-brained, unless the soul of brutes were of a nature wholly different from ours. And we ought not to confound speech with the natural movements which indicate the passions, and can be imitated by machines as well as manifested by animals; nor must it be thought with certain of the ancients, that the brutes speak, although we do not understand their language. For if such were the case, since they are endowed with many organs analogous to ours, they could as easily communicate their thoughts to us as to their fellows. It is also very worthy of remark, that, though there are many animals which manifest more industry than we in certain of their actions, the same animals are yet observed to show none at all in many others: so that the circumstance that they do better than we does not prove that they are endowed with mind, for it would thence follow that they possessed greater reason than any of us, and could surpass us in all things; on the contrary, it rather proves that they are destitute of reason, and that it is nature which acts in them according to the disposition of their organs: thus it is seen, that a clock composed only of wheels and weights can number the hours and measure time more exactly than we with all our skill.

I had after this described the reasonable soul, and shown that it could by no means be educed from the power of matter, as the other things of which I had spoken, but that it must be expressly created; and that it is not sufficient that it be lodged in the human body exactly like a pilot in a ship, unless perhaps to move its members, but that it is necessary for it to be joined and united more closely to the body, in order to have sensations and appetites similar to ours, and thus constitute a real man. I here entered, in conclusion, upon the subject of the soul at considerable length, because it is of the greatest moment: for after the error of those who deny the existence of God, an error which I think I have already sufficiently refuted, there is none that is more powerful in leading feeble minds astray from the straight path of virtue than the supposition that the soul of the brutes is of the same nature with our own; and consequently that after this life we have nothing to hope for or fear, more than flies and ants; in place of which, when we know how far they differ we much better comprehend the reasons which establish that the soul is of a nature wholly independent of the body, and that consequently it is not liable to die with the latter; and, finally, because no other causes are observed capable of destroying it, we are naturally led thence to judge that it is immortal.

René Descartes, 'Discourse V' [1637] in John Veitch (tr) *René Descartes: A Discourse on Method*, Everyman edn (London: Dent, 1912) Part V, pp. 43–6.

6. Animals have no Language

Thomas Hobbes   1588–1679

Speech or language is the connexion of names constituted by the will of men to stand for the series of conceptions of the things about which we think. Therefore, as a name is to an idea or conception of a thing, so is speech to the discourse of the mind. And it seems to be peculiar to man. For even if some brute animals, taught by practice, grasp what we wish and command in words, they do so not through words as words, but as signs; for animals do not know that words are constituted by the will of men for the purpose of signification.

Moreover, the signification that does occur when animals of the same kind call to one another, is not on that account speech, since not by their will, but out of the necessity of nature, these calls by which hope, fear, joy, and the like are signified, are forced out by the strength of these passions. And since among animals there is a limited variety of calls, by changing from one call to another, it comes about that they are warned of danger so that they may flee, are summoned to feeding, aroused to song, solicited to love; yet these calls are not speech since they are not constituted by the will of these animals, but burst forth by the strength of nature from the peculiar fears, joys, desires, and other passions of each of them; and this is not to speak, which is manifest in this, that the calls of animals of the same species are in all lands whatsoever the same, while those of men are diverse.

Therefore other animals also lack understanding. For understanding is a kind of imagination, but one that ariseth from the signification constituted by words.

Because, however, I would say that names have arisen from human invention, someone might possibly ask how a human invention could avail so much as to confer on mankind the benefit speech appears to us to have. For it is incredible that men once came together to take counsel to constitute by decree what all words and all connexions of words would signify. It is more credible, however, that at first there were few names and only of those things that were the most familiar. Thus the first man by his own will imposed names on just a few animals, namely, the ones that God led before him to look at; then on other things, as one or another species of things offered itself to his senses; these names, having been accepted, were handed down from fathers to their sons, who also devised others. But when, in the second chapter of Genesis, God is said to have prohibited the eating of the fruit of the tree of knowledge of good and evil before Adam had given names to anything, in what manner could Adam have understood that command of God, when he did not as yet know what was meant by eating, fruit, tree, knowledge, and lastly, good or evil? It must be, therefore, that Adam understood that divine prohibition not from the meaning of the words, but in some supernatural manner, as is made manifest a little later from this: that God asked him who had told him that he was naked. Similarly, how could Adam, the first mortal, have understood the serpent speaking of death, whereof he could have had no idea? Hence these things could not have been understood in any natural way; and as a consequence, speech could not have had a natural origin except by the will of man himself. This is made even clearer by the confusion of languages at Babel. For from that time the origins of language are diverse and have been brought by single men to single peoples. What others say, however – that names have been imposed on single things according to the nature of those things – is childish. For who could have it so when the nature of things is everywhere the same while languages are diverse? And what relationship hath a call (that is, a sound) with an animal (that is, a body)?

Of the advantages related to language the following are pre-eminent. First, that the power of numeral words enables man not only to count things, but also to measure them, whatsoever they may be; so with bodies (insofar as they have any dimensions), whether they be long, or long and wide, or long, wide, and thick; and similarly he can add, subtract, multiply, divide, and compare them with one another; similarly he can also subject times, motion, weight, and degrees of increase and decrease to calculation. From these things the enormous advantages of human life have far surpassed the condition of other animals. For there is no one that doth not know how much these arts are used in measuring bodies, calculating times, computing celestial motions, describing the face of the earth, navigating, erecting buildings, making engines, and in other necessary things. All of these proceed from numbering, but numbering proceeds from speech. Secondly, one may teach another, that is, communicate his knowledge to another, he can warn, he can advise, all these he hath from speech also; so that a good, great in itself, through communication becomes even greater. Thirdly, that we can command and understand commands is a benefit of speech, and truly the greatest. For without this there would be no society among men, no peace, and consequently no disciplines; but first savagery, then solitude, and for dwellings, caves. For though among certain animals there are seeming polities, these are not of sufficiently great moment for living well; hence they merit not our consideration; and they are largely found among defenseless animals, not in need of many things; in which number man is not included; for just as swords and guns, the weapons of men, surpass the weapons of brute animals (horns, teeth, and stings), so man surpasseth in rapacity and cruelty the wolves, bears, and snakes that are not rapacious unless hungry and not cruel unless provoked, whereas man is famished even by future hunger. From this it is easily understood how much we owe to language, by which we, having been drawn together and agreeing to covenants, live securely, happily, and elegantly; we can so live, I insist, if we so will. But language also hath its disadvantages; namely because man, alone among the animals, on account of the universal signification of names, can create general rules for himself in the art of living just as in the other arts; and so he alone can devise errors and pass them on for the use of others. Therefore man errs more widely and dangerously than can other animals. Also, man if it please him (and it will please him as often as it seems to advance his plans), can teach what he knows to be false from works that he hath inherited; that is, he can lie and render the minds of men hostile to the conditions of society and peace; something that cannot happen in the societies of other animals, since they judge what things are good and bad for them by their senses, not on the basis of the complaints of others, the causes whereof, unless they be seen, they cannot understand. Moreover, it sometimes happens to those that listen to philosophers and Schoolmen that listening becomes a habit, and the words that they hear they accept rashly, even though no sense can be had from them (for such are the kind of words invented by teachers to hide their own ignorance), and they use them, believing that they are saying something when they say nothing. Finally, on account of the ease of speech, the man who truly doth not think, speaks; and what he says, he believes to be true, and he can deceive himself; a beast cannot deceive itself. Therefore by speech man is not made better, but only given greater possibilities.

Science is understood as being concerned with theorems, that is, with the truth of general propositions, that is, with the truth of consequences. Indeed, when one is dealing with the truth of fact, it is not properly called science, but simply knowledge. Therefore it is science when we know a certain proposed theorem to be true, either by knowledge derived from the causes, or from the generation of the subject by right reasoning. On the other hand, when we know (insofar as possible) that such and such a theorem may be true, it is knowledge derived by legitimate reasoning from the experience of effects. Both of these methods of proof are usually called demonstrations; the former kind is, however, preferable to the latter; and rightly so; for it is better to know how we can best use present causes than to know the irrevocable past, whatsoever its nature. Therefore science is allowed to men through the former kind of a *a priori* demonstration only of those things whose generation depends on the will of men themselves.

Therefore many theorems are demonstrable about quantity, the science whereof is called geometry. Since the causes of the properties that individual figures have belong to them because we ourselves draw the lines; and since the generation of the figures depends on our will; nothing more is required to know the phenomenon peculiar to any figure whatsoever, than that we consider everything that follows from the construction that we ourselves make in the figure to be described. Therefore, because of this fact (that is, that we ourselves create the figures), it happens that geometry hath been and is demonstrable. On the other hand, since the causes of natural things are not in our power, but in the divine will, and since the greatest part of them, namely the ether, is invisible; we, that do not see them, cannot deduce their qualities from their causes. Of course, we can, by deducing as far as possible the consequences of those qualities that we do see, demonstrate that such and such *could* have been their causes. This kind of demonstration is called *a posteriori*, and its science, physics. And since one cannot proceed in reasoning about natural things that are brought about by motion from the effects to the causes without a knowledge of those things that follow from that kind of motion; and since cannot proceed to the consequences of motions without a knowledg of quantity, which is geometry; nothing can be demonstrated by physics without something also being demonstrated *a priori*. Therefore physics (I mean true physics), that depends on geometry, is usually numbered among the mixed mathematics. For those sciences are usually called mathematical that are learned not from use and experience, but from teachers and rules. Therefore those mathematics are pure which (like geometry and arithmetic) revolve around quantities in the abstract so that work in the subject requires no knowledge of fact; those mathematics are mixed, in truth, which in their reasoning also consider any quality of the subject, as in the case with astronomy, music, physics, and the parts of physics that can vary on account of the variety of species and the parts of the universe.

Finally, politics and ethics (that is, the sciences of just and unjust, of equity and inequity) can be demonstrated *a priori*; because we ourselves make the principles – that is, the causes of justice (namely laws and covenants) – whereby it is known what justice and equity, and their opposites injustice and inequity, are. For before covenants and laws were drawn up, neither justice nor injustice, neither public good nor public evil, was natural among men any more than it was among beasts.

Thomas Hobbes, 'De Homine' [1658] in Bernard Gert (tr) *Man and Citizen* (London: Harvester, 1976) pp. 37–43.

7. Understanding in Animals

John Locke   1632–1704

Brutes have memory

– This faculty of laying up and retaining the ideas that are brought into the mind, several other animals seem to have to a great degree, as well as man. For to pass by other instances, birds learning of tunes, and the endeavours one may observe in them to hit the notes right, put it past doubt with me, that they have perception and retain ideas in their memories, and use them for patterns. For it seems to me impossible, that they should endeavour to conform their voices to notes (as it is plain they do) of which they had no ideas. For though I should grant sound may mechanically cause a certain motion of the animal spirits, in the brains of those birds, whilst the tune is actually playing; and that motion may be continued on to the muscles of the wings, and so the bird mechanically be driven away by certain noises, because this may tend to the bird's preservation: yet that can never be supposed a reason, why it should cause mechanically, either whilst the tune is playing much less after it has ceased, such a motion of the organs in the bird's voice as should conform it to the notes of a foreign sound; which imitation can be of no use to the bird's preservation. But which is more, it cannot with any appearance of reason be supposed (much less proved) that birds, without sense and memory, can approach their notes nearer and nearer by degrees to a tune played yesterday; which if they have no idea of their memory, is nowhere, nor can be a pattern for them to imitate, or which any repeated essays can bring them nearer to. Since there is no reason why the sound of a pipe should leave traces in their brains, which not at first, but by their after-endeavours, should produce the like sounds; and why the sounds they make themselves, should not make traces which they should follow, as well as those of the pipe, is impossible to conceive.

No knowledge without discernment

– Another faculty we may take notice of in our minds, is that of discerning and distinguishing between the several ideas it has. It is not enough to have a confused perception of something in general; unless the mind had a distinct perception of different objects and their qualities, it would be capable of very little knowledge; though the bodies that affect us were as busy about us as they are now, and the mind were continually employed in thinking. On this faculty of distinguishing one thing from another, depends the evidence and certainty of several, even very general propositions, which have passed for innate truths; because men, overlooking the true cause why those propositions find universal assent, impute it wholly to native uniform impressions; whereas it in truth depends upon this clear discerning faculty of the mind, whereby it perceives two ideas to be the same, or different ...

Brutes compare but imperfectly

– How far brutes partake in this faculty, is not easy to determine: I imagine they have it not in any great degree: for though they probably have several ideas distinct enough, yet it seems to me to be the prerogative of human understanding, when it has sufficiently distinguished any ideas, so as to perceive them to be perfectly different, and so consequently two, to cast about and consider in what circumstances they are capable to be compared: and therefore I think beasts compare not their ideas farther than some sensible circumstances annexed to the objects themselves. The other power of comparing, which may be observed in men, belonging to general ideas, and useful only to abstract reasonings, we may probably conjecture beasts have not.

Compounding

– The next operation we may observe in the mind about its ideas, is composition; whereby it puts together several of those simple ones it has received from sensation and reflection, and combines them into complex ones. Under this of composition may be reckoned also that of enlarging; wherein though the composition does not so much appear as in more complex ones, yet it is nevertheless a putting several ideas together, though of the same kind. Thus by adding several units together, we make the idea of a dozen; and putting together the repeated ideas of several perches, we frame that of a furlong.

Brutes compound but little

– In this also, I suppose, brutes come far short of men: for though they take in and retain together several combinations of simple ideas, as possibly the shape, smell, and voice of his master make up the complex idea a dog has of him, or rather are so many distinct marks whereby he knows him; yet I do not think they do of themselves ever compound them, and make complex ideas. And perhaps even where we think they have complex ideas, it is only one simple one that directs them in the knowledge of several things, which possibly they distinguish less by their sight than we imagine; for I have been credibly informed that a bitch will nurse, play with, and be fond of young foxes, as much as, and in place of, her puppies; if you can but get them once to suck her so long, that her milk may go through them. And those animals which have a numerous brood of young ones at once, appear not to have any knowledge of their number; for though they are mightily concerned for any one of their young that are taken from them whilst they are in sight or hearing; yet if one or two of them be stolen from them in their absence, or without noise, they appear not to miss them, or to have any sense that their number is lessened.

Naming

– When children have, by repeated sensations, got ideas fixed in their memories, they begin by degrees to learn the use of signs. And when they have got the skill to apply the organs of speech to the framing of articulate sounds, they begin to make use of words to signify their ideas to others. These verbal signs they sometimes borrow from others, and sometimes make themselves, as one may observe among the new and unusual names children often give to things in the first use of language.

Abstraction

– The use of words then being to stand as outward marks of our internal ideas, and those ideas being taken from particular things, if every particular idea that we take in should have a distinct name, names must be endless. To prevent this, the mind makes the particular ideas received from particular objects, to become general; which is done by considering them as they are in the mind, such appearances, separate from all other existences, and the circumstances of real existence, as time, place, or any other concomitant ideas. This is called abstraction, whereby ideas, taken from particular beings, become general representatives of all of the same kind, and their names general names, applicable to whatever exists conformable to such abstract ideas. Such precise naked appearances in the mind, without considering how, whence, or with what others they came there, the understanding lays up (with names commonly annexed to them) as the standard to rank real existences into sorts, as they agree with these patterns, and to denominate them accordingly. Thus the same colour being observed today in chalk or snow, which the mind yesterday received from milk, it considers that appearance alone, makes it a representative of all of that kind: and having given it the name whiteness, it by that sound signifies the same quality, wheresoever to be imagined or met with: and thus universals, whether ideas or terms, are made.

Brutes abstract not

– If it may be doubted, whether beasts compound and enlarge their ideas that way to any degree; this, I think, I may be positive in, that the power of abstracting is not at all in them; and that the having of general ideas, is that which puts a perfect distinction betwixt man and brutes, and is an excellency which the faculties of brutes do by no means attain to. For it is evident we observe no footsteps in them of making use of general signs for universal ideas; from which we have reason to imagine, that they have not the faculty of abstracting or making general ideas, since they have no use of words, or any other general signs.

Nor can it be imputed to their want of fit organs to frame articulate sounds, that they have no use or knowledge of general words; since many of them, we find, can fashion such sounds, and pronounce words distinctly enough, but never with any such application. And on the other side, men who, through some defect in the organs want words, yet fail not to express their universal ideas by signs, which serve them instead of general words; a faculty which we see beasts come short in. And therefore I think we may suppose, that it is in this that the species of brutes are discriminated from man; and it is that proper difference wherein they are wholly separated, and which at last widens to so vast a distance: for if they have any ideas at all, and are not bare machines (as some would have them) we cannot deny them to have some reason. It seems as evident to me that they do some of them in certain instances reason, as that they have sense; but it is only in particular ideas, just as they received them from their senses. They are the best of them tied up within those narrow bounds, and have not (as I think) the faculty to enlarge them by any kind of abstraction.

John Locke, *An Essay Concerning Human Understanding* [1690] 29th edn (London: Thomas Tegg, 1841) Book II, pp. 88–91.

8. A Response to Locke

George Berkeley   1685–1753

I proceed to examine what can be alleged in defence of the doctrine of abstraction, and try if I can discover what it is that inclines the men of speculation to embrace an opinion so remote from common sense as that seems to be. There has been a late deservedly esteemed philosopher, who, no doubt, has given it very much countenance by seeming to think the having abstract general ideas is what puts the widest difference in point of understanding betwixt man and beast. 'The having of general ideas,' saith he, 'is that which puts a perfect distinction betwixt man and brutes, and is an excellency which the faculties of brutes do by no means attain unto. For it is evident we observe no footsteps in them of making use of general signs for universal ideas; from which we have reason to imagine that they have not the faculty of abstracting, or making general ideas, since they have no use of words or any other general signs.' And a little after: 'Therefore, I think, we may suppose that it is in this that the species of brutes are discriminated from men and it is that proper difference wherein they are wholly separated, and which at last widens to so wide a distance. For if they have any ideas at all, and are not bare machines (as some would have them), we cannot deny them to have some reason. It seems as evident to me that they do some of them in certain instances reason as that they have sense, but it is only in particular ideas, just as they receive them from their senses. They are the best of them tied up within those narrow bounds, and have not (as I think) the faculty to enlarge them by any kind of abstraction' (Essay on Human Understanding, b. ii, ch. xi, sect. 10, 11). I readily agree with this learned author, that the faculties of brutes can by no means attain to abstraction. But then if this be made the distinguishing property of that sort of animals, I fear a great many of those that pass for men must be reckoned into their number. The reason that is here assigned why we have no grounds to think brutes have abstract general ideas, is that we observe in them no use of words or any other general signs; (which is built on this supposition, to wit, that the making use of words implies the having general ideas.) From which it follows, that men who use language are able to abstract or generalize their ideas. That this is the sense and arguing of the author will further appear by his answering the question he in another place puts. 'Since all things that exist are only particulars, how come we by general terms?' His answer is, 'Words become general by being made the signs of general ideas' (Essay on Human Understanding, b. iii, ch. iii, sect. 6). But it seems that a word becomes general by being made the sign, not of an abstract general idea, but of several particular ideas, any one of which it indifferently suggests to the mind. For example, when it is said the change of motion is proportional to the impressed force, or that whatever has extension is divisible; these propositions are to be understood of motion and extension in general, and nevertheless it will not follow that they suggest to my thoughts an idea of motion without a body moved, or any determinate direction and velocity, or what I must conceive an abstract general idea of extension, which is neither line, surface, nor solid, neither great nor small, black, white, nor red, nor of any other determinate colour. It is only implied that whatever motion I consider, whether it be swift or slow, perpendicular, horizontal, or oblique, or in whatever object, the axiom concerning it holds equally true. As does the other of every particular extension, it matters not whether line, surface, or solid, whether of this or that magnitude or figure.

George Berkeley, 'A Treatise Concerning the Principles of Human Knowledge' [1710] in *A New Theory of Vision and other Select Philosophical Writings*, Everyman edn (London: Dent, 1910) pp. 98–101.

9. Of the Reason of Animals

David Hume   1711–76

Next to the ridicule of denying an evident truth, is that of taking much pains to defend it; and no truth appears to me more evident, than that beasts are endow'd with thought and reason as well as men. The arguments are in this case so obvious, that they never escape the most stupid and ignorant.

We are conscious that we ourselves, in adapting means to ends, are guided by reason and design, and that 'tis not ignorantly nor casually we perform those actions, which tend to self-preservation, to obtaining pleasure, and avoiding pain. When therefore we see other creatures, in millions of instances, perform like actions, and direct them to like ends, all our principles of reason and probability carry us with an invincible force to believe the existence of a like cause. 'Tis needless in my opinion to illustrate this argument by the enumeration of particulars. The smallest attention will supply us with more than are requisite. The resemblance betwixt the actions of animals and those of men is so entire in this respect, that the very first action of the first animal we shall please to pitch on, will afford us an incontestable argument for the present doctrine.

This doctrine is as useful as it is obvious, and furnishes us with a kind of touchstone, by which we may try every system in this species of philosophy. 'Tis from the resemblance of the external actions of animals to those we ourselves perform, that we judge their internal likewise to resemble ours; and the same principle of reasoning, carry'd one step farther, will make us conclude that since our internal actions resemble each other, the causes, from which they are deriv'd, must also be resembling. When any hypothesis, therefore, is advanc'd to explain a mental operation which is common to men and beasts, we must apply the same hypothesis to both; and as every true hypothesis will abide this trial, so I may venture to affirm, that no false one will ever be able to endure it. The common defect of those systems, which philosophers have employ'd to account for the actions of the mind, is, that they suppose such a subtility and refinement of thought, as not only exceeds the capacity of mere animals, but even of children and the common people in our own species; who are notwithstanding susceptible of the same emotions and affections as persons of the most accomplish'd genius and understanding. Such a subtility is a clear proof of the falsehood, as the contrary simplicity of the truth, of any system.

Let us therefore put our present system concerning the nature of the understanding to this decisive trial, and see whether it will equally account for the reasonings of beasts as for these of the human species.

Here we must make a distinction betwixt those actions of animals, which are of a vulgar nature, and seem to be on a level with their common capacities, and those more extraordinary instances of sagacity, which they sometimes discover for their own preservation, and the propagation of their species. A dog, that avoids fire and precipices, that shuns strangers, and caresses his master, affords us an instance of the first kind. A bird, that chooses with such care and nicety the place and materials of her nest, and sits upon her eggs for a due time, and in a suitable season, with all the precaution that a chymist is capable of in the most delicate projection, furnishes us with a lively instance of the second.

As to the former actions, I assert they proceed from a reasoning, that is not in itself different, nor founded on different principles, from that which appears in human nature. 'Tis necessary in the first place, that there be some impression immediately present to their memory or senses, in order to be the foundation of their judgment. From the tone of voice the dog infers his master's anger, and foresees his own punishment. From a certain sensation affecting his smell, he judges his game not to be far distant from him.

Secondly, the inference he draws from the present impression is built on experience, and on his observation of the conjunction of objects in past instances. As you vary this experience, he varies his reasoning. Make a beating follow upon one sign or motion for some time, and afterwards upon another; and he will successively draw different conclusions according to his most recent experience.

Now let any philosopher make a trial, and endeavour to explain that act of the mind, which we call belief, and give an account of the principles, from which it is deriv'd, independent of the influence of custom on the imagination, and let his hypothesis be equally applicable to beasts as to the human species; and after he has done this, I promise to embrace his opinion. But at the same time I demand as an equitable condition, that if my system be the only one, which can answer to all these terms, it may be receiv'd as entirely satisfactory and convincing. And that 'tis the only one, is evident almost without any reasoning. Beasts certainly never perceive any real connexion among objects. 'Tis therefore by experience they infer one from another. They can never by any arguments form a general conclusion, that those objects, of which they have had no experience, resemble those of which they have. 'Tis therefore by means of custom alone, that experience operates upon them. All this was sufficiently evident with respect to man. But with respect to beasts there cannot be the least suspicion of mistake; which must be own'd to be a strong confirmation, or rather an invincible proof of my system.

Nothing shews more the force of habit in reconciling us to any phenomenon, than this, that men are not astonish'd at the operations of their own reason, at the same time, that they admire the instinct of animals, and find a difficulty in explaining it, merely because it cannot be reduc'd to the very same principles. To consider the matter aright, reason is nothing but a wonderful and unintelligible instinct in our souls, which carries us along a certain train of ideas, and endows them with particular qualities, according to their particular situations and relations. This instinct, 'tis true, arises from past observation and experience; but can any one give the ultimate reason, why past experience and observation produces such an effect, any more than why nature alone shou'd produce it? Nature may certainly produce whatever can arise from habit: Nay, habit is nothing but one of the principles of nature, and derives all its force from that origin.

David Hume, *A Treatise of Human Nature* [1739–40] (Oxford: Clarendon Press, 1888) Book I, pp. 176–9.

10. On Animal Souls

Gottfried Wilhelm Leibniz   1646–1716

Philosophers have been much perplexed about the origin of forms, entelechies, or souls; but nowadays it has become known, through careful studies of plants, insects, and animals, that the organic bodies of nature are never products of chaos or putrefaction, but always come from seeds, in which there was undoubtedly some preformation; and it is held that not only the organic body was already there before conception, but also a soul in this body, and, in short, the animal itself; and that by means of conception this animal has merely been prepared for the great transformation involved in its becoming an animal of another kind. Something like this is indeed seen apart from birth as when worms become flies and caterpillars become butterflies.

The animals, of which some are raised by means of conception to the rank of larger animals, may be called spermatic, but those among them which are not so raised but remain in their own kind (that is, the majority) are born, multiply, and are destroyed like the large animals, and it is only a few chosen ones that pass to a greater theatre.

But this is only half of the truth, and accordingly I hold that if an animal never comes into being by natural means no more does it come to an end by natural means; and that not only will there be no birth but also no complete destruction or death in the strict sense. And these reasonings, made *a posteriori* and drawn from experience are in perfect agreement with my principles deduced *a priori*, as above.

Thus, it may be said that not only the soul (mirror of an indestructible universe) is indestructible, but also the animal itself, though its mechanism may often perish in part and take off or put on an organic slough.

These principles have given me a way of explaining naturally the union or rather the mutual agreement of the soul and the organic body. The soul follows its own laws, and the body likewise follows its own laws; and they agree with each other in virtue of the pre-established harmony between all substances, since they are all representations of one and the same universe.

Souls act according to the laws of final causes through appetitions, ends, and means. Bodies act according to the laws of efficient causes or motions. And the two realms, that of efficient causes and that of final causes, are in harmony with one another.

Descartes recognized that souls cannot impart any force to bodies, because there is always the same quantity of force in matter. Nevertheless he was of opinion that the soul could change the direction of bodies. But that is because in his time it was not known that there is a law of nature which affirms also the conservation of the same total direction in matter. Had Descartes noticed this he would have come upon my system of pre-established harmony.

According to this system bodies act as if (to suppose the impossible) there were no souls, and souls act as if there were no bodies, and both act as if each influenced the other.

As regards minds or rational souls, though I find that what I have just been saying is true of all living beings and animals (namely that animals and souls come into being when the world begins and no more come to an end than the world does), yet there is this peculiarity in rational animals, that their spermatic animalcules, so long as they are only spermatic, have merely ordinary or sensuous souls; but when those which are chosen so to speak, attain to human nature through an actual conception, their sensuous souls are raised to the rank of reason and to the prerogative of minds.

Among other differences which exist between ordinary souls and minds some of which differences I have already noted, there is also this: that souls in general are living mirrors or images of the universe of created things, but that minds are also images of the Deity or Author of nature Himself, capable of knowing the system of the universe, and to some extent of imitating it through architectonic ensamples each mind being like a small divinity in its own sphere.

It is this that enables spirits [or minds – *esprits*] to enter into a kind of fellowship with God, and brings it about that in relation to them He is not only what an inventor is to his machine (which is the relation of God to other created things), but also what a prince is to his subjects, and, indeed, what a father is to his children.

Whence it is easy to conclude that the totality of all spirits must compose the City of God, that is to say, the most perfect State that is possible, under the most perfect of Monarchs.

This City of God, this truly universal monarchy, is a moral world in the natural world, and is the most exalted and most divine among the works of God; and it is in it that the glory of God really consists, for He would have no glory were not His greatness and His goodness known and admired by spirits. It is also in relation to this divine City that God specially has goodness, while His wisdom and His power are manifested everywhere.

As we have shown above that there is a perfect harmony between the two realms in nature, one of efficient, and the other of final causes, we should here notice also another harmony between the physical realm of nature and the moral realm of grace, that is to say, between God, considered as Architect of the mechanism of the universe and God considered as Monarch of the divine City of spirits.

A result of this harmony is that things lead to grace by the very ways of nature, and that this globe, for instance, must be destroyed and renewed by natural means at the very time when the government of spirits requires it, for the punishment of some and the reward of others.

It may also be said that God as Architect satisfies in all respects God as Lawgiver, and thus that sins must bear their penalty with them, through the order of nature, and even in virtue of the mechanical structure of things; and similarly that noble actions will attain their rewards by ways which, on the bodily side, are mechanical, although this cannot and ought not always to happen immediately.

Finally, under this perfect government no good action would be unrewarded and no bad one unpunished, and all should issue in the well-being of the good, that is to say, of those who are not malcontents in this great state, but who trust in Providence, after having done their duty, and who love and imitate, as is meet, the Author of all good, finding pleasure in the contemplation of His perfections, as is the way of genuine 'pure love' which takes pleasure in the happiness of the beloved. This it is which leads wise and virtuous people to devote their energies to everything which appears in harmony with the presumptive or antecedent will of God, and yet makes them content with what God actually brings to pass by His secret, consequent and positive will, recognizing that if we could sufficiently understand the order of the universe, we should find that it exceeds all the desires of the wisest men, and that it is impossible to make it better than it is, not only as a whole and in general but also for ourselves in particular, if we are attached, as we ought to be, to the Author of all, not only as to the architect and efficient cause of our being, but as to our master and to the final cause, which ought to be the whole aim of our will, and which can alone make our happiness.

Gottfried Wilhelm Leibniz, *Monadology* [1714] (London: Lowe and Brydone, 1898) pp. 259–71.

11. Freedom of the Will

Jean-Jacques Rousseau   1712–88

I see nothing in any animal but an ingenious machine, to which nature hath given senses to wind itself up, and to guard itself, to a certain degree, against anything that might tend to disorder or destroy it. I perceive exactly the same things in the human machine, with this difference, that in the operations of the brute, nature is the sole agent, whereas man has some share in his own operations, in his character as a free agent. The one chooses and refuses by instinct, the other from an act of free will hence the brute cannot deviate from the rule prescribed to it, even when it would be advantageous for it to do so; and, on the contrary, man frequently deviates from such rules to his own prejudice. Thus a pigeon would be starved to death by the side of a dish of the choicest meats, and a cat on a heap of fruit or grain; though it is certain that either might find nourishment in the foods which it thus rejects with disdain, did it think of trying them. Hence it is that dissolute men run into excesses which bring on fevers and death; because the mind depraves the senses, and the will continues to speak when nature is silent.

Every animal has ideas, since it has senses; it even combines those ideas in a certain degree; and it is only in degree that man differs, in this respect, from the brute. Some philosophers have even maintained that there is a greater difference between one man and another than between some men and some beasts. It is not, therefore, so much the understanding that constitutes the specific difference between the man and the brute, as the human quality of free-agency. Nature lays her commands on every animal, and the brute obeys her voice. Man receives the same impulsion, but at the same time knows himself at liberty to acquiesce or resist: and it is particularly in his consciousness of this liberty that the spirituality of his soul is displayed. For physics may explain, in some measure, the mechanism of the senses and the formation of ideas; but in the power of willing or rather of choosing, and in the feeling of this power, nothing is to be found but acts which are purely spiritual and wholly inexplicable by the laws of mechanism.

However, even if the difficulties attending all these questions should still leave room for difference in this respect between men and brutes, there is another very specific quality which distinguishes them, and which will admit of no dispute. This is the faculty of self-improvement which, by the help of circumstances, generally develops all the rest of our faculties, and is inherent in the species as in the individual: whereas a brute is, at the end of a few months, all he will ever be during his whole life, and his species, at the end of a thousand years, exactly what it was the first year of that thousand. Why is man alone liable to grow into a dotard? Is it not because he returns, in this, to his primitive state; and that, while the brute, which has acquired nothing and has therefore nothing to lose, still retains the force of instinct, man, who loses, by age or accident, all that his perfectibility had enabled him to gain, falls by this means lower than the brutes themselves? It would be melancholy, were we forced to admit that this distinctive and almost unlimited faculty is the source of all human misfortunes; that it is this which, in time, draws man out of his original state, in which he would have spent his days insensibly in peace and innocence; that it is this faculty, which, successively producing in different ages his discoveries and his errors, his vices and his virtues, makes him at length a tyrant both over himself and over nature. It would be shocking to be obliged to regard as a benefactor the man who first suggested to the Oroonoko Indians the use of the boards they apply to the temples of their children, which secure to them some part at least of their imbecility and original happiness.

Savage man, left by nature solely to the direction of instinct, or rather indemnified for what he may lack by faculties capable at first of supplying its place, and afterwards of raising him much above it, must accordingly begin with purely animal functions: thus seeing and feeling must be his first condition, which would be common to him and all other animals. To will, and not to will, to desire and to fear, must be the first, and almost the only operations of his soul, till new circumstances occasion new developments of his faculties.

Whatever moralists may hold, the human understanding is greatly indebted to the passions, which, it is universally allowed, are also much indebted to the understanding. It is by the activity of the passions that our reason is improved; for we desire knowledge only because we wish to enjoy; and it is impossible to conceive any reason why a person who has neither fears nor desires should give himself the trouble of reasoning. The passions, again, originate in our wants, and their progress depends on that of our knowledge; for we cannot desire or fear anything except from the idea we have of it, or from the simple impulse of nature. Now savage man, being destitute of every species of intelligence, can have no passions save those of the latter kind: his desires never go beyond his physical wants. The only goods he recognises in the universe are food, a female, and sleep: the only evils he fears are pain and hunger. I say pain, and not death: for no animal can know what it is to die; the knowledge of death and its terrors being one of the first acquisitions made by man in departing from an animal state.

Jean-Jacques Rousseau, 'A Dissertation on the Origin and Foundation of the Inequality of Mankind' [1754] in *The Social Contract and Discourses*, Everyman edn (London: Dent, 1913) pp. 184–6.

12. Organic Difference

Johann G. Herder   1744–1803

The human species has been praised for possessing in the most perfected form all the powers and capacities of every other species. This is patently untrue. Not only is the assertion incapable of empirical proof; it is also logically insupportable, for it is self-contradictory. Clearly, if it were true, one power would cancel out the other and man would be the most wretched of creatures. For how could man at one and the same time bloom like a flower, feel his way like the spider, build like the bee, suck like the butterfly, and also possess the muscular strength of the lion, the trunk of the elephant and the skill of the beaver? Does he possess, nay does he comprehend, a single one of these powers, with that intensity, with which the animal enjoys and exercises it?

On the other hand, man has also been, I will not say, degraded to the level of the beast, yet altogether denied a character *sui generis*. He has been depicted as a degenerate type of animal who, forever striving for perfection, has in the process wholly lost the characteristics originally peculiar to him. But this, too, flies in the face of truth and of all the evidence that human biology and human history provide. Manifestly, man has qualities which no animal possesses and acts in a manner which, for good or for ill, is entirely his own. No animal devours a member of its species for the sheer fun of it; no animal murders its kind in cold blood at the command of a third party. On the other hand, no animal has a language, still less writings, traditions, religion or rights and law of its own making. Finally, no animal has the education, clothing, habitation, arts, indeterminate mode of life, un-restrained propensities, and fluctuating attitudes, which distinguish almost every human being. We are not enquiring if all this is to the advantage or detriment of our species. It suffices to observe that it constitutes its character. Whilst animals on the whole remain true to the qualities of their kind, man alone has made a goddess of choice in place of necessity. It is this difference which calls for investigation. And the investigation must be as factual as the subject of inquiry. How man came to differ in this way is quite another question, being essentially historical in orientation. And that goes also for the question whether the difference is an original characteristic or an acquired one, whether it is real or only feigned. But that man's perfectibility or corruptibility (a propensity not shared by the animal world) is closely bound up with this distinguishing difference can scarcely be doubted. Let us, however, set aside all metaphysics and approach the problem from an empirical and physiological point of view.

The posture of man is upright; in this he is unique upon earth. Admittedly, the bear has a broad foot and fights in an erect position, and apes and pygmies sometimes run or walk upright. Yet only man is naturally and continuously in the erect position. His foot is firmer and broader than an ape's, with a longer big toe. His heel, too, is on a level with the sole of his foot, and all his bones, organs and muscles are adapted to the upright posture. The calf of his leg is less curved, his pelvis is drawn back and his hips are spread outward from each other. His spine is less curved, his breast wider. His shoulders have clavicles, and his hands have fingers with a sense of feeling. And to crown the structure, his head does not drop forward (like an ape's), but is raised on the muscles of his neck. Man is *anthropos*, a creature looking far above and around him ...

The upright posture of man is natural to him alone; indeed it is the organizing determinant of man's activities and the characteristic which distinguishes him from all other species.

No nation upon earth has been found walking on all fours. However close some aborigines may appear to border on the beast by their mode of thinking and living, they nonetheless walk erect. Even the insensitive beings in Diodorus and other legendary creatures found in ancient or mediaeval writings walk upon two legs ... Had man been a quadruped, and had he been so for thousands of years, surely he would have remained so to the present; and nothing short of a miraculous new creation could have made him what he now is and for what we have come to know him from history and experience.

Why, then, should we give credence to unproved and wholly contradictory paradoxes, when the structure of man, the history of his species, and, as it seems to me, the whole analogy of terrestrial organization point to quite a different hypothesis? No creature, that we know of, has departed from its original organization or has developed in opposition to it. It can operate only with the powers inherent in its organization, and nature knew how to devise sufficient means to confine all living things to the sphere allotted to them. In man everything is adapted to the form he now bears; from it, everything in history is explicable; without it, we are left completely in the dark ...

With grateful eyes let us contemplate the blessing of the hallowed act by which our species became a human species. We cannot but note with a sense of wonder the peculiar organization of powers, deriving from the erect posture of man by which, and by which alone, he became what he is: man.

Johann Gottfried Herder, 'Ideas for a Philosophy of the History of Mankind' [1784–91] in F.M. Barnard (ed) *Herder on Social and Political Culture* (Cambridge University Press, 1969) pp. 255–7.

13. Animals have no Concepts

Artur Schopenhauer   1788–1860

It must be possible to arrive at a complete knowledge of the consciousness of the brutes, for we can construct it by abstracting certain properties of our own consciousness. On the other hand, there enters into the consciousness of the brute instinct, which is much more developed in all of them than in man, and in some of them extends to what we call mechanical instinct.

The brutes have understanding without having reason, and therefore they have knowledge of perception but no abstract knowledge. They apprehend correctly, and also grasp the immediate causal connection, in the case of the higher species even through several links of its chain, but they do not, properly speaking, think. For they lack conceptions, that is, abstract ideas. The first consequence of this, however, is the want of a proper memory, which applies even to the most sagacious of the brutes, and it is just this which constitutes the principal difference between their consciousness and that of men. Perfect intelligence depends upon the distinct consciousness of the past and of the eventual future, as such, and in connection with the present. The special memory which this demands is therefore an orderly, connected, and thinking retrospective recollection. This, however, is only possible by means of general conceptions, the assistance of which is required by what is entirely individual, in order that it may be recalled in its order and connection. For the boundless multitude of things and events of the same and similar kinds, in the course of our life, does not admit directly of a perceptible and individual recollection of each particular, for which neither the powers of the most comprehensive memory nor our time would be sufficient. Therefore all this can only be preserved by subsuming it under general conceptions, and the consequent reference to relatively few principles, by means of which we then have always at command an orderly and adequate survey of our past. We can only present to ourselves in perception particular scenes of the past, but the time that has passed since then and its content we are conscious of only in the abstract by means of conceptions of things and numbers which now represent days and years, together with their content. The memory of the brutes, on the contrary, like their whole intellect, is confined to what they perceive, and primarily consists merely in the fact that a recurring impression presents itself as having already been experienced, for the present perception revivifies the traces of an earlier one. Their memory is therefore always dependent upon what is now actually present. Just on this account, however, this excites anew the sensation and the mood which the earlier phenomenon produced. Thus the dog recognises acquaintances, distinguishes friends from enemies, easily finds again the path it has once travelled, the houses it has once visited, and at the sight of a plate or a stick is at once put into the mood associated with them. All kinds of training depend upon the use of this perceptive memory and on the force of habit, which in the case of animals is specially strong. It is therefore just as different from human education as perception is from thinking. We ourselves are in certain cases, in which memory proper refuses us its service, confined to that merely perceptive recollection, and thus we can measure the difference between the two from our own experience. For example, at the sight of a person whom it appears to us we know, although we are not able to remember when or where we saw him; or again, when we visit a place where we once were in early childhood, that is, while our reason was yet undeveloped, and which we have therefore entirely forgotten, and yet feel that the present impression is one which we have already experienced. This is the nature of all the recollections of the brutes. We have only to add that in the case of the most sagacious this merely perceptive memory rises to a certain degree of phantasy, which again assists it, and by virtue of which, for example, the image of its absent master floats before the mind of the dog and excites a longing after him, so that when he remains away long it seeks for him everywhere. Its dreams also depend upon this phantasy. The consciousness of the brutes is accordingly a mere succession of presents, none of which, however, exist as future before they appear, nor as past after they have vanished; which is the specific difference of human consciousness. Hence the brutes have infinitely less to suffer than we have, because they know no other pains but those which the present directly brings. But the present is without extension, while the future and the past, which contain most of the causes of our suffering, are widely extended, and to their actual content there is added that which is merely possible, which opens up an unlimited field for desire and aversion. The brutes, on the contrary, undisturbed by these, enjoy quietly and peacefully each present moment, even if it is only bearable. Human beings of very limited capacity perhaps approach them in this. Further, the sufferings which belong purely to the present can only be physical. Indeed the brutes do not properly speaking feel death: they can only know it when it appears, and then they are already no more. Thus, then, the life of the brute is a continuous present. It lives on without reflection, and exists wholly in the present; even the great majority of men live with very little reflection. Another consequence of the special nature of the intellect of the brutes, which we have explained is the perfect accordance of their consciousness with their environment. Between the brute and the external world there is nothing, but between us and the external world there is always our thought about it, which makes us often inapproachable to it, and it to us. Only in the case of children and very primitive men is this wall of partition so thin that in order to see what goes on in them we only need to see what goes on round about them. Therefore the brutes are incapable alike of purpose and dissimulation; they reserve nothing. In this respect the dog stands to the man in the same relation as a glass goblet to a metal one, and this helps greatly to endear the dog so much to us, for it affords us great pleasure to see all those inclinations and emotions which we so often conceal displayed simply and openly in him. In general, the brutes always play, as it were, with their hand exposed; and therefore we contemplate with so much pleasure their behaviour towards each other, both when they belong to the same and to different species. It is characterised by a certain stamp of innocence, in contrast to the conduct of men, which is withdrawn from the innocence of nature by the entrance of reason, and with it of prudence or deliberation. Hence human conduct has throughout the stamp of intention or deliberate purpose, the absence of which, and the consequent determination by the impulse of the moment, is the fundamental characteristic of all the action of the brutes. No brute is capable of a purpose properly so-called. To conceive and follow out a purpose is the prerogative of man ...

Artur Schopenhauer, *The World as Will and Idea* [1819] tr. R.B. Haldane and John Kemp, 6th edn (London: Kegan Paul, Trench, Trubner, 1909) vol. II, pp. 228–31; also translated as *The World as Will and Representation*, tr. E.F.J. Payne (New York: Dover Publications, 1969).

14. Animals are not Self-Aware

G.W.F. Hegel   1770–1831

When the spirit strives towards its centre, it strives to perfect its own freedom; and this striving is fundamental to its nature. To say that spirit exists would at first seem to imply that it is a completed entity. On the contrary, it is by nature active, and activity is its essence; it is its own product, and is therefore its own beginning and its own end. Its freedom does not consist in static being, but in a constant negation of all that threatens to destroy freedom. The business of spirit is to produce itself, to make itself its own object, and to gain knowledge of itself; in this way, it exists for itself. Natural objects do not exist for themselves; for this reason they are not free. The spirit produces and realises itself in the light of its knowledge of itself; it acts in such a way that all its knowledge of itself is also realised. Thus everything depends on the spirit's self-awareness; if the spirit knows that it is free, it is altogether different from what it would be without this knowledge. For if it does not know that it is free, it is in the position of a slave who is content with his slavery and does not know that his condition is an improper one. It is the sensation of freedom alone which makes the spirit free, although it is in fact always free in and for itself.

The most immediate knowledge spirit can have of itself when it assumes the shape of a human individual is that it is capable of feeling. It does not as yet have an object, and the individual simply feels himself determined in some particular way. He then tries to distinguish between himself and this determinate quality, and sets about creating an internal division within himself. Thus, my feelings are split up into an external and an internal world. My determinate nature thereby enters a new phase, in that I have a feeling of deficiency or negativity; I encounter a contradiction within myself which threatens to destroy me. But I nevertheless exist; this much I know, and I balance this knowledge against my feeling of negation or deficiency. I survive and seek to overcome the deficiency, so that I am at the same time an impulse. The object towards which my impulse is directed is accordingly the means by which I can attain satisfaction and the restoration of my unity. All living things are endowed with impulses. We are therefore natural beings, and all our impulses are of a sensuous character. Objects, in so far as I am drawn to them by impulse, are means of integration, and this is the entire basis of theory and practice alike. But in our intuitions of the objects to which our impulses are drawn, we are dealing directly with externals and are ourselves external. Our intuitions are discrete units of a sensuous nature, and so also are our impulses, irrespective of their content. By this definition, man would be no different from the animals; for impulses are not conscious of themselves. But man has knowledge of himself, and this distinguishes him from the animals. He is a thinking being. Thought, however, is knowledge of universals, and it simplifies the content of experience, so that man too is simplified by it so as to become something inward and ideal. Or, to be more precise, this inwardness and simplicity is inherent in man, and the content of our experience only becomes universal and ideal if we proceed to simplify it.

What man is in reality, he must also be in ideality. Since he possesses ideal knowledge of reality, he ceases to be merely a natural being at the mercy of immediate intuitions and impulses which he must satisfy and perpetuate. This knowledge leads him to control his impulses; he places the ideal, the realm of thought, between the demands of the impulse and their satisfaction. In the animal, the two coincide; it cannot sever their connection by its own efforts – only pain or fear can do so. In man, the impulse is present before it is satisfied and independently of its satisfaction; in controlling or giving rein to his impulses, man acts in accordance with ends and determines himself in the light of a general principle. It is up to him to decide what end to follow; he can even make his end a completely universal one. In so doing, he is determined by whatever conceptions he has formed of his own nature and volitions. It is this which constitutes man's independence: for he knows what it is that determines him. Thus he can take a simple concept as his end – for example, that of his own positive freedom. The conceptions of the animal are not ideal and have no true reality; it therefore lacks this inner independence. As a living creature, the animal too has its source of movement within itself. But it can only respond to those external stimuli to which it is already inwardly susceptible; anything that does not match its inner being simply does not exist for it. The animal is divided from itself and within itself. It cannot interpose anything between its impulse and the satisfaction of its impulse; it has no will, and cannot even attempt to control itself. Its activating impulses come from within itself, and their operation presupposes that they contain the means of their own fulfilment. Man, however, is not independent because he is the initiator of his own movement, but because he can restrain this movement and thereby master his spontaneity and natural constitution.

The fundamental characteristic of human nature is that man can think of himself as an ego. As a spirit, man does not have an immediate existence but is essentially turned in upon himself. This function of mediation is an essential moment of the spirit. Its activity consists in transcending and negating its immediate existence so as to turn in again upon itself; it has therefore made itself what it is by means of its own activity. Only if it is turned in upon itself can a subject have true reality. Spirit exists only as its own product. The example of the seed may help to illustrate this point. The plant begins with the seed, but the seed is also the product of the plant's entire life, for it develops only in order to produce the seed. We can see from this how impotent life is, for the seed is both the origin and the product of the individual; as the starting point and the end result, it is different and yet the same, the product of one individual and the beginning of another. Its two sides fall asunder like the simple form within the grain and the whole course of the plant's development.

Every individual has an example even closer to hand in the shape of his own person. Man can only fulfil himself through education and discipline; his immediate existence contains merely the possibility of self-realisation (i.e. of becoming rational and free) and simply imposes on him a vocation and obligation which he must himself fulfil. The animal's education is soon complete; but this should not be seen as a blessing bestowed on the animal by nature. Its growth is merely a quantitative increase in strength. Man, on the other hand, must realise his potential through his own efforts, and must first acquire everything for himself, precisely because he is a spiritual being; in short, he must throw off all that is natural in him. Spirit, therefore, is the product of itself.

Georg Wilhelm Friedrich Hegel, *Lecture on the Philosophy of World History* [1830] ed Maurice Cowling *et al.* (Cambridge University Press, 1975) pp. 48–51.

15. An Animal is not a Species Being

Karl Marx   1818–83

Man is a species-being, not only because in practice and in theory he adopts the species (his own as well as those of other things) as his object, but – and this is only another way of expressing it – also because he treats himself as the actual, living species; because he treats himself as a universal and therefore a free being.

The life of the species, both in man and in animals, consists physically in the fact that man (like the animal) lives on inorganic nature; and the more universal man (or the animal) is, the more universal is the sphere of inorganic nature on which he lives. Just as plants, animals, stones, air, light, etc. constitute theoretically a part of human consciousness, partly as objects of natural science, partly as objects of art – his spiritual inorganic nature, spiritual nourishment which he must first prepare to make palatable and digestible – so also in the realm of practice they constitute a part of human life and human activity. Physically man lives only on these products of nature, whether they appear in the form of food, heating, clothes, a dwelling, etc. The universality of man appears in practice precisely in the universality which makes all nature his inorganic body – both inasmuch as nature is (1) his direct means of life, and (2) the material, the object, and the instrument of his life activity. Nature is man's inorganic body – nature, that is, insofar as it is not itself human body. Man lives on nature – means that nature is his body, with which he must remain in continuous interchange if he is not to die. That man's physical and spiritual life is linked to nature means simply that nature is linked to itself, for man is a part of nature.

In estranging from man, (1) nature, and (2) himself, his own active functions, his life activity, estranged labour estranges the species from man. It changes for him the life of the species into a means of individual life. First it estranges the life of the species and individual life, and secondly it makes individual life in its abstract form the purpose of the life of the species, likewise in its abstract and estranged form.

For labour, life activity, productive life itself, appears to man in the first place merely as a means of satisfying a need – the need to maintain physical existence. Yet the productive life is the life of the species. It is life-engendering life. The whole character of a species – its species-character – is contained in the character of its life activity; and free, conscious activity is man's species-character. Life itself appears only as a means to life.

The animal is immediately one with its life activity. It does not distinguish itself from it. It is its life activity. Man makes his life activity itself the object of his will and of his consciousness. He has conscious life activity. It is not a determination with which he directly merges. Conscious life activity distinguishes man immediately from animal life activity. It is just because of this that he is a species-being. Or it is only because he is a species-being that he is a conscious being, i.e. that his own life is an object for him. Only because of that is his activity free activity. Estranged labour reverses this relationship, so that it is just because man is a conscious being that he makes his life activity, his essential being, a mere means to his existence.

In creating a world of objects by his practical activity, in his work upon inorganic nature, man proves himself a conscious species-being, i.e. as a being that treats the species as its own essential being, or that treats itself as a species-being. Admittedly animals also produce. They build themselves nests, dwellings, like the bees, beavers, ants, etc. But an animal only produces what it immediately needs for itself or its young. It produces one-sidedly, whilst man produces universally. It produces only under the dominion of immediate physical need, whilst man produces even when he is free from physical need and only truly produces in freedom therefrom. An animal produces only itself, whilst man reproduces the whole of nature. An animal's product belongs immediately to its physical body, whilst man freely confronts his product. An animal forms objects only in accordance with the standard and the need of the species to which it belongs, whilst man knows how to produce in accordance with the standard of every species, and knows how to apply everywhere the inherent standard to the object. Man therefore also forms objects in accordance with the laws of beauty.

It is just in his work upon the objective world, therefore, that man really proves himself to be a species-being. This production is his active species-life. Through this production, nature appears as his work and his reality. The object of labour is, therefore, the objectification of man's species-life: for he duplicates himself not only, as in consciousness, intellectually, but also actively, in reality, and therefore he sees himself in a world that he has created. In tearing away from man the object of his production, therefore, estranged labour tears from him his species-life, his real objectivity as a member of the species, and transforms his advantage over animals into the disadvantage that his inorganic body, nature, is taken away from him.

Karl Marx, 'Economic and Philosophical Manuscripts' [1844] in *Collected Works* (London: Lawrence and Wishart, 1975) vol. 3, pp. 275–7.

16. On the Genius of Species

Friedrich Nietzsche   1844–1900

The problem of consciousness (or more correctly: of becoming conscious of oneself) meets us only when we begin to perceive in what measure we could dispense with it: and it is at the beginning of this perception that we are now placed by physiology and zoology (which have thus required two centuries to overtake the hint thrown out in advance by Leibniz). For we could in fact think, feel, will, and recollect, we could likewise 'act' in every sense of the term, and nevertheless nothing of it all would require to 'come into consciousness' (as one says metaphorically). The whole of life would be possible without its seeing itself, as it were, in a mirror: as in fact even at present the far greater part of our life still goes on without this mirroring – and even our thinking, feeling, volitional life as well, however painful this statement may sound to an older philosopher. What then is the purpose of consciousness generally, when it is in the main superfluous? Now it seems to me, if you will hear my answer and its perhaps extravagant supposition, that the subtlety and strength of consciousness are always in proportion to the capacity for communication of a man (or an animal), the capacity for communication in its turn being in proportion to the necessity for communication: the latter not to be understood as if precisely the individual himself who is master in the art of communicating and making known his necessities would at the same time have to be most dependent upon others for his necessities. It seems to me, however, to be so in relation to whole races and successions of generations: where necessity and need have long compelled men to communicate with their fellows and understand one another rapidly and subtly, a surplus of the power and art of communication is at last acquired, as if it were a fortune which had gradually accumulated, and now waited for an heir to squander it prodigally (the so-called artists are these heirs, in like manner the orators, preachers, and authors: all of them men who come at the end of a long succession, 'late-born' always, in the best sense of the word, and as has been said, squanderers by their very nature). Granted that this observation is correct, I may proceed further to the conjecture that consciousness generally has only been developed under the pressure of the necessity for communication – that from the first it has been necessary and useful only between man and man (especially between those commanding and those obeying), and has only developed in proportion to its utility. Consciousness is properly only a connecting network between man and man – it is only as such that it has had to develop; the recluse and wild-beast species of men would not have needed it. The very fact that our actions, thoughts, feelings and motions come within the range of our consciousness – at least a part of them – is the result of a terrible, prolonged 'must' ruling man's destiny: as the most endangered animal he *needed* help and protection; he needed his fellows, he was obliged to express his distress, he had to know how to make himself understood – and for all this he needed 'consciousness' first of all, consequently, to 'know' himself what he lacked, to 'know' how he felt and to 'know' what he thought. For, to repeat it once more, man, like every living creature, thinks unceasingly, but does not know it; the thinking which is becoming conscious of itself is only the smallest part thereof, we may say, the most superficial part, the worst part: for this conscious thinking alone is done in words, that is to say, in the symbols for communication, by means of which the origin of consciousness is revealed. In short, the development of speech and the development of consciousness (not of reason, but of reason becoming self-conscious) go hand in hand. Let it be further accepted that it is not only speech that serves as a bridge between man and man, but also the looks, the pressure and the gestures; our becoming conscious of our sense impressions, our power of being able to fix them, and as it were to locate them outside of ourselves, has increased in proportion as the necessity has increased for communicating them to *others* by means of signs. The sign-inventing man is at the same time the man who is always more acutely self-conscious; it is only as a social animal that man has learned to become conscious of himself – he is doing so still, and doing so more and more. As is obvious, my idea is that consciousness does not properly belong to the individual existence of man, but rather to the social and gregarious nature in him; that, as follows therefrom, it is only in relation to communal and gregarious utility that it is finely developed; and that consequently each of us, in spite of the best intention of understanding himself as individually as possible, and of 'knowing himself', will always just call into consciousness the non-individual in him, namely, his 'averageness' – that our thought itself is continuously as it were outvoted by the character of consciousness – by the imperious 'genius of the species' therein – and is translated back into the perspective of the herd. Fundamentally our actions are in an incomparable manner altogether personal, unique and absolutely individual – there is no doubt about it; but as soon as we translate them into consciousness, they do not appear so any longer ... This is the proper phenomenalism and perspectivism as I understand it: the nature of animal consciousness involves the notion that the world of which we can become conscious is only a superficial and symbolic world, a generalised and vulgarised world: that everything which becomes conscious becomes just thereby shallow, meagre, relatively stupid – a generalisation, a symbol, a characteristic of the herd; that with the evolving of consciousness there is always combined a great, radical perversion, falsification, superficialisation, and generalisation. Finally, the growing consciousness is a danger, and whoever lives among the most conscious Europeans knows even that it is a disease.

Friedrich Wilhelm Nietzsche, *The Joyful Wisdom (The Gay Science)* [1882] tr Thomas Common (London: T.N. Foulis, 1910) pp. 296–300, no. 354.

17. The Lure of the Simple Distinction

Mary Midgley

Man has always had a good opinion of himself, and with reason. What, however, is essentially the ground of it? What finally (you may ask) does distinguish man from the animals?

Nearly everything is wrong with this question.

First – as I have been saying – unless we take man to be a machine or an angel, it should read 'distinguish man *among* the animals,' and animals of this planet at that, with no extraterrestrial nonsense to give us all the drawbacks of religion and none of its benefits.

Second, as the question is usually put, it asks for a single, simple, final distinction, and for one that confers praise. This results, I suppose, from the old tradition of defining things by genus and differentia; that is, by naming first the class to which each thing belongs, and then the characteristic which marks it out from other members of that class. This rather hopeful scheme is supposed to enable us to find a formula stating the essence of each thing (or rather of each natural kind). And the differentia ought indeed to be in some way the thing's characteristic excellence, its central function – since that, and not just some chance quality (as in 'featherless biped'), is useful in helping us to place it sensibly, in telling us, therefore, what it is really like. The old, more or less Aristotelian, definition of man as a rational animal follows this pattern and is its best-known example.[1]

Now most people today would with good reason reject this scheme as too ambitious to use outside the human scene. We cannot expect (they would agree) that things not made by man will necessarily have an essence we can grasp and a simple characteristic excellence we can see the point of. Evaluating snails from the human point of view is a fallible process and should be taken as such. We can certainly find marks that will help us to classify and understand them. But we had better not claim that by doing so we have finally expressed their true nature in a simple formula.

People are slower, however, to see that the same obstacle blocks us when we ask 'What is the characteristic excellence of Man?' If we mean 'What would seem distinctive about him to a nonhuman observer?' we would need first to know that observer's frame of reference, and what contrasts would strike him. If we mean 'What is the best and most important thing within human life?' the question is a real one, and we can try to answer it. But it is not about biological classification. It is a question in moral philosophy. And we do not help ourselves at all in answering it if we decide in advance that the answer ought to be a single, simple characteristic, unshared by other species, such as the differentia is meant to be. Why should a narrow morality necessarily be the right one? Why should not our excellence involve our whole nature? The Platonic exaltation of the intellect above all our other faculties is a particular moral position and must be defended as such against others; it cannot ride into acceptance on the back of a crude method of taxonomy.

Oversimplicity, in fact, is what wrecks the notion of essence. Grading qualities as *more* and *less essential* – that is, more and less important to the species concerned – is not silly at all. Aristotle was doing this when he rejected two-footedness as a proper genus for man. It simply was not central enough in the life of the species; 'Bird and Man for instance are two-footed, but their two-footedness is diverse and differentiated.'[2] Birds and men, in fact, have dispensed with the support of forefeet for distinct though parallel reasons; if one mentioned those reasons, calling birds winged or flying animals and men handed or manipulative ones, one would be saying things of much greater interest. Flying and having hands are fairly essential properties, in that they make a great difference in the characteristic life of the creature. They are helpful in explaining it, where the negative 'two-footed' is not. Similarly, Lorenz criticizes Desmond Morris for 'over-emphasizing, in his book *The Naked Ape*, the beastliness of man ... He minimizes the unique properties and faculties of man in an effectively misleading manner. The outstanding and biologically relevant property of the human species is neither its partial hairlessness nor its 'sexiness', but its capacity for conceptual thought.'[3]

Lorenz's point is that conceptual thought is a *structural* property, one affecting the whole organization of the life of the species, while hairlessness and 'sexiness' in his view are minor, more local properties that affect it much less pervasively. And because each species does have its own way of life, structural properties can indeed be unique to a species. But not all of them are, and even where they are unique, that does not prove them excellent, even from the species' own point of view. Any species can have pervasive and characteristic bad habits. Conversely, what is good does not have to be unique to a species. For instance, in describing beavers, we should certainly say that their engineering capacity was one of their most outstanding features. But this does not isolate them. The elements of this capacity are present in their heritage: beavers are rodents, and gnawing, burrowing, and building industriously are a part of rodent life. And termites build, moles burrow, bees are industrious. What makes beavers special is a particular *combination and further development* of these basic faculties. Again, if we consider the extraordinarily keen and effective eyes of birds of prey, we are not forced to isolate them. We need to know that all birds have pretty good sight, which is necessary to flying, and that predators in general have to be sharper and better equipped than their prey. Or again, if the talk is of elephants, we can do justice to the miracle of the trunk without pretending that nobody else has a nose.

Structural properties, then, do not have to be exclusive or necessarily excellent. Nor do they have to be black-or-white, yes-or-no matters. And certainly no one of them is enough alone to define or explain a species. We commonly employ a cluster of them, whose arrangements as *more* or *less essential* can be altered from time to time for many reasons. And what is really characteristic is the shape of the whole cluster.

The various things that have been proposed as differentia for man – conceptual thought or reason, language, culture, self-consciousness, tool using, productivity, laughter, a sense of the future, and all the rest – form part of such a cluster, but none of them can monopolize it or freeze it into finality. There are always more that we have not thought of mentioning yet, and among them the most obvious. What would we say about someone who had all the characteristics just mentioned, but none of the normal human affections? These, of course, are plainly very like those of many other species, so they do not get named as the differentiae. But shortage of them is the commonest reason for calling people inhuman. Because of this sort of thing, it is really not possible to find a mark that distinguishes man from 'the animals' without saying *which* animals. We resemble different ones in different ways. It is also essential to remember how immensely they differ from one another. In certain central respects, all social mammals, including us, are far more like one another than any is like a snake or a codfish, or even a bee.

The logical point is simply that, in general, living creatures are quite unlike mathematical terms, whose essence really can be expressed in a simple definition. A triangle without three sides ceases to be a triangle. But a flightless bird does not cease to be a bird, nor a flying fish a fish. What is special about each creature is not a single, unique quality but a rich and complex arrangement of powers and qualities, some of which it will certainly share with its neighbors. And the more complex the species, the more true this is. To expect a single differentia is absurd.

And it is not even effectively flattering to the species, since it obscures our truly characteristic richness and versatility.

Mary Midgley, *The Beast and Man – The Roots of Human Nature* (London: Methuen, 1980) pp. 203–7.

1. Aristotle himself did not give this definition, though his argument at *Ethics* 1.7 and elsewhere does suggest it. Nor (certainly) did he ever proclaim that everything should be defined in the way described. He disliked such sweeping schemes and, if asked how things should be defined, would probably have answered that 'it is the mark of an educated man to expect in each subject the sort of precision of which it is capable' (*Ethics* 1.3).
2. *De Partibus Animalium* 1.3
3. *Studies in Animal and Human Behaviour*, tr. R.D. Martin (London, 1970), vol. I, p. 14.

Part II
Dominion and the Limits to Power

1. The Golden Age

Plato   427–347 B.C.

Stranger: ... The life about which you ask, when all the fruits of the earth sprang up of their own accord for men, did not belong at all to the present period of revolution, but this also belonged to the previous one. For then, in the beginning, God ruled and supervised the whole revolution, and so again, in the same way, all the parts of the universe were divided by regions among gods who ruled them, and, moreover, the animals were distributed by species and flocks among inferior deities as divine shepherds, each of whom was in all respects the independent guardian of the creatures under his own care, so that no creature was wild, nor did they eat one another, and there was no war among them, nor any strife whatsoever. To tell all the other consequences of such an order of the world would be an endless task. But the reason for the story of the spontaneous life of mankind is as follows: God himself was their shepherd, watching over them, just as man, being an animal of different and more divine nature than the rest, now tends the lower species of animals. And under his care there were no states, nor did men possess wives or children; for they all came to life again out of the earth, with no recollection of their former lives. So there were no states or families, but they had fruits in plenty from the trees and other plants, which the earth furnished them of its own accord, without help from agriculture. And they lived for the most part in the open air, without clothing or bedding; for the climate was tempered for their comfort, and the abundant grass that grew up out of the earth furnished them soft couches. That, Socrates, was the life of men in the reign of Cronus; but the life of the present age, which is said to be the age of Zeus, you know by your own experience. Would you be able and willing to decide which of them is the more blessed?
Young Socrates: Certainly not.
Stranger: Shall I, then, make some sort of a judgement for you?
Young Socrates: Do so, by all means.
Stranger: Well, then, if the foster children of Cronus, having all this leisure and the ability to converse not only with human beings but also with beasts, made full use of all these opportunities with a view to philosophy, talking with the animals and with one another and learning from every creature that, through possession of some peculiar power he may have had in any respect beyond his fellows' perceptions tending towards an increase of wisdom, it would be easy to decide that

the people of those old times were immeasurably happier than those of our epoch. Or if they merely ate and drank till they were full and gossiped with each other and the animals, telling such stories as are even now told about them in that case, too, it would, in my opinion, be very easy to reach a decision. However, let us pass those matters by, so long as there is no one capable of reporting to us what the desires of the people in those days were in regard to knowledge and the employment of speech. The reason why we revived this legend must be told, in order that we may get ahead afterwards. For when the time of all those conditions was accomplished and the change was to take place and all the earth-born race had at length been used up, since every soul had fulfilled all its births by falling into the earth as seed its prescribed number of times, then the helmsman of the universe dropped the tiller and withdrew to his place of outlook, and fate and innate desire made the earth turn backwards. So, too, all the gods who shares, each in his own sphere, the rule of the Supreme Spirit, promptly perceiving what was taking place, let go the parts of the world which were under their care. And as the universe was turned back and there came the shock of collision, as the beginning and the end rushed in opposite directions, it produced a great earthquake within itself and caused a new destruction of all sorts of living creatures. But after that, when a sufficient time had elapsed, there was rest now from disturbance and confusion, calm followed the earthquakes, and the world went on its own accustomed course in orderly fashion, exercising care and rule over itself and all within itself, and remembering and practising the teachings of the Creator and Father to the extent of its power, at first more accurately and at last more carelessly; and the reason for this was the material element in its composition, because this element, which was inherent in the primeval nature, was infected with great disorder before the attainment of the existing orderly universe. For from its Composer the universe has received only good things; but from its previous condition it retains in itself and creates in the animals all the elements of harshness and injustice which have their origin in the heavens. Now as long as the world was nurturing the animals within itself under the guidance of the Pilot, it produced little evil and great good; but in becoming separated from him it always got on most excellently during the time immediately after it was let go, but as time went on and it grew forgetful, the ancient condition of disorder prevailed more and more and towards the end of the time reached its height, and the universe, mingling but little good with much of the opposite sort, was in danger of destruction for itself and those within it. Therefore at that moment God, who made the order of the universe, perceived was in dire trouble, and fearing that it might founder in the tempest confusion and sink in the boundless sea of diversity, he took again his place as its helmsman, reversed whatever had become unsound and unsettled in the previous period when the world was left to itself, set the world in order, restored it and made it immortal and ageless.

So now the whole tale is told; but for our purpose of exhibiting the nature of the king it will be enough to revert to the earlier part of the story. For when the universe was turned again into the present path of generation, the age of individuals came again to a stop, and that led to new processes, the reverse of those which had gone before. For the animals which had grown so small as almost to disappear grew larger, and those newly born from the earth with hoary hair died and passed below the earth again. And all other things changed, imitating the condition of the universe and conforming to it, and so too pregnancy and birth and nurture necessarily imitated and conformed to the rest; for no living creature could any longer come into being by the union of other elements, but just as the universe was ordered to be the ruler of its own course, so in the same way the parts were ordered, so far as they could, to grow and beget and give nourishment of themselves under the same guidance.

And now we have come at last to the point for the sake of which this whole discourse was begun. For much might be said, and at great length, about the other animals, their previous forms and the causes of their several changes; but about mankind there is less to say and it is more to our purpose. For men, deprived of the care of the deity who had possessed and tended us, since most of the beasts who were by nature unfriendly had grown fierce, and they themselves were feeble and unprotected, were ravaged by the beasts and were in the first ages still without resources or skill; the food which had formerly offered itself freely had failed them, and they did not yet know how to provide for themselves, because no necessity had hitherto compelled them.

Plato, 'The Statesman' in Harold N. Fowler and W.R.M. Lamb (tr) *Plato* (London: Heinemann, 1925) 271d–4c.

...ls are for Our Use

384–322 B.C.

But whether any person is such by nature, and whether it is advantageous and just for any one to be a slave or no, or whether all slavery is contrary to nature, shall be considered hereafter; not that it is difficult to determine it upon general principles, or to understand it from matters of fact; for that some should govern, and others be governed, is not only necessary but useful, and from the hour of their birth some are marked out for those purposes, and others for the other, and there are many species of both sorts. And the better those are who are governed the better also is the government, as for instance of man, rather than the brute creation: for the more excellent the materials are with which the work is finished, the more excellent certainly is the work; and wherever there is a governor and a governed, there certainly is some work produced; for whatsoever is composed of many parts, which jointly become one, whether conjunct or separate, evidently show the marks of governing and governed; and this is true of every living thing in all nature; nay, even in some things which partake not of life, as in music; but this probably would be a disquisition too foreign to our present purpose. Every living thing in the first place is composed of soul and body, of these the one is by nature the governor, the other the governed; now if we would know what is natural, we ought to search for it in those subjects in which nature appears most perfect, and not in those which are corrupted; we should therefore examine into a man who is most perfectly formed both in soul and body, in whom this is evident, for in the depraved and vicious the body seems to rule rather than the soul, on account of their being corrupt and contrary to nature. We may then, as we affirm, perceive in an animal the first principles of herile and political government; for the soul governs the body as the master governs his slave; the mind governs the appetite with a political or a kingly power, which shows that it is both natural and advantageous that the body should be governed by the soul, and the pathetic part by the mind, and that part which is possessed of reason; but to have no ruling power, or an improper one, is hurtful to all; and this holds true not only of man, but of other animals also, for tame animals are naturally better than wild ones, and it is advantageous that both should be under subjection to man; for this is productive of their common safety: so is it naturally with the male and the female; the one is superior, the other inferior; the one governs, the other is governed; and the same rule must necessarily hold good with respect to all mankind. Those men therefore who are as much inferior to others as the body is to the soul, are to be thus disposed of, as the proper use of them is their bodies, in which their excellence consists; and if what I have said be true, they are slaves by nature, and it is advantageous to them to be always under government. He then is by nature formed a slave who is qualified to become the chattel of another person, and on that account is so, and who has just reason enough to know that there is such a faculty, without being indued with the use of it; for other animals have no perception of reason, but are entirely guided by appetite, and indeed they vary very little in their use from each other; for the advantage which we receive, both from slaves and tame animals, arises from their bodily strength administering to our necessities; for it is the intention of nature to make the bodies of slaves and freemen different from each other, that the one should be robust for their necessary purposes, the others erect, useless indeed for what slaves are employed in, but fit for civil life, which is divided into the duties of war and peace; though these rules do not always take place, for slaves have sometimes the bodies of freemen, sometimes the souls; if then it is evident that if some bodies are as much more excellent than others as the statues of the gods excel the human form, every one will allow that the inferior ought to be slaves to the superior; and if this is true with respect to the body, it is still juster to determine in the same manner, when we consider the soul; though it is not so easy to perceive the beauty of the soul as it is of the body. Since then some men are slaves by nature, and others are freemen, it is clear that where slavery is advantageous to any one, then it is just to make him a slave ...

But as there are many sorts of provision, so are the methods of living both of man and the brute creation very various; and as it is impossible to live without food, the difference in that particular makes the lives of animals so different from each other. Of beasts, some live in herds, others separate, as is most convenient for procuring themselves food; as some of them live upon flesh, others on fruit, and others on whatsoever they light on, nature having so distinguished their course of life, that they can very easily procure themselves subsistence; and as the same things are not agreeable to all, but one animal likes one thing and another another, it follows that the lives of those beasts who live upon flesh must be different from the lives of those who live on fruits; so is it with men, their lives differ greatly from each other; and of all these the shepherd's is the idlest, for they live upon the flesh of tame animals, without any trouble, while they are obliged to change their habitations on account of their flocks, which they are compelled to follow, cultivating, as it were, a living farm. Others live exercising violence over living creatures, one pursuing this thing, another that, these preying upon men; those who live near lakes and marshes and rivers, or the sea itself, on fishing, while others are fowlers, or hunters of wild beasts; but the greater part of mankind live upon the produce of the earth and its cultivated fruits; and the manner in which all those live who follow the direction of nature, and labour for their own subsistence, is nearly the same, without ever thinking to procure any provision by way of exchange or merchandise, such are shepherds, husbandmen, robbers, fishermen, and hunters: some join different employments together, and thus live very agreeably; supplying those deficiencies which were wanting to make their subsistence depend upon themselves only: thus, for instance, the same person shall be a shepherd and a robber, or a husbandman and a hunter; and so with respect to the rest, they pursue that mode of life which necessity points out. This provision then nature herself seems to have furnished all animals with, as well immediately upon their first origin as also when they are arrived at a state of maturity; for at the first of these periods some of them are provided in the womb with proper nourishment, which continues till that which is born can get food for itself, as is the case with worms and birds; and as to those which bring forth their young alive, they have the means for their subsistence for a certain time within themselves, namely milk. It is evident then that we may conclude of those things that are, that plants are created for the sake of animals, and animals for the sake of men; the tame for our use and provision; the wild, at least the greater part, for our provision also, or for some other advantageous purpose, as furnishing us with clothes, and the like. As nature therefore makes nothing either imperfect or in vain, it necessarily follows that she has made all these things for men: for which reason what we gain in war is in a certain degree a natural acquisition; for hunting is a part of it, which it is necessary for us to employ against wild beasts; and those men who being intended by nature for slavery are unwilling to submit to it, on which occasion such a war is by nature just: that species of acquisition then only which is according to nature is part of economy; and this ought to be at hand, or if not, immediately procured, namely, what is necessary to be kept in store to live upon, and which are useful as well for the state as the family.

Aristotle, 'Politics' in William Ellis (tr) *The Politics of Aristotle*, Everyman edn (London: Dent, 1912) 1254b2–6b12.

3. Rational Domination

St Augustine   354–430

It is not without significance, that in no passage of the holy canonical books there can be found either divine precept or permission to take away our own life, whether for the sake of entering on the enjoyment of immortality, or of shunning, or ridding ourselves of anything whatever. Nay, the law, rightly interpreted, even prohibits suicide, where it says, 'Thou shalt not kill.' This is proved specially by the omission of the words 'thy neighbour', which are inserted when false witness is forbidden: 'Thou shalt not bear false witness against thy neighbour.' Nor yet should any one on this account suppose he has not broken this commandment if he has borne false witness only against himself. For the love of our neighbour is regulated by the love of ourselves, as it is written, 'Thou shalt love thy neighbour as thyself.' If, then, he who makes false statements about himself is not less guilty of bearing false witness than if he had made them to the injury of his neighbour; although in the commandment prohibiting false witness only his neighbour is mentioned, and persons taking no pains to understand it might suppose that a man was allowed to be a false witness to his own hurt; how much greater reason have we to understand that a man may not kill himself, since in the commandment, 'Thou shalt not kill,' there is no limitation added nor any exception made in favour of any one, and least of all in favour of him on whom the command is laid! And so some attempt to extend this command   even to beasts and cattle, as if it forbade us to take life from any creature. But if so, why not extend it also to the plants, and all that is rooted in and nourished by the earth? For though this class of creatures have no sensation, yet they also are said to live, and consequently they can die; and therefore, if violence be done them, can be killed. So, too, the apostle, when speaking of the seeds of such things as these, says, 'That which thou sowest is not quickened except it die;' and in the Psalm it is said, 'He killed their vines with hail.' Must we therefore reckon it a breaking of this commandment, 'Thou shalt not kill,' to pull a flower? Are we thus insanely to countenance the foolish error of the Manichæans? Putting aside, then, these ravings, if, when we say, Thou shalt not kill, we do not understand this of the plants, since they have no sensation, nor of the irrational animals that fly, swim, walk, or creep, since they are dissociated from us by their want of reason, and are therefore by the just appointment of the Creator subjected to us to kill or keep alive for our own uses; if so, then it remains that we understand that commandment simply of man. The commandment is, 'Thou shalt not kill man;' therefore neither another nor yourself, for he who kills himself still kills nothing else than man.

St Augustine, *The City of God*, tr Marcus Dods (Edinburgh: T.T. Clark, 1877) Book 1, pp. 30–2.

4. Unrestricted Dominion

St Thomas Aquinas   1225–74

OF THE MASTERSHIP BELONGING TO MAN IN THE STATE OF INNOCENCE

(In four articles)
We next consider the mastership which belonged to man in the state of innocence. Under this head there are four points of inquiry: (1) Whether man in the state of innocence was master over the animals? (2) Whether he was master over all creatures? (3) Whether in the state of innocence all men were equal? (4) Whether in that state man would have been master over men?

First Article
Whether Adam in the State of Innocence had
Mastership over the Animals?

We proceed thus to the first article:
Objection 1. It would seem that in the state of innocence Adam had no mastership over the animals. For Augustine says (Genesis ix, 14), that the animals were brought to Adam, under the direction of the angels, to receive their names from him. But the angels need not have intervened thus, if man himself were master over the animals. Therefore in the state of innocence man had no mastership of the animals.
Objection 2. Further, it is unfitting that elements hostile to one

another should be brought under the mastership of one. But many animals are hostile to one another, as the sheep and the wolf. Therefore all animals were not brought under the mastership of man.

Objection 3. Further, Jerome says: 'God gave man mastership over the animals, although before sin he had no need of them: for God foresaw that after sin animals would become useful to man.' Therefore at least before sin, it was unfitting for man to make use of his mastership.

Objection 4. Further, it is proper to a master to command. But a command is not given rightly save to a rational being. Therefore man had no mastership over the irrational animals.

On the contrary, it is written (Genesis i. 26): 'Let him have dominion over the fishes of the sea, and the birds of the air, and the beasts of the earth' (Vulgate, 'and the whole earth').

I answer that, as above stated (Q. xcv., A. I) for his disobedience to God, man was punished by the disobedience of those creatures which should be subject to him. Therefore in the state of innocence, before man had disobeyed, nothing disobeyed him that was naturally subject to him. Now all animals are naturally subject to man. This can be proved in three ways. First, from the order observed by nature; for just as in the generation of things we perceive a certain order of procession of the perfect from the imperfect (thus matter is for the sake of form; and the imperfect form, for the sake of the perfect), so also is there order in the use of natural things; thus the imperfect are for the use of the perfect; as the plants make use of the earth for their nourishment, and animals make use of plants, and man makes use of both plants and animals. Therefore it is in keeping with the order of nature, that man should be master over animals. Hence the Philosopher says (Politics i. 5) that the hunting of wild animals is just and natural, because man thereby exercises a natural right. Secondly, this is proved from the order of Divine Providence which always governs inferior things by the superior. Wherefore, as man, being made to the image of God, is above other animals, these are rightly subjected to his government. Thirdly, this is proved from a property of man and of other animals. For we see in the latter a certain participated prudence of natural instinct, in regard to certain particular acts; whereas man possesses a universal prudence as regards all practical matters. Now whatever is participated is subject to what is essential and universal. Therefore the subjection of other animals to man is proved to be natural.

Reply Objection 1. A higher power can do many things that an inferior power cannot do to those which are subject to them. Now an angel is naturally higher than man. Therefore certain things in regard to animals could be done by angels, which could not be done by man; for instance, the rapid gathering together of all the animals.

Reply Objection 2. In the opinion of some, those animals which now are fierce and kill others, would, in that state, have been tame, not only in regard to man, but also in regard to other animals. But this is quite unreasonable. For the nature of animals was not changed by man's sin, as if those whose nature now it is to devour the flesh of others, would then have lived on herbs, as the lion and falcon. Nor does Bede's gloss on Genesis i.30, say that trees and herbs were given as food to all animals and birds, but to some. Thus there would have been a natural antipathy between some animals. They would not, however, on this account have been excepted from the mastership of man: as neither at present are they for that reason excepted from the mastership of God, Whose Providence has ordained all this. Of this Providence man would have been the executor, as appears even now in regard to domestic animals, since fowls are given by men as food to the trained falcon.

Reply Objection 3. In the state of innocence man would not have had any bodily need of animals – neither for clothing, since then they were naked and not ashamed, there being no inordinate motions of concupiscence – nor for food, since they fed on the trees of paradise – nor to carry him about, his body being strong enough for that purpose. But man needed animals in order to have experimental knowledge of their natures. This is signified by the fact that God led the animals to man, that he might give them names expressive of their respective natures.

Reply Objection 4. All animals by their natural instinct have a certain participation of prudence and reason: which accounts for the fact that cranes follow their leader, and bees obey their queen. So all animals would have obeyed man of their own accord, as in the present state some domestic animals obey him.

Second Article
Whether Man had Mastership over all Other Creatures?

We proceed thus to the Second Article:

Objection 1. It would seem that in the state of innocence man would not have had mastership over all other creatures. For an angel naturally has a greater power than man. But, as Augustine says (De Trin. iii, 8), 'corporeal matter would not have obeyed even the holy angel.' Much less therefore would it have obeyed man in the state of innocence.

Objection 2. Further, the only powers of the soul existing in plants are nutritive, augmentative, and generative. Now these do not naturally obey reason; as we can see in the case of any one man. Therefore, since it is by his reason that man is competent to have mastership, it seems that in the state of innocence man had no dominion over plants.

Objection 3. Further, whosoever is master of a thing, can change it. But man could not have changed the course of the heavenly bodies; for this belong to God alone, as Dionysius says (Ep. ad Polycarp. vii). Therefore man had no dominion over them.

On the contrary, it is written (Genesis 1, 26): 'That he may have dominion over ... every creature.'

I answer that, man in a certain sense contains all things; and so according as he is master of what is within himself, in the same way he can have mastership over other things. Now we may consider four things in man: his reason, which makes him like to the angels; his sensitive powers, whereby he is like the animals; his natural forces, which liken him to the plants; and the body itself, wherein he is like to inanimate things. Now in man reason has the position of a master and not of a subject. Wherefore man had no mastership over the angels in the primitive state; so when we read 'all creatures', we must understand the creatures which are not made to God's image. Over the sensitive powers, as the irascible and concupiscible, which obey reason in some degree, the soul has mastership by commanding. So in the state of innocence man had mastership over the animals by commanding them. But of the natural powers and the body itself man is master not by commanding, but by using them. Thus also in the state of innocence man's mastership over plants and inanimate things consisted not in commanding or in changing them, but in making use of them without hindrance.

The answers to the objections appear from the above.

St Thomas Aquinas, 'Summa Theologica' in Fathers of the English Dominican Providence (trs) *The Summa Theologica of St Thomas Aquinas*, 2nd edn rev (London: Burns, Oates and Washbourne, 1922) Question 96.

5. Difference does Not Justify Domination

Michel E. de Montaigne   1533–92

We are neither superior nor inferior to the rest. All that is under heaven, says the sage, is subject to one law and one fate:

> Enshackled in the gruesome bonds of doom. (Lucretius)

Some difference there is; there are orders and degrees, but uner the aspect of one same Nature:

> But each sole thing
> Proceeds according to its proper wont,
> And all conserve their own distinctions, based
> In Nature's fixed decree. (Lucretius)

Man must be forced and lined up within the barriers of this organization. The poor wretch has no mind really to step over them. He is shackled and entangled, he is subjected to the same obligation as the other creatures of his order, and is of a very mediocre condition, without any real and essential prerogative and pre-eminence. That which he thinks and imagines himself to possess, neither has body nor can it be perceived. And if it be so that he alone of all the animals has this freedom of imagination, this licence of thought, which represents to him that which is, that which is not, that which he wills, the false and the true; it is an advantage sold to him very dearly, and of which he has very little cause to boast. For from it springs the principal source of all the ills that press upon him, sin, sickness, irresolution, affliction, despair.

I say then, to return to my theme, that there is no reason to image that the beasts do, through a natural and enforced instinct, the same things that we do by choice and skill. From like results we must infer like faculties (and from more abundant results, more abundant faculties); and we must consequently confess that the same reason, the same methods, that we employ in working are also employed by the animals (if not some other and better ones). Why do we imagine in them that natural compulsion, although we experience no such thing in ourselves? Besides that it is more honourable, and nearer allied to the Divinity, to be guided and obliged to act rightly by a natural and irresistible condition, than to act rightly by an impulsive and fortuitous liberty; and safer to leave the reins of our conduct in the hands of Nature than to keep them in our own. In the vanity of our presumption we prefer to owe our superiority to our own powers rather than to Nature's bounty. We endow the other animals with natural gifts and renounce them in their favour, in order to honour and ennoble ourselves with acquired gifts. And we do all this, it seems to me, in all simplicity, for I should prize as highly gifts that are purely and naturally my own, as those I had begged and collected from education. It is not in our power to acquire a higher recommendation than to be favoured by God and Nature.

Take the case of the fox, which the inhabitants of Thrace employ before they attempt to cross a frozen river, by letting it loose before them. If we saw him at the edge of the water approaching his ear very near to the ice in order to listen if, at a distance or near by, he can hear the noise of the water running underneath, and recoiling or advancing according as he perceives the ice to be thick or thin, should we not be justified in assuming that the same ideas pass through his head as would pass through ours, and that his natural sense has taught him to reason and conclude somewhat as follows: 'That which makes a noise, moves; that which moves is not frozen; that which is not frozen is liquid, and yields under a weight'? For to attribute that merely to an acute sense of hearing, without any reasoning or concluding, is an absurd notion, and not to be imagined. We must judge in like manner of the many wiles and strategems that the animals employ to defend themselves from our attacks upon them.

And if we would claim any superiority from the fact that we have it in our power to seize them, employ them in our service and use them at our pleasure, it is but the same advantage we have over one another. On these terms we have our slaves. Were there not women in Syria called Climacides, who, crouching on all fours, served as footstools or step-ladders to enable the ladies to mount into their coaches? And the majority of free people, for a very slight consideration, surrender their life and being into the power of others. The wives and concubines of the Thracians plead to be chosen to die upon their husbands' tombs ...

We condemn everything that appears strange to us and which we do not understand; and we do the same in our judgement of the animals. They resemble us in many ways, and from them we may, by comparison, draw some conclusions; but what can we know of those things that are peculiar to them?

Michel Eyquem de Montaigne, 'Apology for Raymond Sebond' [c.1592] in E.J. Trechman (tr) *Essays of Montaigne* (London: Oxford University Press, 1927) pp. 451–2, 460.

6. Animals in the Cosmic Hierarchy

Richard Hooker   1554–1600

In the matter of knowledge, there is between the angels of God and the children of men this difference: angels already have full and complete knowledge in the highest degree that can be imparted unto them; men, if we view them in their spring, are at the first without understanding or knowledge at all. Nevertheless from this utter vacuity they grow by degrees, till they come at length to be even as the angels themselves are. That which agreeth to the one now, the other shall attain unto in the end; they are not so far disjoined and severed, but that they come at length to meet. The soul of man being therefore at the first as a book, wherein nothing is and yet all things may be imprinted; we are to search by what steps and degrees it riseth unto perfection of knowledge.

Unto that which hath been already set down concerning natural agents this we must add, that albeit therein we have comprised as well creatures living as void of life, if they be in degree of nature beneath men; nevertheless a difference we must observe between those natural agents that work altogether unwittingly, and those which have though weak yet some understanding what they do, as fishes, fowls, and beasts have. Beasts are in sensible capacity as ripe even as men themselves, perhaps more ripe. For as stones, though in dignity of nature inferior unto plants, yet exceed them in firmness of strength or durability of being; and plants, though beneath the excellency of creatures endued with sense, yet exceed them in the faculty of vegetation and of fertility: so beasts, though otherwise behind men, may notwithstanding in actions of sense and fancy go beyond them; because the endeavours of nature, when it hath a higher perfection to seek, are in lower the more remiss, not esteeming thereof so much as those things do, which have no better proposed unto them.

The soul of man therefore being capable of a more divine perfection, hath (besides the faculties of growing unto sensible knowledge which is common unto us with beasts) a further ability, whereof in them there is no show at all, the ability of reaching higher than unto sensible things. Till we grow to some ripeness of years, the soul of man doth only store itself with conceits of things of inferior and more open quality, which afterwards do serve as instruments unto that which is greater; in the meanwhile above the reach of meaner creatures it ascendeth not.

Richard Hooker, *Laws of Ecclesiatical Polity* [1594] (London: Dent, 1907) Book 1, pp. 166–7.

7. The Right of Nature

Thomas Hobbes   1588–1679

We get a right over irrational creatures, in the same manner that we do over the persons of men; to wit, by force and natural strength. For if in the state of nature it is lawful for every one, by reason of that war which is of all against all, to subdue and also to kill men as oft as it shall seem to conduce unto their good; much more will the same be lawful against brutes; namely, at their own discretion to reduce those to servitude, which by art may be tamed and fitted for use, and to persecute and destroy the rest by a perpetual war as dangerous and noxious. Our dominion therefore over beasts, hath its original from the right of nature, not from divine positive right. For if such a right had not been before the publishing of the Sacred Scriptures, no man by right might have killed a beast for his food, but he to whom the divine pleasure was made manifest by holy writ; a most hard condition for men indeed, whom the beasts might devour without injury, and yet they might not destroy them. Forasmuch therefore as it proceeds from the right of nature, that a beast may kill a man, it is also by the same right that a man may slay a beast.

Thomas Hobbes, 'De Cive' [1642] in Sir William Molesworth (ed) *The English Works of Thomas Hobbes of Malmesbury* (London: John Bohn, 1841) vol. II, pp. 113–14.

8. Dominion is Subject to Law

Samuel Pufendorf   1632–92

We observe that brute beasts, which are below our condition of life, also enjoy liberty to some degree. But with them it is only of a low kind, since their strength and the dullness of their senses is confined within narrow limits, while their appetite is so base that it concerns itself with but few objects and with them in a very cursory manner, and is stirred only by the crude and everywhere obvious things which serve the belly. They have, furthermore, no customs, or law, or right which they are obligated to observe, either among themselves or towards men. Among a few there are some rudiments of marriage, but it is found only in the mere act of bodily conjunction, and some show of affection, but not in any bond of fidelity. As for the most of them no vestige remains of affection, once their desire has been satisfied, nor any care for shame or kinship. Many of them have a strong love for their offspring, which, however, lasts only until it can shift for itself; after this the parents take no further thought for their offspring, their love is entirely forgotten, nor do the offspring make any return to their parents, as if from a feeling of obligation, or bother themselves to render them any assistance. The beasts which live on flesh, tear and devour without scruple whatever pleases their appetite, and many of them in their savagery are brought to mutual destruction. Since they know no laws of ownership, on the gnawings of hunger they often fight fiercely for what is common to all, and no sense of propriety prevents their seizing what others had stored up for their own use. There is, indeed, no regard among them, no honour, no rule, no prerogative other than that acquired by mere superiority in strength.

Among some animals, indeed, likeness of kind often begets a form of friendship and society, and many, therefore, are accustomed to live in herds, while some, more ferocious than others, give vent to their savagery on other species rather than on their own. So Juvenal says:

The wild beast of similar genus spares his kindred spots. When did ever lion, though stronger, deprive his fellow-lion of life? In what woods did ever boar perish by the tusks of a boar larger than himself? The tigress of India maintains unbroken harmony with each tigress that ravens. Bears, savage to others, are yet at peace among themselves.

But aside from the fact that the above sentiment is expressed with considerable poetic licence, this relationship is scarcely a strong bond of lasting peace, since, forsooth, it is broken the instant a consideration of the belly interposes. Puppies play happily together, but throw a piece of meat among them, and at once you will see them fighting with one another. When some animals seem to show obedience, love, faithfulness, or gratitude towards me, it is due to mere habit, or the enticement of food. Remove these, and when their strength is sufficient, or there be something about a man to excite their appetite, they will not spare him. The conclusion is that no internal and moral restraint curtails the liberty of animals, but, on the other hand, their external movements are very often controlled by man through the use of force.

If, now, one asks why animals enjoy a liberty unrestrained by law, the simplest reply is, because God did not endow them with a mind that can comprehend law. For there seemed no need of great care in fostering and guarding the security of animals, which are not only produced by nature, in such great numbers, with high fecundity and little effort, but which also are without an immortal soul, their life coming only from a minute disposition and motion of particles of matter. And the Creator is pleased to manifest His power in producing and destroying them. Nor was there any great need of restraining the brute creation by laws, since their appetites are aroused only by hunger, thirst, and sexual passion, and can be slaked by the ready and copious provisions of nature; while man has strength and wit enough to prevent their licence, as it were, from doing him too great harm.

Now why the Creator was unwilling to endow man with a lawless liberty of this kind, and why such liberty would be utterly inappropriate to him is clear for many reasons drawn from the natural or acquired condition of human nature. The dignity of man's nature, and that excellence of his in which he surpasses other creatures, required that his actions should be made to conform to a definite rule, without which there can be no recognition of order, seemliness, or beauty. And so man has that supreme dignity, the possession of an immortal soul, furnished with the light of intellect and the faculty of judgement and choice, and most highly endowed for many an art. For this reason he is called 'a creature above all others precious and endowed with lofty reason, fitted to rule over the lower animals'. Solinus calls man an animal 'which the nature of things has set over all other animals by virtue of his passing judgement upon sense perceptions and his capacity for reason' ...

Now if we consider this faculty of mankind in its relation to things and animals which man uses and misuses, the proof that such use carries with it no injury to the animals can be found both in the nature of man, and in the concession of the Creator. For it is not likely that a most Good and Wise Creator should lay upon man, the first of earthly creatures, such a necessity that he cannot preserve his life without doing another creature an injury, which cannot avoid being associated with sin. There is the further express concession of God, which leaves no scruple that might arise in any way from the slaughter of animals. If this seems to raise any question of humanity that can be entirely removed by the mere consideration that God has assigned to them such a condition, and has given the race of men that faculty; and man in using this right, whether reposing in him by the act of God or conceded him, works no injury. Regarding plants and such other things as lack sense, there seems to be no difficulty, since it cannot be seen how they suffer any ill in being consumed by man; especially since they would be destroyed in any event by beasts or in the early change of seasons, while many of them would not flourish at all without the aid of man. We will not pause over the superstition of the Egyptians regarding abstinence from certain herbs.

Now regarding animate beings endowed with consciousness, to which loss of life is attended with suffering, many who have considered the licence of men over brutes from the point of pure reason, feel that some question may be raised. For it does not at once and without question follow that, because the Creator gave the first of men dominion over animals, He thereby granted him full licence so that he could even kill them for unnecessary uses ... Man has also dominion over man, yet he can exercise no such licence as that over his fellow man. Nor would men have had grounds to complain that the divine indulgence had been niggardly towards them, or that their necessities had been scantily provided for, if they had been denied power over the lives of animals, at least of such as offer no danger to human existence. For the labour performed by animals in cultivating the field, and the other things that come from them, such as milk, eggs, that are not necessary to continue the species, wool, and the like, would have been enough to support men after a fashion. Nor did man receive the power to use them at his pleasure for food, because of the fact that God commanded him to sacrifice them in His worship. For what is allowed men by a special command of God can still be unlawful except in that case. And this is the reason why many ancient philosophers disapproved of such slaughter. For why should man for the sake of superfluous pleasure take from a harmless animal the life given it by the Creator of them both, especially since men cannot excuse themselves by the example even of lions, wolves, or other carnivores? For nature has so formed these last that they cannot exist upon other than bloody food, and they reject the products of the soil; while the very opposite is true of man, who is nourished by other food, meat having to be prepared by cooking and seasoning before it agrees with his stomach.

Samuel Pufendorf, *The Law of Nature and Nations* [1688] trs. C.H. and W.A. Oldfather (New York: Oceana, 1931) vol. II, pp. 147–8 and 526–7.

9. The Workmanship Model

John Locke   1632–1704

But though this be a state of liberty, yet it is not a state of licence; though man in that state have an uncontrollable liberty to dispose of his person or possessions, yet he has not liberty to destroy himself, or so much as any creature in his possession, but where some nobler use than its bare preservation calls for it. The state of nature has a law of nature to govern it, which obliges every one; and reason, which is that law, teaches all mankind who will but consult it, that, being all equal and independent, no one ought to harm another in his life, health, liberty, or possessions. For men being all the workmanship of one omnipotent and infinitely wise Maker – all the servants of one sovereign Master, sent into the world by his order, and about his business – they are his property, whose workmanship they are, made to last during his, not one another's pleasure; and being furnished with like faculties, sharing all in one community of nature, there cannot be supposed any such subordination among us, that may authorize us to destroy one another, as if we were made for one another's uses, as the inferior ranks of creatures are for ours. Every one, as he is bound to preserve himself, and not to quit his station wilfully, so, by the like reason, when his own preservation comes not in competition, ought he, as much as he can, to preserve the rest of mankind, and may not, unless it be to do justice on an offender, take away or impair the life, or what tends to the preservation of the life, the liberty, health, limb, or goods of another.

John Locke, 'The Second Treatise of Government' in *John Locke; Two Treatises of Government*, ed Peter Laslett (Cambridge: Cambridge University Press, 1988) pp. 270–1.

10. Responsibility to the Weak

Alexander Pope   1688–1744

I cannot think it extravagant to imagine, that mankind are no less, in proportion, accountable for the ill use of their dominion over creatures of the lower rank of beings, than for the exercise of tyranny over their own species. The more entirely the inferior creation is submitted to our power, the more answerable we should seem for our mismanagement of it; and the rather, as the very condition of nature renders these creatures incapable of receiving any recompense in another life, for their ill treatment in this.

'Tis observable of those noxious animals, which have qualities most powerful to injure us, that they naturally avoid mankind, and never hurt us unless provoked, or necessitated by hunger. Man, on the other hand, seeks out and pursues even the most inoffensive animals on purpose to prosecute and destroy them.

Montaigne thinks it some reflection upon human nature itself, that few people take delight in seeing beasts caress or play together, but almost every one is pleased to see them lacerate and worry one another. I am sorry this temper is become almost a distinguishing character of our own nation, from the observation which is made by foreigners of our beloved pastimes, bear-baiting, cock-fighting, and the like. We should find it hard to vindicate the destroying of any thing that has life, merely out of wantonness; yet in this principle our children are bred up, and one of the first pleasures we allow them is the licence of afflicting pain upon poor animals; almost as soon as we are sensible what life is ourselves, we make it our sport to take it from other creatures. I cannot but believe a very good use might be made of the fancy which children have for birds and insects. Mr Locke takes notice of a mother who permitted them to her children, but rewarded or punished them as they treated them well or ill. This was no other than entering them betimes into a daily exercise of humanity, and improving their very diversion to a virtue.

I fancy, too, some advantage might be taken of the common notion, that 'tis ominous or unlucky to destroy some sorts of birds, as swallows or martins; this opinion might possibly arise from the confidence these birds seem to put in us by building under our roofs, so that it is a kind of violation of the laws of hospitality to murder them. As for robin-redbreasts in particular, 'tis not improbable they owe their security to the old ballad of 'The Children in the Wood'. However it be, I don't know, I say, why this prejudice, well improved and carried as far as it would go, might not be made to conduce to the preservation of many innocent creatures, which are now exposed to all the wantonness of an ignorant barbarity.

There are other animals that have the misfortune, for no manner of reason, to be treated as common enemies wherever found. The conceit that a cat has nine lives, has cost at least nine lives in ten of the whole race of 'em; scarce a boy in the streets but has in this point outdone Hercules himself, who was famous for killing a monster that had but three lives. Whether the unaccountable animosity against this useful domestic may be any cause of the general persecution of owls (who are a sort of feather'd cats) or whether it be only an unreasonable pique the moderns have taken to a serious countenance, I shall not determine. Tho' I am inclined to believe the former; since I observe the sole reason alleged for the destruction of frogs is because they are like toads. Yet amidst all the misfortunes of these unfriended creatures, 'tis some happiness that we have not yet taken a fancy to eat them: for should our countrymen refine upon the French never so little, 'tis not to be conceived to what unheard-of torments owls, cats and frogs may be yet reserved.

When we grow up to men, we have another succession of sanguinary sports; in particular hunting. I dare not attack a diversion which has such authority and custom to support it, but must have leave to be of opinion, that the agitation of that exercise, with the example and number of the chasers, not a little contribute to resist those checks, which compassion would naturally suggest in behalf of the animal pursued. Nor shall I say with Monsieur Fleury, that this sport is a remain of the Gothic barbarity; but I must animadvert upon a certain custom yet in use with us, and barbarous enough to be derived from the Goths, or even the Scythians; I mean that savage compliment our huntsmen pass upon ladies of quality, who are present at the death of a stag, when they put the knife in their hands to cut the throat of a helpless, trembling and weeping creature

... Questuque cruentus,
Atque imploranti similis ...

But if our sports are destructive, our gluttony is more so, and in a more inhuman manner. Lobsters roasted alive, pigs whipt to death, fowls sewed up, are testimonies of our outrageous luxury. Those who (as Seneca expresses it) divide their lives betwixt an anxious conscience and a nauseated stomach, have a just reward of their gluttony in the diseases it brings with it: for human savages, like other wild beasts, find snares and poison in the provisions of life, and are allured by their appetite to their destruction. I know nothing more shocking or horrid, than the prospect of one of their kitchens cover'd with blood, and filled with the cries of creatures expiring in tortures. It gives one an image of a giant's den in a romance, bestrow'd with scattered heads and mangled limbs of those who were slain by his cruelty.

The excellent Plutarch (who has more strokes of good-nature in his writings than I remember in any author) cites a saying of Cato to this effect, that 'tis no easie task to preach to the belly, which has no ears. 'Yet if (says he) we are ashamed to be so out of fashion as not to offend, let us at least offend with some discretion and measure. If we kill an animal for our provision, let us do it with the meltings of compassion, and without tormenting it. Let us consider, that 'tis in its own nature cruelty to put a living creature to death; we at least destroy a soul that has sense and perception ...' In the life of Cato the Censor, he takes occasion from the severe disposition of that man to discourse in this manner: 'It ought to be esteem'd a happiness to mankind, that our humanity has a wider sphere to exert itself in, than bare justice. It is no more than the obligation of our very birth to practise equity to our own kind, but humanity may be extended thro' the whole order of creatures, even to the meanest: Such actions of charity are the overflowing of a mild good-nature on all below us. It is certainly the part of a well-natured man to take care of his horses and dogs, not only while they are foals and whelps, but even when their old age has made them incapable of service.'

History tells us of a wise and polite nation that rejected a person of the first quality, who stood for a judicatory office, only because he had been observed, in his youth, to take pleasure in tearing and murdering of birds. And of another that expelled a man out of the Senate, for dashing a bird against the ground which had taken shelter in his bosom. Every one knows how remarkable the Turks are for their humanity in this kind: I remember an Arabian author, who has written a treatise to show, how far a man, supposed to have subsisted in a desert island, without any instruction, or so much as the sight of any other man, may, by the pure light of nature, attain the knowledge of philosophy and virtue. One of the first things he makes him observe is, that universal benevolence of nature in the protection and perservation of its creatures. In imitation of which, the first act of virtue he thinks his self-taught philosopher would of course fall into is, to relieve and assist all the animals about him in their wants and distresses.

Ovid has some very tender and pathetic lines applicable to this occasion.

Quid merutistis oves, placidum pecus, inque regendos
Natum homines, pleno qua fertis in Ubere nectar?
Mollia qua nobis vestras velamina lanas
Prabetis; vitaque magis quam morte juvatis.
Quid meruëre boves, animal sine fraude dobisque,
Innocuum, simplex, natum tolerare labores:
Qui potuit, curvi dempto modo pondere aratri,
Ruricolam mastare suum ...
Quam male consuevit, quam se parat ille cruori
Impius himano, Vituli qui guttura cultro
Rumpit, & immotas prabet mugitibus aures!
Aut qui vagitus similes puerilibus hoedum
Edentem jugulare potest!

Perhaps that voice or cry so nearly resembling the human, with which Providence has endued so many different animals, might purposely be given them to move our pity, and prevent those cruelties we are too apt to inflict on our fellow-creatures.

There is a passage in the book of Jonas, when God declares his unwillingness to destroy Nineveh, where methinks that compassion of the Creator, which extends to the meanest rank of his creatures, is expressed with wonderful tenderness – 'Should I not spare Nineveh the great city, wherein are more than six-score thousand persons – and also much cattel?' And we have in Deuteronomy a precept of great good-nature of this sort, with a blessing in form annexed to it, in those words: 'If thou shalt find a bird's nest in the way, thou shalt not take the damm with the young; But thou shalt in any wise let the damm go; that it may be well with thee, and that thou may'st prolong thy days.'

To conclude, there is certainly a degree of gratitude owing to those animals that serve us; as for such as are mortal or noxious, we have a right to destroy them; and for those that are neither of advantage or prejudice to us, the common enjoyment of life is what I cannot think we ought to deprive them of.

This whole matter, with regard to each of these considerations, is set in a very agreeable light in one of the Persian fables of Pilpay, with which I shall end this paper.

A traveller passing thro' a thicket, and feeling a few sparks of a fire, which some passengers had kindled as they went that way before, made up to it. On a sudden the sparks caught hold of a bush, in the midst of which lay an adder, and set it in flames. The adder entreated the traveller's assistance, who tying a bag to the end of his staff, reached it, and drew him out: He then bid him go where he pleased, but never more be hurtful to men, since he owed his life to a man's compassion. The adder, however, prepared to sting him, and when he expostulated how unjust it was to retaliate good with evil, I shall do no more (said the adder) than what you men practise every day, whose custom it is to requite benefits with ingratitude. If you cannot deny this truth, let us refer it to the first we meet. The man consented, and seeing a tree, put the question to it in what manner a good turn was to be recompensed: If you mean according to the usage of men (replied the tree) by its contrary: I have been standing here these hundred years to protect them from the scorching sun, and in requital they have cut down my branches, and are going to saw my body into planks. Upon this the adder insulting the man, he appealed to a second evidence, which was granted, and immediately they met a cow. The same demand was made, and much the same answer given, that among men it was certainly so. I know it (said the cow) by woeful experience; for I have served a man this long time with milk, butter and cheese, and brought him besides a calf every year: but now I am old, he turns me into this pasture, with design to sell me to a butcher, who will shortly make an end of me. The traveller upon this stood confounded, but desired of courtesy one trial more, to be finally judged by the next beast they should meet. This happened to be a fox, who upon hearing the story in all its circumstances, could not be persuaded it was possible for the adder to enter in so narrow a bag. The adder to convince him went in again; when the fox told the man he had now his enemy in his power, and with that he fastened the bag, and crushed him to pieces.

Alexander Pope, 'Of Cruelty to Animals' [1713] in Rosalind Vallance (ed) *A Hundred English Essays* (London: Thomas Nelson, 1950) pp. 159–65.

11. Animals do Not Make War on Humans

Jean-Jacques Rousseau   1712–88

Accustomed from their infancy to the inclemencies of the weather and the rigour of the seasons, inured to fatigue, and forced, naked and unarmed, to defend themselves and their prey from other ferocious animals, or to escape them by flight, men would acquire a robust and almost unalterable constitution. The children, bringing with them into the world the excellent constitution of their parents, and fortifying it by the very exercises which first produced it, would thus acquire all the vigour of which the human frame is capable. Nature in this case treats them exactly as Sparta treated the children of her citizens: those who come well formed into the world she renders strong and robust, and all the rest she destroys; differing in this respect from our modern communities, in which the State, by making children a burden to their parents, kills them indiscriminately before they are born.

The body of a savage man being the only instrument he understands, he uses it for various purposes, of which ours, for want of practice, are incapable: for our industry deprives us of that force and agility, which necessity obliges him to acquire. If he had had an axe, would he have been able with his naked arm to break so large a branch from a tree? If he had had a sling, would he have been able to throw a stone with so great velocity? If he had had a ladder, would he have been so nimble in climbing a tree? If he had had a horse, would he have been himself so swift of foot? Give civilised man time to gather all his machines about him, and he will no doubt easily beat the savage; but if you would see a still more unequal contest, set them together naked and unarmed, and you will soon see the advantage of having all our forces constantly at our disposal, of being always prepared for every event, and of carrying one's self, as it were, perpetually whole and entire about one.

Hobbes contends that man is naturally intrepid, and is intent only upon attacking and fighting. Another illustrious philosopher holds the opposite, and Cumberland and Puffendorf also affirm that nothing is more timid and fearful than man in the state of nature; that he is always in a tremble, and ready to fly at the least noise or the slightest movement. This may be true of things he does not know; and I do not doubt his being terrified by every novelty that presents itself, when he neither knows the physical good or evil he may expect from it, nor can make a comparison between his own strength and the dangers he is about to encounter. Such circumstances, however, rarely occur in a state of nature, in which all things proceed in a uniform manner, and the face of the earth is not subject to those sudden and continual changes which arise from the passions and caprices of bodies of men living together. But savage man, living dispersed among other animals, and finding himself betimes in a situation to measure his strength with theirs, soon comes to compare himself with them; and, perceiving that he surpasses them more in adroitness than they surpass him in is to be no longer afraid of them. Set a bear, or a wolf, ...oust, agile, and resolute savage, as they all are, armed with ...d a good cudgel, and you will see that the danger will be at ...both sides, and that, after a few trials of this kind, wild beasts, wh...n are not fond of attacking each other, will not be at all ready to attack man, whom they will have found to be as wild and ferocious as themselves. With regard to such animals as have really more strength than man has adroitness, he is in the same situation as all weaker animals, which notwithstanding are still able to subsist; except indeed that he has the advantage that, being equally swift of foot, and finding an almost certain place of refuge in every tree, he is at liberty to take or leave it at every encounter, and thus to fight or fly, as he chooses. Add to this that it does not appear that any animal naturally makes war on man, except in case of self-defence or excessive hunger, or betrays any of those violent antipathies, which seem to indicate that one species is intended by nature for the food of another.

Jean-Jacques Rousseau, 'Second Discourse' [1755] in *The Social Contract and Discourses,* Everyman edn (London: Dent, 1913) pp. 178–80.

12. Animals may be Used

Immanuel Kant   1724–1804

In any country, there are, of course, various products of nature that nevertheless, because of their abundance, must be regarded as artifacts (*artefacta*) of the state, inasmuch as the land would not have produced so much had there been no state or powerful government, but the inhabitants had, instead, remained in a state of nature. For example, because of shortage of feed or beasts of prey, hens (the most useful species of bird), sheep, swine, cattle, and the like would either not exist at all in the country in which I live or would be exceedingly rare if there were no government to safeguard the acquisitions and possessions of its inhabitants. The same is true of the number of people in a country, for without a government it can only remain small, just as it is in the American wilderness; indeed, the people would still remain small in numbers even if we were to assume that they are much more industrious than those who live under a government (as, of course, they are not). The inhabitants of such a country would be very sparse, since they would be unable to spread themselves out on the land with their households, because of the danger of devastation by other men, by savages, or by beasts of prey. Consequently, under such circumstances, there would be no adequate means of livelihood for such a great number of people as now populate a country. Inasmuch as crops (for example, potatoes) and domestic animals are products of human labour, at least as far as their quantity is concerned, we can say that they may be used, consumed, or destroyed (killed). In the same vein, it might seem that we could say that the supreme authority in the state, the sovereign, also has the right to lead his subjects into a war as though it were a hunting expedition and to march them onto a field of battle as though it were a pleasure excursion on the grounds that they are for the most part products of his own activity.

This kind of argument for a right (which in all likelihood hovers darkly in the minds of monarchs) is indeed valid with respect to animals, which can be owned by human beings, but it absolutely cannot be applied to a human being, and especially not to a citizen. A citizen must always be regarded as a colegislative member of the state (that is, not merely as a means, but at the same time as an end in itself), and as such he must give his free consent through his representatives, not only to the waging of war in general, but also to any particular declaration of war. It is only under this limiting condition that the state may demand and dispose of a citizen's services if they involve being exposed to danger.

Immanuel Kant, *Metaphysics of Morals* [1797] tr John Ladd (New York: Bobbs-Merrill, 1965) pp. 345–6.

13. Dominion and Property

Johann Gottlieb Fichte   1762–1814

There are also animals upon the earth who may be useful to men in their accidences, or whose substances may be useful to men; their meat to eat, their skin for various purposes, etc. If any citizen intends to subject only the accidences of such animals to his ends, he must first make the animal subservient to him. Moreover, since the animals are fed and kept alive only by organized matter, and since it is not to be expected that nature will take care of them after they have once been made art-products, he must replace nature in becoming their nourisher. This, again, is conditioned by the *exclusive possession* of the animal; only *I* must feed and attend the animal always, and only I, therefore, must be allowed to enjoy the advantages it may confer.

There is no reason why each one should not have the same right to take possession of an animal. Hence, exclusive property in animals can be obtained only through the original property-compact in a state.

There is, however, this difference between property in land and property in animals, that the land can always be designated by the place in space which it occupies, whereas the animal has free motion and can not be so specified. How then is it to be made known what particular animal belongs to a certain person and to no one else?

If it should, firstly, be the case that only certain kinds of animals are ever made exclusive property of persons, it would be, above all, necessary to specify to what kinds of animals the right of property can extend. This would enable every one to know at once whether an animal, coming within his reach, is the property of anybody or not. For instance, if I have a right to hunt, I may shoot the deer, because it is a deer; but I may not shoot the horse, although I do not know who owns it. Why not? Simply because I know that horses have been declared property by the state, and that, hence, some one is surely the owner of the horse, although I do not know who. If some one should tame a deer, it doubtless becomes his property. But if the deer runs away and I shoot it, am I, therefore, responsible for it as for the horse? Clearly not, since the state has not declared that the right of property extends to deer. The right of the original owner of an animal remains, although the animal may run away from him, because in the original compact it has been agreed upon in what kinds of animals the right of property may rest. Such animals are called tame animals. The ground why precisely these kinds of animals have been declared property in a state and none others, lies in their fitness for serving the needs of men in their accidences, in the possibility of taming them, and in the necessity of taking care of them.

But let no one believe that this taming and feeding of the animals is the true legal ground of the right of property in them. That legal ground is to be found only in the property-compact. Hence, if any one should introduce a new kind of tamed animals, for instance, buffaloes or kangaroos, the state would first have to declare them animals to which the right of property should extend, since otherwise they would be properly treated like wild animals. If they were kept locked up in such a one's house or yard, they would, of course, thereby become part of his house property. It is also clear, from the foregoing, that the state has a perfect right to prohibit the keeping of certain animals, for instance, of lions, bears, monkeys, and unnecessary dogs.

But the next question is: to whom does this or that animal which in its kind had been declared property, belong? These animals may either remain under the immediate supervision of their proprietor, so that he can at any moment prove them to be his – unless, indeed, they be unlawfully in his possession – or they may be feeding in a common pasture with the animals of other proprietors. How, in the latter case, can ownership be proved? Happily, animal instinct has supplied the neglect of the lawgiver. Tame animals accustom themselves to their stables, and the judge decides according to the instinct of the animal as to who is its owner. Yet, would it not be proper to have all tame animals marked in some way, the marks to be as inviolable as those which designate the several pieces of landed property, and thus to place them under the direct protection of the law? (In the armies the horses are, indeed, so marked.) Each bill of sale of an animal ought to be accompanied by a specification of the mark upon the animal, so as to guarantee perfect safety to the purchaser.

In reference to some animals, the right of property is determined by the space they occupy, to wit, when they are of a kind which can be confined to a certain locality, and must be so confined to serve their end. In such cases the owner is proprietor of the animals, because he is proprietor of the locality wherein they exist (fish-lakes, bird-houses, etc.) When the fish is out of the lake, or the bird out of the cage, they have no owner.

The right of property is always granted with reference to the end to be accomplished by it; so, likewise, the right of property in animals. Now, most animals are useful, not only in their accidences (as milk, eggs, and their labour) but also in their substance; we eat their meat, make use of their skins, etc.

It may, perhaps, be deemed expedient to limit this right of property in the *substance* of the animals, and to specify this limit in the original property-compact. Such a limitation would not invalidate the right of property in the animals, so far as it has reference to their accidences, but it would restrict the right to do with the substance of the animals as might please the owner. The state, for instance, might provide that a certain number of cattle shall always be kept in the state, and that, therefore, only a limited number may be slaughtered. If such a law is passed in a state, another law must be passed, of course, providing that, at all times, a certain amount of food for cattle shall be raised and set aside, since otherwise the former legislation would cancel itself.

Animals propagate themselves, and their young ones are their accidences. The ownership of the old animals involves the ownership of their whole future breed, precisely as the ownership of a grain of wheat involves that of all the future wheat which may grow out of it.

It may be lawful, however, to limit the number of cattle which shall be kept in a commonwealth.

The animals have free movement and feed from the products of the field. Hence, when an animal trespasses upon the fields of a farmer, there arises this dispute between the agriculturist and the cattle-raiser:

The former says: 'I have the right to cultivate land in this state, and the products of the field are mine.' The latter replies: 'I have the right to raise cattle in the same state, and the state knows well enough that animals are determined by their nature to hunt food.'

This dispute the state has to settle by establishing laws, based on the original property-compact, whereby either the one party alone is compelled to keep his cattle in a closed pasture, or, which is more fair, the other party is also compelled to fence in his fields. Whosoever neglects to do his duty in this respect, must not only repay damages, but also makes himself liable to an additional fine. If accidents happen in spite of all precautions, they are to be considered as misfortunes for which neither party is liable, and which the state has to repair.

Wild animals are animals the accidences whereof can not be subjected to the use of men. Their substance, however, may be useful, only through the death of such animals. In so far they belong to the whole state, or are undivided property. They become the property of individuals only by being caught or killed.

There is, however, one great distinction between these animals. Some of them are inclosed in an element which is not subject to men, at least in so far as these animals live in and of it, namely, the fishes in rivers and seas. Hence, they do no harm to men. It is the same with some other animals, which, though they live in and of the same element as men, the earth, yet do so little damage to it, that they are not materially injurious; namely, the birds. The harm which they do to the crops, etc, is amply repaid by their killing off injurious insects.

It is quite different with another class of wild animals, which are injurious to men and destroy man's labours. All kinds of game belong to this class. Now, since the state guarantees to each person his property, it must protect that of the agriculturist against the devastation of these animals. Everywhere wilderness must give way to culture, and the irregular modes of living, which cannot be surely known to suffice for man's subsistence, must give way to regular pursuits.

Hence, the state must make fishing a lawful pursuit, which is best accomplished – with a view to make it an orderly business – by assigning specific districts of rivers and lakes to fishermen, who thus become the proprietors of these districts in the manner of agriculturists, of course only in regard to the use of these districts.

They would not have the right, for instance, to prevent navigation within their districts, since that would not interfere with their pursuits in the same localities.

But all wild animals of the second class must be regarded by the state as absolutely injurious; not as a source of emolument, but as a class of enemies. The first object of hunting is not, therefore, to possess the game, but to protect the farmer; and the state must undertake this protection precisely as it undertakes to protect property against thieves and incendiaries, namely, by appointing men especially intrusted with this duty. Of course, the agriculturist retains the right to shoot any piece of game or wild animal which may stray within his fence, and does not need to wait for the official gamekeeper's arrival, precisely as each citizen retains the right to quench the flames, if his house should be put on fire, without waiting for the arrival of the official firemen.

Now, since the chase affords considerable profits, it is not to be assumed that the people ought to pay taxes for sustaining it; rather, it ought to pay itself. For this reason it will be most advantageous to grant to a certain class of persons, game-keepers, the right of chase in specified districts – as in the case of the fishermen – which right thus becomes their property. Let it be well understood, that the right of property is not vested in the animals, as such, but only in the killing of this class of animals within the specified district. Nevertheless, since it is the chief object of the chase to protect the agriculturist, the game-keeper can receive this right only on the express condition that the game is truly kept harmless by him, and that he holds himself responsible for all the damages farmers may receive by reason of such game.

No one but the gamekeeper can possibly have the intention to take care of or protect the game, and this end is granted to him only in so far as the game is not injurious to the purposes of culture; or in so far as the game remains in the forest. Whoever kills them there, trespasses upon the property of the gamekeeper; whereas, he who kills them upon his fields is perfectly justified. For the life of the game is not guaranteed by the state; indeed, the game has no end for the state; on the contrary, their death is the end which the state has in view. The killed game belongs to the gamekeeper of the district; the damage they have inflicted whilst at large must be paid by him, whether the animals be worth much or nothing at all.

The first end of the chase is to protect culture; all other ends are accidental. Hence, it is properly made the duty of the gamekeeper to exterminate, likewise, wild animals, from which he himself derives no benefit, and which may not be immediately injurious to himself; as, for instance, eagles, hawks, sparrows, nay, even caterpillars and other injurious insects. Other animals, which are immediately injurious to himself, because they destroy his game, such as foxes, wolves, etc, he will exterminate of his own accord.

If the chase were a burden without profit, government would have to undertake it. But since it is combined with considerable advantages, which generally increase in value the less attention the gamekeeper pays to his proper business – and herein lies the root of the chief difficulty – and since, therefore, complaints will often be preferred against the gamekeepers, it is expedient to keep them under the close supervision of the government. The right of keeping game, being combined with emoluments, cannot remain, therefore, in the hands of the government. Government would always be an interested party as the possessor of the game, and the agriculturist would have no impartial judge.

Johann Gottlieb Fichte, *The Science of Rights* [1798] tr. A.E. Kroeger (London: Routledge and Kegan Paul, 1970) pp. 302–11.

14. The Limits to Power

John Stuart Mill   1806–73

In a Mansion-House report of last week, it is stated that one William Burn was charged before the Lord Mayor 'with having most cruelly beaten one of the horses he was driving in a waggon. He had been sitting on the middle horse, which was without reins, and he struck one of the poor animals most desperately about the head with the butt-end of his whip. The horse fell, and the prisoner struck it even more brutally when down. The Lord Mayor expressed great indignation at the conduct of the defendant, and was about to fine him to the utmost extent, when he suddenly learned that he had a large family,' whereupon he said to him 'You deserve the highest punishment; but I cannot think of punishing your wife and children. The sentence of the court upon you is, that you pay a fine of ten shillings, or be confined in the House of Correction for fourteen days.' The defendant 'thanked his lordship, and paid the fine.'

We regard this leniency, together with the reason assigned for it, as a match for the most unthinking and ill-judged exercises of magisterial discretion with which the London police-courts have lately favoured us. 'A large family' has long been familiar as an excuse for begging, and recommendation to the benevolent electors whose suffrages confer the responsible office of parish beadle. Hereafter, it seems it is to be a licence for violating the law, and, worse than that, for committing acts of savage brutality, which excite not merely regret but indignation that such a creature should have a wife and children in his power to treat in the same manner.

Let us look at the thing first on the general principles of the administration of justice. The Lord Mayor thought the man deserved the full penalty, and was about to inflict it. He thought, therefore, that the highest fine which the law authorised, forty shillings, or in default of payment fourteen days in the House of Correction (for the law actually allows no longer term), would not have been more than enough to make some impression upon the man's obdurate nature, and induce him and others like him to put some restraint upon their brutality. And who will not agree with the Lord Mayor in so thinking? Rather, who will not go far beyond him? Who does not see that the maximum penalty ought to be much higher, that it is ridiculously and lamentably inadequate; that it was fixed so low, not because it was thought sufficient, but because the promoters of the bill were too happy to get the consent of the Legislature to any penalty at all, in order at least to establish the fact that the law disapproves and stigmatises ferocious abuse of power against the helpless? This recognition, we suspect, is the chief part of the good which the Act against Cruelty to Animals has yet done; and even that, the insignificance of the penalties in a great measure neutralizes, for if those who commit the crime are now aware that their superiors think it wrong, they cannot suppose that it is thought to be anything very bad by people who are so very much more than gentle in their repression of it.

But to return to the Lord Mayor. He thought, at any rate, that forty shillings, or imprisonment for fourteen days, was not more than sufficient severity to give the man a salutary lesson. If forty shillings were not more than enough, ten shillings are less than enough; and the man is let off with a penalty which the magistrate knows to be insufficient to correct his own vicious habits and to deter others. And this because the Lord Mayor 'cannot think of punishing' the wife and children. In the first place, the instantaneous payment of the ten shillings renders it more than probable that ample means existed for a fortnight's support. In the second place, did the law intend that the inconvenience which a man's wife and children may suffer, from penalties imposed on himself, should be a reason for not inflicting the punishment which he has merited by his misdeeds? Would the Lord

Mayor have given him the benefit of this excuse if he had stolen a handkerchief? No, truly; there would have been no thought then of hardship to the family, although in that case the offence might actually have been committed to relieve their hunger; and at any rate, the offender would not have proved to be the kind of man from whom it would be a mercy to have separated them.

Real consideration for the wife and children would have spoken a very different language to the magistrate. It would have said something like this – A man capable of the act of which this man is found guilty, must be one of two things. He is either a wretch who wantonly ill-treats a helpless being, for the pleasure of tyranny, because it is in his power and cannot resist; or an irritable, violent creature, who on the smallest provocation (provocation from the unconscious dumb animal who slaves to death for his benefit!) flies into an uncontrollable rage, and cannot restrain himself from wreaking a savage vengeance. One of these two characters the man must be; and on either supposition we may infer what sort of a taskmaster he is to the unfortunate woman and the unfortunate children, who are as much in his power, and much more liable to rouse his ferocious passions than the animal over whom he tyrannised. It really seems to us, that they are more objects of pity for being compelled to live with such a man than they would have been for being deprived during a whole fortnight of his agreeable society, and that it would have been a greater kindness to them to have seized the opportunity of giving a severe lesson to one who had the power of making so many human creatures miserable. If he could have been made less brutal to his horses it would have made him less brutal to his human victims likewise. Disgusting enough it is that animals like these should have wives and children; and disgusting that, merely because they are of the male sex, they should have the whole existence of these dependants as much under their absolute control as slave masters in any modern slave country have that of their slaves; and without even the wretched compensation of supporting them – for in that rank the wife always, and the children by the time they are seven or eight years old, take part, to the full measure of their physical strength, in the labours for the support of the family. But as if all this was not enough, the man is told by a magistrate, that because he has a family to ill-use, he may indulge himself in ill-using any other creatures who come in his way, and may practise on them the amiable propensities of which his family are to reap the full enjoyment. We have no doubt the Lord Mayor meant kindly; but the tender mercies of thoughtless people are cruel; and we wish that, instead of being thanked by the ruffian whom he let off, he had deserved the thanks of the public for a rigorous exercise of the most important moral power a magistrate possesses –

that of putting down strongly and manfully, by word and deed, the brutal vices of the worst part of the populace.

John Stuart Mill, 'The Case of William Burn', in *The Morning Chronicle*, 17 November 1846.

15. Animals as Utilities

Henry Sidgwick   1838–1900

To whatever extent the surface of the earth is appropriated to the exclusive occupation of individuals, its vegetable products will, of course, belong primarily to the occupier, as – generally speaking – no one else can enjoy them without his consent. Often, of course, their growth is altogether due to his exertion and care, or admits of being materially aided thereby; in fact the encouragement of such production is, as we have seen, the chief end that justifies the appropriation of the soil. So again, where the labour and care of the occupier is directly applied to tame animals that feed on the natural produce of the soil, the appropriation to him of the progeny of the animals is justified on similar grounds. By 'tame' animals we mean such as are normally within the control of some man, so that they can at any time be physically taken into possession by him: if they stray beyond his control, it is through accident or the enticement of other men, and their ownership is normally ascertainable by some natural or artificial mark. It is obvious that the exclusive use of such animals may be appropriated to individuals without much more difficulty than that of inanimate things. The case is different with animals which we call 'wild', i.e. which require some process of capture, uncertain in its results, before a man can take possession of them. Still, if their existence is entirely or largely due to the labour and care of the landowner or his employees, our general principle would seem to justify us in prohibiting other men from taking possession of them, so far as their ownership is clearly ascertainable, as e.g. if they belong to a particular rare species. Where this ascertainment is practically impossible, the prohibition would be futile: but even then, so far as they can be prevented from straying, their exclusive use is indirectly secured by appropriating the land. It is, however, obvious that in the case of land whose only useful produce consists in wild animals and vegetables, capable of living and thriving without human labour or protection, one main argument for allowing appropriation is absent. Still, the appropriation of such land – assuming a fair compensation for the utilities thus withdrawn from the community – seems to be as legitimate an application of the individualistic principle as its appropriation for agricultural use; provided that its appropriation tends materially to increase the utility obtainable from such land: in considering which we have to take into account the enjoyment derived from hunting wild animals, as well as the utility of the animals when captured. If the whole *quantum* of utility obtainable in these two, and any other, ways, when the land is allotted to the exclusive use of individuals, is clearly greater than the whole *quantum* of utility that may be expected to result from leaving it common, appropriation, whether by sale outright, or lease for a term of years, seems clearly expedient: if it is clearly less, the utilitarian legislator will unhesitatingly decide to prohibit such exclusive use; but, of course, in any concrete case the balance of utilities may be difficult to ascertain.

Henry Sidgwick, *The Elements of Politics* [1891] (London: Macmillan, 1891) pp. 70–2.

16. Nature Teaches Mutual Aid

Peter Kropotkin   1842–1921

That life in societies is the most powerful weapon in the struggle for life, taken in its widest sense, has been illustrated by several examples on the foregoing pages, and could be illustrated by any amount of evidence, if further evidence were required. Life in societies enables the feeblest insects, the feeblest birds, and the feeblest mammals to resist, or to protect themselves from, the most terrible birds and beasts of prey; it permits longevity; it enables the species to rear its progeny with the least waste of energy and to maintain its numbers albeit a very slow birth-rate; it enables the gregarious animals to migrate in search of new abodes. Therefore, while fully admitting that force, swiftness, protective colours, cunningness, and endurance to hunger and cold, which are mentioned by Darwin and Wallace, are so many qualities making the individual, or the species, and fittest under certain circumstances, we maintain that under *any* circumstances sociability is the greatest advantage in the struggle for life. Those species which willingly or unwillingly abandon it are doomed to decay; while those animals which know best how to combine, have the greatest chances of survival and of further evolution although they may be inferior to others in *each* of the faculties enumerated by Darwin and Wallace, save the intellectual faculty. The highest vertebrates, and especially mankind, are the best proof of this assertion. As to the intellectual faculty, while every Darwinist will agree with Darwin that it is the most powerful arm in the struggle for life, and the most powerful factor of further evolution, he also will admit that intelligence is an eminently social faculty. Language, imitation, and accumulated experience are so many elements of growing intelligence of which the unsociable animal is deprived. Therefore we find, at the top of each class of animals, the ants, the parrots, and the monkeys, all combining the greatest sociability with the highest development of intelligence. The fittest are thus the most sociable animals and sociability appears as the chief factor of evolution, both directly, by securing the well-being of the species while diminishing the waste of energy, and indirectly, by favouring the growth of intelligence.

Moreover, it is evident that life in societies would be utterly impossible without a corresponding development of social feelings and, especially, of a certain collective sense of justice growing to become a habit. If every individual were constantly abusing its personal advantages without the others interfering in favour of the wronged, no society-life would be possible. And feelings of justice develop, more or less, with all gregarious animals. Whatever the distance from which the swallows or the cranes come, each one returns to the nest it has built or repaired last year. If a lazy sparrow intends appropriating the nest which a comrade is building, or even steals from it a few sprays of straw, the group interferes against the lazy comrade; and it is evident that without such interference being the rule, no nesting associations of birds could exist. Separate groups of penguins have separate resting-places and separate fishing abodes, and do not fight for them. The droves of cattle in Australia have particular spots to which each group repairs to rest, and from which it never deviates; and so on. We have any number of direct observations of the peace that prevails in the nesting associations of birds, the villages of the rodents, and the herds of grass-eaters; while, on the other side, we know of few sociable animals which so continually quarrel as the rats in our cellars do, or as the morses, which fight for the possession of a sunny place on the shore. Sociability thus puts a limit to physical struggle, and leaves room for the development of better moral feelings. The high development of parental love in all classes of animals, even with lions and tigers, is generally known ...

Compassion is a necessary outcome of social life. But compassion

also means a considerable advance in general intelligence and sensibility. It is the first step towards the development of higher moral
sentiments. It is, in its turn, a powerful factor of further evolution ...

Happily enough, competition is not the rule either in the animal
world or in mankind. It is limited among animals to exceptional
periods, and natural selection finds better fields for its activity.
Better conditions are created by the elimination of competition by
means of mutual aid and mutual support. In the great struggle for
life – for the greatest possible fulness and intensity of life with the
least waste of energy – natural selection continually seeks out the
ways precisely for avoiding competition as much as possible. The
ants combine in nests and nations; they pile up their stores, they rear
their cattle – and thus avoid competition; and natural selection picks
out of the ants' family the species which know best how to avoid
competition, with its unavoidably deleterious consequences. Most
of our birds slowly move southwards as the winter comes, or gather
in numberless societies and undertake long journeys – and thus
avoid competition. Many rodents fall asleep when the time comes
that competition should set in; while other rodents store food for
the winter, and gather in large villages for obtaining the necessary
protection when at work. The reindeer, when the lichens are dry in
the interior of the continent, migrate towards the sea. Buffaloes
cross an immense continent in order to find plenty of food. And the
beavers, when they grow numerous on a river, divide into two
parties, and go, the old ones down the river, and the young ones up
the river – and avoid competition. And when animals can neither fall
asleep, nor migrate, nor lay in stores, nor themselves grow their
food like the ants, they do what the titmouse does, and what
Wallace has so charmingly described: they resort to new kinds of
food – and thus, again, avoid competition.

'Don't compete! – competition is always injurious to the species,
and you have plenty of resources to avoid it!' That is the *tendency* of
nature, not always realized in full, but always present. That is the
watchword which comes to us from the bush, the forest, the river, the
ocean. 'Therefore combine – practise mutual aid! That is the surest
means for giving to each and to all the greatest safety, the best
guarantee of existence and progress, bodily, intellectual, and moral.'
That is what Nature teaches us; and that is what all those animals
which have attained the highest position in their respective classes have
done.

Prince Peter Kropotkin, *Mutual Aid; A Factor of Evolution* (Harmondsworth:
    Penguin, 1939) pp. 60–2, 72–3.

17. Dominion as Power

Bertrand Russell   1872–1970

I met recently a mountain climber of considerable skill and first-rate intellect, in fact a man of international eminence in the world of learning, who somewhat surprised me by a theory to which, he said, his observations had led him. Mountains, he said, are made to be climbable: on rocks, foot-holds and handholds are found just at such distances as are necessary for a full-grown man. He contended that, if men were twice the size they are, existing climbs would become too easy to be interesting, but few new ones would be possible, so that mountain climbing would no longer be interesting. Apparently he believed that, in the remote geological ages when rocks were formed, they were fashioned with a view to the pleasure of those few eccentrics who like to risk their lives by walking up precipices as if they were flies. It seemed to me that the mountain goat, the ibex and the chamois might have other views on this subject. If they had a parliament, they would congratulate each other on the clumsiness of this horrid creature Man, and would render thanks that his cunning is impeded by such a clumsy body. Where they skip, he crawls; where they bound freely, he clings to a rope. Their evidence of beneficence in nature would be the opposite of the mountain climber's and yet every bit as convincing.

There was an eighteenth-century divine who gravely maintained that rabbits have white tails for the convenience of those who wish to shoot them. What would rabbits have said to him if they could speak? Imagine the punishment that would have been inflicted on him if, in the course of some Gulliver's travels, he had come across a country where the rabbits held the government. Imagine the district attorney, a rabbit selected for his powers of eloquent invective, addressing the jury of rabbits. 'This degraded creature', he would thunder, 'who, incredible as it may appear, has been regarded with respect by his own abominable species, solemnly maintains that there is no wickedness in the wanton destruction of our noblest citizens to satisfy the gross appetites of so-called human beings. Nay, worse, he is so perverted as to suppose that our white tails, which, as every right-thinking rabbit knows, serve the purpose of aesthetic delight, were given us in order that it might be the easier to assassinate us.' I cannot doubt that the eminent divine would suffer the utmost rigour of the law.

I have often wondered what turkeys would think of Christmas if they were capable of thought. I am afraid they would hardly regard it as a season of peace and goodwill.

An eminent biologist of my acquaintance looks forward to the day when rats will hold the primacy among animals and human beings will have been deposed.

There is no impersonal reason for regarding the interests of human beings as more important than those of animals. We can destroy animals more easily than they can destroy us; that is the only solid basis of our claim to superiority. We value art and science and literature, because these are things in which we excel. But whales might value spouting, and donkeys might maintain that a good bray is more exquisite than the music of Bach. We cannot prove them wrong except by the exercise of arbitrary power. All ethical systems, in the last analysis, depend upon weapons of war.

Bertrand Russell, 'If Animals Could Talk' [1932] in Henry Ruja (ed) *Mortals and Others; Bertrand Russell's American Essays 1931–1935* (London: Allen and Unwin, 1975) vol. 1, pp. 120–1.

18. Critique of the Principle of Domination

Max Horkheimer   1895–1973

Modern insensitivity to nature is indeed only a variation of the pragmatic attitude that is typical of western civilization as a whole. The forms are different. The early trapper saw in the prairies and mountains only the prospects of good hunting; the modern business-man sees in the landscape an opportunity for the display of cigarette posters. The fate of animals in our world is symbolized by an item printed in newspapers of a few years ago. It reported that landings of planes in Africa were often hampered by herds of elephants and other beasts. Animals are here considered simply as obstructors of traffic. This mentality of man as the master can be traced back to the first chapters of Genesis. The few precepts in favour of animals that we encounter in the Bible have been interpreted by the most outstanding religious thinkers, Paul, Thomas Aquinas and Luther, as pertaining only to the moral education of man, and in no wise to any obligation of man toward other creatures. Only man's soul can be saved; animals have but the right to suffer. 'Some men and women', wrote a British churchman a few years ago, 'suffer and die for the life, the welfare, the happiness of others. This law is continually seen in operation. The supreme example of it was shown to the world (I write with reverence) on Calvary. Why should animals be exempted from the operation of this law or principle?' Pope Pius IX did not permit a society for the prevention of cruelty to animals to be founded in Rome because, as he declared, theology teaches that man owes no duty to any animal. National Socialism, it is true, boasted of its protection of animals, but only in order to humiliate more deeply those 'inferior races' whom they treated as mere nature.

These instances are quoted only in order to show that pragmatic reason is not new. Yet, the philosophy behind it, the idea that reason, the highest intellectual faculty of man, is solely concerned with instruments, nay, is a mere instrument itself, is formulated more clearly and accepted more generally today than ever before. The principle of domination has become the idol to which everything is sacrificed.

The history of man's efforts to subjugate nature is also the history of man's subjugation by man. The development of the concept of the ego reflects this twofold history.

It is very hard to describe precisely what the languages of the western world have at any given time purported to connote in the term ego – a notion steeped in vague associations. As the principle of the self endeavouring to win in the fight against nature in general, against other people in particular, and against its own impulses, the ego is felt to be related to the functions of domination, command, and organization. The ego principle seems to be manifested in the outstretched arm of the ruler, directing his men to march or dooming the culprit to execution. Spiritually, it has the quality of a ray of light. In penetrating the darkness, it startles the ghosts of belief and feeling, which prefer to lurk in shadows. Historically, it belong pre-eminently to an age of caste privilege marked by a cleavage between intellectual and manual labour, between conquerors and conquered. Its dominance is patent in the patriarchal epoch. It could scarcely have played a decisive role in matriarchal days – to recall Bachofen and Morgan – when chthonic deities were worshiped. Nor may one properly ascribe ego or self to the slave of antiquity, to the amorphous mass at the base of the social pyramid.

The principle of domination, based originally on brute force, acquired in the course of time a more spiritual character. The inner voice took the place of the master in issuing commands. The history of western civilization could be written in terms of the growth of the ego as the underling sublimates, that is internalizes, the commands of his master who has preceded him in self-discipline. From this standpoint, the leader and the elite might be described as having effected coherence and logical connection between the various transactions of daily life. They enforced continuity, regularity, even uniformity in the productive process, primitive though it was. The ego within each subject became the embodiment of the leader. It established a rational nexus between the variegated experiences of different persons. Just as the leader groups his men as foot soldiers and mounted troops, just as he charts the future, so the ego classifies experiences by categories or species and plans the life of the individual. French sociology has taught that the hierarchical arrangement of primitive general concepts reflected the organization of the tribe and its power over the individual. It has shown that the whole logical order, the ranking of concepts according to priority and posteriority, inferiority and superiority, and the marking out of their respective domains and boundaries, mirror social relations and the division of labour ...

In traditional theology and metaphysics, the natural was largely conceived as the evil, and the spiritual or supernatural as the good. In popular Darwinism, the good is the well-adapted, and the value of that to which the organism adapts itself is unquestioned or is measured only in terms of further adaptation. However, being well adapted to one's surroundings is tantamount to being capable of coping success-fully with them, of mastering the forces that beset one. Thus the theoretical denial of the spirit's antagonism to nature – even as implied in the doctrine of interrelation between the various forms of organic life, including man – frequently amounts in practice to subscribing to the principle of man's continuous and thoroughgoing domination of nature. Regarding reason as a natural organ does not divest it of the trend to domination or invest it with greater potentialities for recon-ciliation. On the contrary, the abdication of the spirit in popular Darwinism entails the rejection of any elements of the mind that transcend the function of adaptation and consequently are not instru-ments of self-preservation. Reason disavows its own primacy and professes to be a mere servant of natural selection. On the surface, this new empirical reason seems more humble toward nature than the reason of the metaphysical tradition. Actually, however, it is arrogant, practical mind riding roughshod over the 'useless spiritual', and dismissing any view of nature in which the latter is taken to be more than a stimulus to human activity. The effects of this view are not confined to modern philosophy.

The doctrines that exalt nature or primitivism at the expense of spirit do not favour reconciliation with nature; on the contrary, they emphasize coldness and blindness toward nature. Whenever man deliberately makes nature his principle, he regresses to primitive urges. Children are cruel in mimetic reactions, because they do not really understand the plight of nature. Almost like animals, they often treat one another coldly and carelessly, and we know that even gregarious animals are isolated when they are together. Obviously, individual isolation is much more marked among nongregarious animals and in groups of animals of different species. All this, however, seems to a certain extent innocent. Animals, and in a way even children, do not reason. The philosopher's and politician's abdication of reason by a surrender to reality extenuates a much worse form of regression and inevitably culminates in a confusing of philosophical truth with ruthless self-preservation and war.

In summary, we are the heirs, for better or worse, of the Enlightenment and technological progress. To oppose these by regressing to more primitive stages does not alleviate the permanent crisis they have brought about. On the contrary, such expedients lead from historically reasonable to utterly barbaric forms of social domination. The sole way of assisting nature is to unshackle its seeming opposite, independent thought.

Max Horkheimer, *Eclipse of Reason* [1946] (London: Oxford University Press, 1947) pp. 104–6, 126–7.

19. Dominion is Social

Rosalind Coward

There is in fact nothing in nature which permits a reading of male aggression as inevitable, female passivity and weakness as eternal. Certainly, animals mate, animals breed and animals sometime fight (often male animals, but not always). But it is an illegitimate leap of thought to deduce that the same *meanings* can be derived from the same acts in both the human and animal worlds.

There can be no way in which aggression, dominance, mating and so on have the same place within human society as they do in animal society. There are crucial differences between human and animal societies; in human societies divisions between the sexes and between groups have enmeshed with specifically *human* history, where dominance and power are closely associated with the control of resources and therefore imply that other members of society are placed in 'subordinate' and weak positions.

As far as can be deduced, animals have not yet instituted a division of labour geared towards the production of surplus resources for the future. As a result, there's no evidence that certain groups either create or appropriate a surplus of resources and then control the distribution of these resources for future profit. Indeed, as far as the evidence goes, immediate survival is the name of the game. Complex societies, complex ecologies exist, but food is consumed as it appears or at most stored for the ensuing winter. As far as we know, when squirrels bury acorns, they do not have in mind harvesting from the resulting trees in twenty years' time, and selling acorns at vastly inflated prices to the hedgehogs.

Some human societies, though not all, do just this.[1] Food and goods are produced and accumulated not to ensure immediate survival but to be used for exchange for other goods. And in some societies, this process of exchange is linked to the creation of profit – profit from the control of surplus goods and resources. In these societies, the creation of profit has also developed linked to unequal distribution of the resources: one group controls how the surplus is distributed, and in short has power over other groups.

In animal society there's a startling absence of complex accumulation and unequal distribution of resources. Of course, scientists, not to be daunted by the shocking absence of bourgeois traits among animals, have found what they regard as a solution. 'Genes', they say, are every animal's natural property. Thus all mating, parenting and territorial behaviour is seen as a sort of economic calculation for the future. Both animals and humans share this common concern – to perpetuate their genes.

Whatever animals are up to when they mate, it is ridiculous to establish a logical connection between the activities of the selfish gene and a complex society where control of the surplus produces certain groups in dominance and others in positions of inferiority.[2] Genes can go on for ever without a bean in their pocket. But in some human societies, the activity of reproduction has been harnessed to the control of property. In some hierarchical societies, property is appropriated and controlled, and transmitted to the future via biological families, thus ensuring the reproduction of inequalities in the future. In such societies, women's reproduction capacities are linked to one particular family. Thus some hierarchies are based on reproductive relationship (kinship relations or what we call family relations); certain groups appropriate and control the surplus to their own advantage, and against the interests of other members of that society.

The history of this process of accumulation is none other than the specific history of *property* relations. In some cases, like our own, it has led to the capitalist mode of production. This history of property relations is not the same as territoriality, mating and male aggression. The history of property relations belongs to human history not as an inevitable aspect of humanity but as a chance by-product whose outcome has been the inequitable control of resources. Now in the animal world some animals do suffer or get destroyed – a harsh winter might wipe out the wren population; one species may find its access to a watering hole limited by the aggression of another; there may be a shortage of food due to natural failure. But as far as anyone can tell animals do not have an inequitable distribution of available resources within species, or a system of biological reproduction ensuring that the inequitable distribution as well as the genes continue in perpetuity.

Now the point of this argument is to demonstrate that aggression, dominance and power in our society do not occur as in nature. They occur in a society based on divisions and on divisions which have overwhelming consequences for what a person's position in that society will be. Among others, the division between men and women has fatal consequences for the *social* position of those sexes. For in the end, men and women do have an unequal relation to the distribution of resources. The issue has been horrendously confused because virtually all political arguments – from the left and the right alike – insist on seeing men and women as one. We are led to believe that because men and women marry, they therefore make up one family, with identical access to social resources. But the truth is that, whatever the class, men and women do have a different relation to social resources. Because of inequalities in the job market, because of how care for children and the elderly is arranged, and because of the way the state treats women, women rarely have the same relation to resources as men. And in a hierarchical society, this separation of groups from the control of resources is not a neutral event. Groups separated from the means of production are viewed as inferior by those in control. We're not in the same situation as animals. Male animals may fight; dominant males may sit on their dung heaps. But it is illegitimate to assume that the female of the species is therefore 'inferior', 'weaker', 'subordinate'. Indeed, this whole language of inferiority, weakness, subordination, dominance and power is a *human* language. It arises from certain societies where some groups have been disadvantaged to the benefit of others.

Rosalind Coward, *Female Desire* (London: Paladin, 1984) pp. 236–9.
1. Not all societies create a surplus which is then distributed inequitably. Certain societies produce surplus resources which are then distributed equitably between the whole society.
2. See Richard Dawkins, *The Selfish Gene* (London: Paladin, 1978).

Part III
Justice, Rights and Obligations

1. Justice Requires Friendship

Aristotle   384–322 B.C.

Each of the constitutions may be seen to involve friendship just in so far as it involves justice. The friendship between a king and his subjects depends on an excess of benefits conferred; for he confers benefits on his subjects if being a good man he cares for them with a view to their well-being, as a shepherd does for his sheep (whence Homer called Agamemnon: 'shepherd of the peoples'). Such too is the friendship of a father, though this exceeds the other in the greatness of the benefits conferred; for he is responsible for the existence of his children, which is thought the greatest good, and for their nurture and upbringing. These things are ascribed to ancestors as well. Further, by nature a father tends to rule over his sons, ancestors over descendants, a king over his subjects. These friendships imply superiority of one party over the other, which is why ancestors are honoured. The justice therefore that exists between persons so related is not the same on both sides but is in every case proportioned to merit; for that is true of the friendship as well. The friendship of man and wife, again, is the same that is found in an aristocracy; for it is in accordance with virtue – the better gets more of what is good, and each gets what befits him; and so, too, with the justice in these relations. The friendship of brothers is like that of comrades; for they are equal and of like age, and such persons are for the most part like in their feelings and their character. Like this, too, is the friendship appropriate to timocratic government; for in such a constitution the ideal is for the citizens to be equal and fair; therefore rule is taken in turn, and on equal terms; and the friendship appropriate here will correspond.

But in the deviation-forms, as justice hardly exists, so too does friendship. It exists least in the worst form; in tyranny there is little or no friendship. For where there is nothing common to ruler and ruled, there is not friendship either, since there is not justice; e.g. between craftsman and tool, soul and body, master and slave; the latter in each case is benefited by that which uses it, but there is no friendship nor justice towards lifeless things. But neither is there friendship towards a horse or an ox, nor to a slave *qua* slave. For there is nothing common to the two parties; the slave is a living tool and the tool a lifeless slave. *Qua* slave then, one cannot be friends with him. But *qua* man one can; for there seems to be some justice between any man and any other who can share in a system of law or be a party to an agreement;

re there can also be friendship with him in so far as he is a man.
ore while in tyrannies friendship and justice hardly exist, in
democracies they exist more fully; for where the citizens are equal
they have much in common.

Aristotle, 'Nicomachean Ethics' in W.D. Ross (tr) *The Works of Aristotle* (London: Oxford University Press, 1915) vol. IX, 1161a–b.

2. No Friendship with Irrational Creatures

St Thomas Aquinas   1225–74

Whether It Is Unlawful to Kill Any Living Thing

We proceed thus to the First Article:

Objection 1. It would seem unlawful to kill any living thing. For the Apostle says (Romans xiii, 2): 'They that resist the ordinance of God purchase to themselves damnation.' Now Divine providence has ordained that all living things should be preserved, according to Psalms cxlvi, 8, 9, 'Who maketh grass to grow on the mountains ... Who giveth to beasts their food'. Therefore it seems unlawful to take the life of any living thing.

Objection 2. Further, murder is a sin because it deprives a man of life. Now life is common to all animals and plants. Hence for the same reason it is apparently a sin to slay dumb animals and plants.

Objection 3. Further, in the Divine law a special punishment is not appointed save for a sin. Now a special punishment had to be inflicted, according to the Divine law, on one who killed another man's ox or sheep (Exodus xxii, 1). Therefore the slaying of dumb animals is a sin.

On the contrary. Augustine says (De Civ. Dei i, 20): 'When we hear it said, "Thou shalt not kill," we do not take it as referring to trees, for they have no sense, nor to irrational animals, because they have no fellowship with us. Hence it follows that the words, "Thou shalt not kill" refer to the killing of a man.'

I answer that, there is no sin in using a thing for the purpose for which it is. Now the order of things is such that the imperfect are for the perfect, even as in the process of generation nature proceeds from imperfection to perfection. Hence it is that just as in the generation of a man there is first a living thing, then an animal, and lastly a man, so too things, like the plants, which merely have life, are all alike for animals, and all animals are for man. Wherefore it is not unlawful if man use plants for the good of animals, and animals for the good of man, as the Philosopher states (Politics i. 3).

Now the most necessary use would seem to consist in the fact that animals use plants, and men use animals, for food, and this cannot be done unless these be deprived of life: wherefore it is lawful both to take life from plants for the use of animals, and from animals for the use of men. In fact this is in keeping with the commandment of God Himself: for it is written (Genesis i, 29, 30): 'Behold I have given you every herb .. and all trees ... to be your meat, and to all beasts of the earth;' and again (ix, 3): 'Everything that moveth and liveth shall be meat to you'.

Reply Objection 1. According to the Divine ordinance the life of animals and plants is preserved not for themselves but for man. Hence, as Augustine says (De Civ. Dei i, 20), 'by a most just ordinance of the Creator, both their life and their death are subject to our use'.

Reply Objection 2. Dumb animals and plants are devoid of the life of reason whereby to set themselves in motion; they are moved, as it were by another, by a kind of natural impulse, a sign of which is that they are naturally enslaved and accommodated to the uses of others.

Reply Objection 3. He that kills another's ox, sins, not through killing the ox, but through injuring another man in his property. Wherefore this is not a species of the sin of murder but of the sin of theft or robbery.

Whether Irrational Creatures also Ought to be Loved out of Charity

We proceed thus to the Third Article:

Objection 1. It would seem that irrational creatures also ought to be loved out of charity. For it is chiefly by charity that we are conformed to God. Now God loves irrational creatures out of charity, for He loves 'all things that are' (Wisdom of Solomon xi, 25), and whatever He loves, He loves by Himself Who is charity. Therefore we also should love irrational creatures out of charity.

Objection 2. Further, charity is referred to God principally, and extends to other things as referable to God. Now just as the rational creature is referable to God, in as much as it bears the resemblance of image, so too, are the irrational creatures, in as much as they bear the resemblance of a trace. Therefore charity extends also to irrational creatures.

Objection 3. Further, just as the object of charity is God, so is the object of faith. Now faith extends to irrational creatures, since we believe that heaven and earth were created by God, that the fishes and birds were brought forth out of the waters, and animals that walk, and plants, out of the earth. Therefore charity extends also to irrational creatures.

On the contrary, the love of charity extends to none but God and our neighbour. But the word neighbour cannot be extended to irrational creatures, since they have no fellowship with man in the rational life. Therefore charity does not extend to irrational creatures.

I answer that, according to what has been stated above (Q. XIII, A. I) charity is a kind of friendship. Now the love of friendship is twofold: first, there is the love for the friend to whom our friendship is given, secondly, the love for those good things which we desire for our friend. With regard to the first, no irrational creature can be loved out of charity; and for three reasons. Two of these reasons refer in a general way to friendship, which cannot have an irrational creature for its object: first because friendship is towards one to whom we wish good things. While properly speaking, we cannot wish good things to an irrational creature, because it is not competent, properly speaking, to possess good, this being proper to the rational creature which, through its free-will, is the master of its disposal of the good it possesses. Hence the Philosopher says (Physics ii, 6) that we do not speak of good or evil befalling suchlike things, except metaphorically. Secondly, because all friendship is based on some fellowship in life; since 'nothing is so proper to friendship as to live together,' as the Philosopher proves (Ethics, viii, 5). Now irrational creatures can have no fellowship in human life which is regulated by reason. Hence friendship with irrational creatures is impossible, except metaphorically speaking. The third reason is proper to charity, for charity is based on the fellowship of everlasting happiness, to which the irrational creature cannot attain. Therefore we cannot have the friendship of charity towards an irrational creature.

Nevertheless we can love irrational creatures out of charity, if we regard them as the good things that we desire for others, in so far, to wit, as we wish for their preservation, to God's honour and man's use; thus too does God love them out of charity.

Wherefore the Reply to the First Objection is evident.

Reply Objection 2. The likeness by way of trace does not confer the capacity for everlasting life, whereas the likeness of image does: and so the comparison fails.

Reply Objection 3. Faith can extend to all that is in any way true, whereas the friendship of charity extends only to such things as have a natural capacity for everlasting life; wherefore the comparison fails.

St Thomas Aquinas, 'Summa Theologica' in Fathers of the English Dominican
    Providence (trs) *The Summa Theologica of St Thomas Aquinas* (New York:
    Benzinger Bros, 1918) Part 1, Questions 64.1 and 65.3.

3. Exclusion from Friendship is Not Rational

Michel E. de Montaigne   1533–92

If it be justice to give every one his due, the beasts which serve, love
and defend their benefactors, and that pursue and injure strangers and
those who hurt them, by doing so reflect some of our notions of
justice; as they do also in observing a very just equality in distributing
their goods among their young.

With regard to friendship, that of animals is without comparison
more passionate and more constant than that of man. King Lysi-
machus' dog, Hyrcanus, when his master was dead, obstinately remained in his bed, refusing to eat and drink; on the day when the body
was burned, he started off and leapt into the fire, where he was
consumed. As did also the dog of one named Pyrrhus, who would not
budge from off his master's bed after he was dead; and, when his body
was removed, let himself be carried with it, and finally flung himself
on the funeral pyre on which his master was burned.

There are certain affectional tendencies that sometimes arise within
us without the consent of our reason, which are the result of
unreasoning chance which others call sympathy; of this the animals are
as capable as ourselves. We may see horses forming a sort of attachment
to each other, to such a degree that we have much ado to make them
live and travel separately. We may observe them taking a particular
fancy to a colour in those of their kind, as we might to a particular
type of face, and, when they meet with a horse of that colour, hasten
to make its acquaintance with great joy and demonstrations of good
will; at the same time taking a dislike and hatred of some other colour.

Animals, like ourselves, exercise a choice in their amours, and are
particular in selecting their mates. Like ourselves they are not free
from extreme and implacable jealousy and envy.

Desires are either natural and necessary, as eating and drinking, or
natural and not necessary, as intercourse with females; or again they
are neither natural nor necessary. Of this latter kind are almost all
those of human beings. They are all superfluous and artificial; for it is

marvellous how little Nature needs for her satisfaction, how little she has left us to desire. Our culinary dressings are not of her ordaining. The Stoics say that a man should be able to subsist on an olive a day. Our delicate choice of wines is no part of her teaching, nor are the additional refinements of our amorous desires:

> Are her kisses sweeter
> Though she be daughter to a mighty consul? (Horace)

Those exotic desires which have crept into us in consequence of wrong ideas and ignorance of the good, are so numerous that they drive out almost all the natural ones. No more nor less than if foreigners had entered a city in such numbers as to thrust out the native inhabitants, or to suppress their ancient authority and power, seizing and usurping it entirely to themselves.

Animals are much more self-controlled than we are, and keep with greater moderation within the limits that Nature has prescribed. Not so strictly however but that they sometimes share our sensualities. And just as we have heard of men being impelled by furious lusts to animal loves, these have sometimes been known to be enamoured of human beings, and to indulge their abnormal affections for others of a different species. Witness the elephant which was a rival with Aristophanes the grammarian in the affection of a young flower-girl in the city of Alexandria, and in no wise yielded to him in the attentions of a very passionate suit; for, going through the market-place where they sold fruits, this beast would seize some of them with his trunk and offer them to her. He would not lose sight of her more than he possibly could, and would occasionally thrust his trunk into her bosom under her cape to feel her breasts. They tell also of a dragon in love with a maid, of a goose enamoured of a boy in the town of Asopus, and of a ram that danced attendance on Glaucia the flute-player. Barbary apes are constantly known to be madly enamoured of women.

Among certain animals the males are known to be addicted to loving those of their own sex. Oppianus and others cite examples to show how animals, in their marriages, respect the laws of kinship: but experience very often shows us the contrary:

> The heifer thinks no shame her sire to bear
> On willing back; the horse his filly leaps;
> The goat will pair with them he has begot;
> Birds breed by them by whom themselves are bred. (Ovid)

Can there be a more evident example of sly cunning than that of the mule of the philosopher Thales? Fording a river, when laden with salt, she chanced to stumble, so that the sacks she carried were saturated with wet. Having observed that by the dissolving of the salt her burden was lightened, she never failed, as soon as she came to a stream, to plunge into it with her load, until her master, discovering her roguery, ordered her to be laden with wool; after that, finding herself nonplussed, she gave up that trick.

There are some in which our vice of avarice is naïvely reflected; for we may see them very diligent to appropriate by stealth and carefully to conceal all they can, although they may have no use for it.

As to husbandry, they surpass us, not only in that foresight which makes them store up and save for the future; they also possess much of the knowledge necessary to that end. The ants carry their grains and seeds out of their barns and spread them out to air, to cool and dry them, whenever they find they are beginning to turn mouldy and smell rank, lest they should rot and spoil. But the precaution and foresight they exercise in gnawing their grains of wheat exceeds all that can be imagined in man's prudence. Because the wheat does not always remain dry and wholesome, but dissolves, becomes soft and as if steeped in milk, being on the way to sprout and germinate; lest it should shoot and so lose its nature and property as a store of food, they nibble off the end where it usually sprouts.

With regard to war, which is the greatest and most pompous of human activities, I would fain know whether we should regard it as arguing some prerogative, or, on the contrary, as a testimony of our imbecility and imperfection; as indeed the science of defeating and killing one another, of ruining and destroying our own race, seems to have little to recommend it to the animals that have it not ...

Concerning the rights of familiarity and agreement, formed by intercourse, it is quite usual to accustom cats, dogs and hares to live in harmony.

But that which experience teaches those who travel by sea, and especially on the Sicilian sea, of the condition of the halcyon or king-fisher, surpasses all human imagination. What kind of animal was ever so honoured by Nature in its breeding, birth and deliverance? For the poets say indeed that one island, that of Delos, being once a wanderer, was made firm for the sake of the lying-in of Latona; but God willed that the whole sea should be arrested, made firm and smooth, without waves, without wind or rain, whilst the halcyon is breeding, which is just about the time of the solstice, the shortest day in the year. And by this privilege of hers we have seven days and seven nights, in the very heart of winter, when we may safely navigate. The female never knows any other male but her own mate; she keeps company with him all her life, and never forsakes him. When he becomes weak and broken with age she will bear him on her back, carry him everywhere and wait on him till death.

No wit of man could ever attain to the knowledge of that marvellous fabric, the nest which the halcyon constructs for its young, nor guess what material it is made of. Plutarch, who saw and handled many of them, thinks it consists of the bones of some fish bound and joined together and interlaced, some being placed lengthwise, the others laid across, with ribs and hoops added in such a manner as to form a round vessel ready to float. Then, the construction being completed, it is carried to the edge of the sea, where the tide, gently beating upon it, shows where the parts that are not well joined are to be mended, and where those are to be strengthened which are loosened and have come apart through the beating of the waves. On the other hand those parts which are well knit are tightened and closed up by the beat of the sea, in such a way that it cannot break or come to pieces, nor be damaged by the throwing of stones or iron, except with great force. And what is more wonderful is the proportion and the shape of the cavity within; for it is composed and proportioned in such a way that it cannot receive or admit anything but the bird that had built it. For it is closed, locked and impenetrable to any other thing, so that nothing can enter, not even the sea-water.

There we have a very clear description of this structure, and borrowed from a good source; yet it seems to me that it does not make the difficulty of the architecture sufficiently clear. Now, what vanity can that be that makes us consider beneath us, and interpret disdainfully, these actions that we can neither comprehend nor imitate?

To pursue a little further this equality and correspondence between men and animals. The privilege that our soul glories in of reducing to her own condition all that she apprehends, of stripping all things that come to her of their mortal and corporeal qualities, of compelling the things she deems worthy of her notice to put off and divest themselves of their corruptible qualities, and make them lay aside, like so many mean and superfluous garments, their thickness, length, depth, weight, colour, smell, roughness, smoothness, hardness, softness and all palpable properties, in order to make them conform to her own immortal and spiritual condition; so that the Rome and Paris that I have in my soul, the Paris that I have in my imagination, I imagine and conceive to be without size and without place, without stones, plaster or wood. This same privilege, I say, seems very evidently to be shared by the beasts. For when we see a horse, accustomed to trumpets and battles and the rattle of musketry, shaking and trembling in his sleep while stretched on his litter, as if he were in the fray, it is certain that in his soul he imagines the beat of the drum without noise, an army without body and without arms:

> Thou'lt see the sturdy horses, though outstretched,
> Yet sweating in their sleep, and panting ever,
> And straining utmost strength, as if for prize. (Lucretius)

This hare that a greyhound imagines in a dream, after which we see him panting in his sleep, stretching out his tail, moving his legs convulsively, exactly reproducing the motion of running is a hare without skin and bones ...

... Nature has not privileged us in that any more than in any other respect, above her common laws. And, if we judge ourselves aright, we shall find that, if there be some animals less favoured in that respect than we, there are others, and they are very numerous, that are more so; 'many animals surpass us in beauty' (Seneca), even among our terrestrial compatriots. For, as regards the denizens of the sea (leaving aside the shape as a whole, in which there can be no comparison, so much does it differ from ours), in colour, neatness, smoothness, and agility, we sufficiently yield place to them; and no less in all qualities to those of the air. And that prerogative, on which the poets lay so much stress, of our erect stature, which makes us look to heaven, whence it came,

> Whilst other creatures, prone, the earth regard,
> Sublime the front he gave to man, and bade him
> Raise his eyes to heaven's majestic vault
> And contemplate the stars ... (Ovid)

is poetical indeed; for there are many little creatures whose sight is turned wholly skywards. Camels and ostriches appear to me to have their necks set up straighter and more upright than ours. What animals are there that have not their face high and in front, that do not look forward, as we do, and discover, in their normal posture, as much of heaven and earth, as man? And what qualities of our bodily constitution, described by Plato and Cicero, are not at the service of a thousand kinds of animals? Those that most resemble us are the ugliest and meanest of the whole herd: the apes in external appearance and facial shape:

The Simian how similar, the ugly beast, to us! (Ennius)

the pig for inward and vital parts.

In truth, when I imagine man quite naked, yea, even in that sex that seems to have the greater share of beauty, his blemishes, his natural limitations, his imperfections, I find that we have more reason than any other animal to cover ourselves. We are to be excused for having borrowed from those that have been more favoured by Nature than ourselves, for having decked ourselves with their beauty, and concealed ourselves under their spoils of wool, feathers, hair, silk.

Observe moreover that we are the only animal that is offended by the defects in our fellow-creatures, and that we alone have to withdraw and hide ourselves in our natural actions, from our kind. It is in truth also a fact worthy of consideration that the masters of the craft prescribe as a cure for amorous passions a full and open sight of the body we desire; and that, to cool our love, it only needs entire liberty to see the object of it:

Full oft the man who viewed the secret parts
Was stayed in full career, and felt his passions cool. (Ovid)

And, although this recipe may proceed from a rather squeamish and frigid disposition, yet it is a wonderful sign of our imperfection that acquaintance and familiarity should make us distasteful to one another. It is not modesty so much as discretion and artfulness that makes our ladies so circumspect in refusing admittance to their boudoir before they are dressed up and painted for public view;

And these our Venuses are 'ware of this.
Wherefore the more are they at pains to hide
All the behind-the-scenes of life from those
Whom they desire to keep in bonds of love. (Lucretius)

Whereas in many animals there is nothing that we do not love, and that does not gratify our senses; so that from their very excrements and discardings we obtain not only dainties to eat, but our richest ornaments and perfumes.

These remarks concern only the common run of mortals, and we are not so sacrilegious as to include in them those divine, supernatural and extraordinary beauties we sometimes see refulgent among us, like stars under a corporeal and terrestrial veil.

Moreover, the very share in the bounties of Nature which, by our own confession, we allow the animals, is much to their advantage. We ourselves assume imaginary and fanciful advantages, advantages which are to come and non existent, which human capacity itself cannot guarantee, or advantages which we erroneously attribute to ourselves in the freedom of our opinions, such as reason, knowledge, honour. And to them we leave for their share essential, tangible and attainable advantages, as peace, repose, security, innocence and health: health, I say, the richest and finest gift that Nature can bestow upon us.

Therefore Philosophy, even that of the Stoics, is so bold as to say that Heraclitus and Pherecydes, if they had been allowed to give their wisdom in exchange for health, and by this transaction rid themselves, the one of the dropsy, the other of the lousy disease that afflicted him, they would have done well. By which admission they set a still greater store by wisdom, since they compare it and put it into the scales with health, than they do in this other proposition, which is also one of theirs: They say that if Circe had offered Ulysses two potions, the one to make a madman wise, and the other to make a wise man mad, Ulysses would rather have taken the cup of madness than consent to Circe's transforming his human shape into that of a beast; and they add that Wisdom herself would have spoken to him in this wise: 'Forsake me, let me alone, rather than allow me to dwell in the body and shape of an ass.'

What! will the philosophers then abandon this great and divine Wisdom for this corporeal and terrestrial covering? Then it is not by our reason, our speech and our soul that we are superior to the animals; it is by our beauty, our fair complexion and the fine symmetry of our limbs, for which our intelligence, our wisdom and all the rest are to be set at naught!

Well, I accept this frank and naïve confession. Assuredly they knew that these qualities that we make such a boast of, are but a vain imagination. Even though the beasts had all the virtue, knowledge, wisdom and perfection of the Stoics, they would still be beasts; and yet they would not be comparable to a poor, wretched, witless man.

In short, whatever is not as we are, is not worth a rap. And God himself, to be any good, must be like us, as we shall presently show. From which it is clear that it is not upon any true ground of reason, but from a foolish arrogance and stubbornness, that we put ourselves before the other animals, and remove ourselves from their condition and fellowship.

Michel Eyquem de Montaigne, 'Apology for Raymond Sebond' [c.1592] in E.J.
Trechman (tr) *Essays of Montaigne* (London: Oxford University Press, 1927)
pp. 464–80.

4. The Government of Animals

Thomas Hobbes   1588–1679

It is of itself manifest that the actions of men proceed from the will,
and the will from hope and fear, insomuch as when they shall see a
greater good or less evil likely to happen to them by the breach than
observation of the laws, they will wittingly violate them. The hope
therefore which each man hath of his security and self-preservation,
consists in this, that by force or craft he may disappoint his neighbour,
either openly or by stratagem. Whence we may understand, that the
natural laws, though well understood, do not instantly secure any man
in their practice; and consequently, that as long as there is no caution
had from the invasion of others, there remains to every man that same
primitive right of self-defence by such means as either he can or will
make use of, that is, a right to all things, or the right of war. And it is
sufficient for the fulfilling of the natural law, that a man be prepared in
mind to embrace peace when it may be had.

It is a trite saying, that all laws are silent in the time of war, and it is
a true one, not only if we speak of the civil, but also of the natural
laws, provided they be referred not to the mind, but to the actions of
men, by chapter iii, article 27. And we mean such a war, as is of all
men against all men; such as is the mere state of nature; although in the
war of nation against nation, a certain mean was wont to be observed.
And therefore in old time, there was a manner of living, and as it were
a certain economy, which they called, living by rapine; which was
neither against the law of nature (things then so standing), nor void of
glory to those who exercised it with valour, not with cruelty. Their
custom was, taking away the rest, to spare life, and abstain from oxen
fit for plough, and every instrument serviceable to husbandry. Which
yet is not so to be taken, as if they were bound to do thus by the law
of nature; but that they had regard to their own glory herein, lest by
too much cruelty they might be suspected guilty of fear.

Since therefore the exercise of the natural law is necessary for the
preservation of peace, and that for the exercise of the natural law
security is no less necessary; it is worth considering what that is which

affords such a security. For this matter nothing else can be imagined, but that each man provide himself or such meet helps, as the invasion of one on the other may be rendered so dangerous, as either of them may think it better to refrain than to meddle. But first, it is plain that the consent of two or three cannot make good such a security; because that the addition but of one, or some few on the other side, is sufficient to make the victory undoubtedly sure, and heartens the enemy to attack us. It is therefore necessary, to the end the security sought for may be obtained, that the number of them who conspire in a mutual assistance be so great, that the accession of some few to the enemy's party may not prove to them a matter of moment sufficient to assure the victory.

Furthermore, how great soever the number of them is who meet on self-defence, if yet they agree not among themselves of some excellent means whereby to compass this, but every man after his own manner shall make use of his endeavours, nothing will be done; because that, divided in their opinions, they will be a hinderance to each other; or if they agree well enough to some one action, through hope of victory, spoil, or revenge, yet afterward, through diversity of wits and counsels, or emulation and envy, with which men naturally contend, they will be so torn and rent, as they will neither give mutual help nor desire peace, except they be constrained to it by some common fear. Whence it follows that the consent of many (which consists in this only, as we have already defined in the foregoing section, that they direct all their actions to the same end and the common good), that is to say, that the society proceeding from mutual help only, yields not that security which they seek for, who meet and agree in the exercise of the above-named laws of nature; but that somewhat else must be done, that those who have once consented for the common good to peace and mutual help, may by fear be restrained lest afterwards they again dissent, when their private interest shall appear discrepant from the common good.

Aristotle reckons among those animals which he calls politic, not man only, but divers others, as the ant, the bee, etc; which, though they be destitute of reason, by which they may contract and submit to government, notwithstanding by consenting, that is to say, ensuing or eschewing the same things, they so direct their actions to a common end, that their meetings are not obnoxious unto any seditions. Yet is not their gathering together a civil government, and therefore those animals not to be termed political; because their government is only a consent, or many wills concurring in one object, not (as is necessary in civil government) one will. It is very true, that in those creatures living only by sense and appetite, their consent of minds is so durable, as there is no need of anything more to secure it, and by consequence to preserve peace among them, than barely their natural inclination. But among men the case is otherwise. For, first, among them there is a contestation of honour and preferment; among beasts there is none: whence hatred and envy, out of which arise sedition and war, is among men; among beasts no such matter. Next, the natural appetite of bees, and the like creatures, is conformable; and they desire the common good, which among them differs not from their private. But man scarce esteems anything good, which hath not somewhat of eminence in the enjoyment, more than that which others do possess. Thirdly, those creatures which are void of reason, see no defect, or think they see none, in the administration of their commonweals; but in a multitude of men there are many who, supposing themselves wiser than others, endeavour to innovate, and divers innovators innovate divers ways; which is a mere distraction and civil war. Fourthly, these brute creatures, howsoever they may have the use of their voice to signify their affections to each other, yet want they that same art of words which is necessarily required to those motions in the mind, whereby good is represented to it as being better, and evil as worse than in truth it is. But the tongue of man is a trumpet of war and sedition: and it is reported of Pericles, that he sometimes by his elegant speeches thundered and lightened, and confounded whole Greece itself. Fifthly, they cannot distinguish between injury and harm; thence it happens that as long as it is well with them, they blame not their fellows. But those men are of most trouble to the republic, who have most leisure to be idle; for they use not to contend for public places, before they have gotten the victory over hunger and cold. Last of all, the consent of those brutal creatures is natural; that of men by compact only, that is to say, artificial. It is therefore no matter of wonder, if somewhat more be needful for men to the end they may live in peace. Wherefore consent or contracted society, without some common power whereby particular men may be ruled through fear of punishment, doth not suffice to make up that security, which is requisite to the exercise of natural justice.

Since therefore the conspiring of many wills to the same end doth not suffice to preserve peace, and to make a lasting defence, it is requisite that, in those necessary matters which concern peace and self-defence, there be but one will of all men. But this cannot be done, unless every man will so subject his will to some other one, to wit, either man or council, that whatsoever his will is in those things which are necessary to the common peace, it be received for the wills of all men in general, and of every one in particular. Now the gathering together of many men, who deliberate of what is to be done or not to be done for the common good of all men, is that which I call a council.

This submission of the wills of all those men to the will of one man or one council, is then made, when each one of them obligeth himself by contract to every one of the rest, not to resist the will of that one man or council, to which he hath submitted himself; that is, that he refuse him not the use of his wealth and strength against any others whatsoever; for he is supposed still to retain a right of defending himself against violence: and this is called union. But we understand that to be the will of the council, which is the will of the major part of those men of whom the council consists.

But though the will itself be not voluntary, but only the beginning of voluntary actions (for we will not to will, but to act); and therefore falls least of all under deliberation and compact; yet he who submits his will to the will of another, conveys to that other the right of his strength and faculties. Insomuch as when the rest have done the same, he to whom they have submitted, hath so much power, as by the terror of it he can conform the wills of particular men unto unity and concord.

Now union thus made, is called a city or civil society; and also a civil person. For when there is one will of all men, it is to be esteemed for one person; and by the word *one*, it is to be known and distinguished from all particular men, as having its own rights and properties. Insomuch as neither any one citizen, nor all of them together (if we except him, whose will stands for the will of all), is to be accounted a city. A city therefore, (that we may define it), is one person, whose will, by the compact of many men, is to be received for the will of them all; so as he may use all the power and faculties of each particular person to the maintenance of peace, and for common defence.

But although every city be a civil person, yet every civil person is not a city; for it may happen that many citizens, by the permission of the city, may join together in one person, for the doing of certain things. These now will be civil persons; as the companies of merchants, and many other convents. But cities they are not, because they have not submitted themselves to the will of the company simply and in all things, but in certain things only determined by the city, and on such terms as it is lawful for any one of them to contend in judgment against the body itself of the sodality; which is by no means allowable to a citizen against the city. Such like societies, therefore, are civil persons subordinate to the city.

In every city, that man or council, to whose will each particular man hath subjected his will so as hath been declared, is said to have the supreme power, or chief command, or dominion. Which power and right of commanding, consists in this, that each citizen hath conveyed all his strength and power to that man or council; which to have done, because no man can transfer his power in a natural manner, is nothing else than to have parted with his right of resisting. Each citizen, as also every subordinate civil person, is called the subject of him who hath the chief command.

By what hath been said, it is sufficiently showed in what manner and by what degrees many natural persons, through desire of preserving themselves and by mutual fear, have grown together into a civil person, whom we have called a city. But they who submit themselves to another for fear, either submit to him whom they fear, or some other whom they confide in for protection. They act according to the first manner, who are vanquished in war, that they may not be slain; they according to the second, who are not yet overcome, that they may not be overcome. The first manner receives its beginning from natural power, and may be called the natural beginning of a city; the latter from the council and constitution of those who meet together, which is a beginning by institution. Hence it is that there are two kinds of cities; the one natural, such as the paternal and despotical; the other institutive, which may be also called political. In the first, the lord acquires to himself such citizens as he will; in the other, the citizens by their own wills appoint a lord over themselves, whether he be one man or one company of men, endued with the command in chief. But we will speak, in the first place, of a city political or by institution; and next, of a city natural.

Thomas Hobbes, 'De Cive' [1642] in Sir William Molesworth (ed) *The English Works of Thomas Hobbes of Malmesbury* (London: John Bohn, 1841) vol. II, pp. 63–75.

5. Animals have no Intrinsic Rights

Samuel Pufendorf   1632–92

The Roman Jurisconsults used to define the law of nature as 'what nature taught all animals', not, therefore, what is peculiar to man alone, but 'what other animals as well are supposed to know'. And so, on this hypothesis, whatever brutes and men are understood to be attracted to in common, or in common to avoid, belongs to the law of nature, and consequently a law is postulated which is common both to men and brutes. This opinion probably arose from that theory, proclaimed by certain ancients, regarding the soul of the universe, of which soul all others are but particles, which are in themselves of the same nature, but operate differently, according as they take their lodging in different bodies, and are assigned different organs through which to function. A theory related to this was that of metempsychosis according to which men and brutes differ only in bodily forms, but have similar souls, which pass from one animal to another. But learned men in general reject the idea that such a law is common to man and beasts, since, indeed, it cannot be thought that a being which has no power of reason, should have any right. As Hesiod writes 'For the son of Cronos has ordained this law for men, that fishes and beasts and winged fowls should devour one another, for right is not in them; but to mankind he gave right.'

Now although many actions of men and beasts are very much alike, by the performance of which a man is said to have satisfied the law, as a matter of fact there is a great difference between them, since among beasts they come from the simple inclination of their nature, while man performs them from a sense, as it were, of obligation, a sense which brutes do not have. So writers must be supposed to be using figures of speech, when they attribute to some brutes, mere animate creatures, justice, bravery, pity, gratitude, or chastity, because something resembling these virtues can be seen in certain actions of brutes. For things which appear on their face similar are by no means the same, if they proceed from a different internal principle. Now Grotius maintains that some acts of lower animals, such as ants and bees, are in a special way ordered by measure of reason, or some internal intelligent principle, and that some of them show a real regard for their proper interests in the case of their offspring and kind ...

We might say in defence of the Roman Jurisconsults that they used the term 'natural law' improperly of course, of the ordering by God of such things as serve to preserve nature herself, that is, to preserve species and individual animals. A reason for this is that in the particular section of their law they discuss only the conjunction of sexes, the procreation and education of offspring, and self-defence. Many others have in almost the same way used the term improperly.

Plutarch has written to the point on this matter, *On the Love of Offspring* (iii, 495 BC):

For, as in wild plants, such as wild vines, figs, and olives, Nature has implanted the principles of cultivated fruit, though crude and imperfect; so she has endowed beasts with a love of their young, though imperfect and not attaining to justice, nor proceeding further than utility. But in man, whom she produced a rational and political being, inclining him to justice, law, religion, building of cities and friendship, she hath placed the seed of those things that are generous, fair, and fruitful – that is, the love of their children, following the first principles which entered into the very constitution of their bodies.

Some writers constitute as the object of natural law such acts as contain in themselves a moral necessity or baseness, which are, therefore, in their own nature either required or unlawful, and hence necessarily understood to be commanded or forbidden by God. And in this respect, they say, natural law is distinguished not only from human law, but from the divine voluntary or positive law, which does not command or forbid things which are of their own proper nature obligatory or unlawful, but makes them by its forbidding unlawful, or by its command obligatory. But things forbidden by natural law are not improper because God forbade them, but God forbade them because they were of themselves improper; while in the same way things commanded by the same law are not proper or necessary because they are commanded by God, but they were commanded because they are of themselves proper ...

For we do not understand that the law of nature by its absolute authority enjoins us to cultivate friendship and society with brutes, nor are they capable of sustaining an obligation arising from a pact with men. From this defect of a common right there follows a practical state of war between those who can mutually injure each other, and are understood on probable reasons to be able so to desire. In this state every one has the faculty to do to another, with whom he is at war, whatever will seem to his advantage. And yet this state of war with brutes is very different from that war in which men meet at times, the latter being neither universal nor perpetual, and not extending promiscuously to every kind of licence. This state is most clearly to be seen in the case of large animals which, as opportunity is offered, turn also even upon men; and the person who wishes to spare them requires that men live in a worse state than the beasts. But domestic animals give themselves to the service of men, not from any obligation, but because they are either captivated by the choice food offered them, or restrained by force, upon the removal of which they will soon return to their liberty, while some will even turn against man himself. Some also reproduce in such numbers that they must be exterminated, if men themselves are not to find their living-space circumscribed and inconvenient.

But it is vain for some to deny that it follows from the lack common right between men and brutes, that a man may injure the and use them for food; and to maintain that even though no injury is done to the brutes, yet it is done to their Creator, unless there is certainty of His consent, or even to the owners of the animals. But surely that is an idle exception. For it is a safe conclusion from the fact that the Creator established no common right between man and brutes, that no injury is done brutes if they are hurt by man, since God himself made such a state exist between man and brutes. It is, furthermore, one thing to question whether a man may injure a brute, and another whether a man may injure a second person by the use of a brute. Only the former is denied in our argument, and not the latter.

Samuel Pufendorf, *The Law of Nature and Nations* [1688] trs. C.H. and W.A. Oldfather (New York: Oceana, 1931) vol. II, pp. 180–3 and 530–1.

6. Cruelty is Not Natural

John Locke   1632–1704

One thing I have frequently observed in children, that, when they have got possession of any poor creature, they are apt to use it ill; they often torment and treat very roughly young birds, butterflies, and such other poor animals, which fall into their hands, and that with a seeming kind of pleasure. This, I think, should be watched in them; and if they incline to any such cruelty, they should be taught the contrary usage; for the custom of tormenting and killing beasts will, by degrees, harden their minds even towards men; and they who delight in the suffering and destruction of inferior creatures, will not be apt to be very compassionate or benign to those of their own kind. Our practice takes notice of this, in the exclusion of butchers from juries of life and death. Children should from the beginning be bred up in an abhorrence of killing or tormenting any living creature, and be taught not to spoil or destroy any thing unless it be for the preservation or advantage of some other that is nobler. And truly, if the preservation of all mankind, as much as in him lies, were every one's persuasion, as indeed it is every one's duty, and the true principle to regulate our religion, politics, and morality by, the world would be much quieter, and better-natured, than it is. But to return to our present business; I cannot but commend both the kindness and prudence of a mother I knew, who was wont always to indulge her daughters, when any of them desired dogs, squirrels, birds, or any such things, as young girls use to be delighted with: but then, when they had them, they must be sure to keep them well, and look diligently after them, that they wanted nothing, or were not ill used; for, if they were negligent in their care of them, it was counted a great fault, which often forfeited their possession; or at least they failed not to be rebuked for it, whereby they were early taught diligence and good-nature. And indeed I think people should be accustomed, from their cradles, to be tender to all sensible creatures, and to spoil or waste nothing at all.

This delight they take in doing of mischief (whereby I mean spoiling of any thing to no purpose, but more especially the pleasure they take to put any thing in pain that is capable of it) I cannot persuade myself to be any other than a foreign and introduced disposition, an habit borrowed from custom and conversation. People teach children to strike, and laugh when they hurt, or see harm come to others; and they have the examples of most about them to confirm them in it. All the entertainment of talk and history is of nothing almost but fighting and killing; and the honour and renown that is bestowed on conquerors (who for the most part are but the great butchers of mankind) farther mislead growing youths, who by this means come to think slaughter the laudable business of mankind, and the most heroic of virtues. By these steps unnatural cruelty is planted in us; and what humanity abhors, custom reconciles and recommends to us, by laying it in the way to honour. Thus, by fashion and opinion, that comes to be a pleasure, which in itself neither is, nor can be any. This ought carefully to be watched, and early remedied, so as to settle and cherish the contrary and more natural temper of benignity and compassion in the room of it; but still by the same gentle methods, which are to be applied to the other two faults before mentioned. It may not perhaps be unreasonable here to add this farther caution, viz. that the mischiefs or harms that come by play, inadvertency, or ignorance, and were not known to be harms, or designed for mischief's sake, though they may perhaps be sometimes of considerable damage, yet are not at all, or but very gently, to be taken notice of. For this, I think, I cannot too often inculcate, that whatever miscarriage a child is guilty of, and whatever be the consequence of it, the thing to be regarded in taking notice of it, is only what root it springs from, and what habit it is like to establish; and to that the correction ought to be directed, and the child not to suffer any punishment for any harm which may have come by his play or inadvertency. The faults to be amended lie in the mind; and if they are such as either age will cure, or no ill habits will follow from, the present action, whatever displeasing circumstances it may have, is to be passed by without any animadversion.

Another way to instil sentiments of humanity, and to keep them lively in young folks, will be, to accustom them to civility, in their language and deportment towards their inferiors, and the meaner sort of people, particularly servants. It is not unusual to observe the children, in gentlemen's families, treat the servants of the house with domineering words, names of contempt, and an imperious carriage; as if they were of another race, and species beneath them. Whether ill example, the advantage of fortune, or their natural vanity, inspire this haughtiness, it should be prevented, or weeded out; and a gentle, courteous, affable carriage towards to the lower ranks of men, placed in the room of it. No part of their superiority will be hereby lost, but the distinction increased, and their authority strengthened, when love in inferiors is joined to outward respect, and an esteem of the person has a share in their submission; and domestics will pay a more ready and cheerful service, when they find themselves not spurned, because fortune has laid them below the level of others, at their master's feet. Children should not be suffered to lose the consideration of human nature in the shufflings of outward conditions: the more they have, the better-humoured they should be taught to be, and the more compassionate and gentle to those of their brethren, who are placed lower, and have scantier portions. If they are suffered from their cradles to treat men ill and rudely, because, by their father's title, they think they have a little power over them; at best it is ill-bred; and, if care be not taken, will, by degrees, nurse up their natural pride into an habitual contempt of those beneath them: and where will that probably end, but in oppression and cruelty?

John Locke, 'Some Thoughts Concerning Education' [1693] in *The Works of John Locke in Ten Volumes*, 10th edn (London, 1801) vol. 9, pp. 112–15.

7. No Justice Without Equality

David Hume   1711–76

This poetical fiction of the golden age is, in some respects, of a piece with the philosophical fiction of the state of nature; only that the former is represented as the most charming and most peaceable condition, which can possibly be imagined; whereas the latter is painted out as a state of mutual war and violence, attended with the most extreme necessity. On the first origin of mankind, we are told, their ignorance and savage nature were so prevalent, that they could give no mutual trust, but must each depend upon himself and his own force or cunning for protection and security. No law was heard of: no rule of justice known: no distinction of property regarded: power was the only measure of right; and a perpetual war of all against all was the result of men's untamed selfishness and barbarity.

Whether such a condition of human nature could ever exist, or if it did, could continue so long as to merit the appellation of a state, may justly be doubted. Men are necessarily born in a family-society, at least; and are trained up by their parents to some rule of conduct and behaviour. But this must be admitted, that, if such a state of mutual war and violence was ever real, the suspension of all laws of justice, from their absolute inutility, is a necessary and infallible consequence.

The more we vary our views of human life, and the newer and more unusual the lights are in which we survey it, the more shall we be convinced, that the origin here assigned for the virtue of justice is real and satisfactory.

Were there a species of creatures intermingled with men, which, though rational, were possessed of such inferior strength, both of body and mind, that they were incapable of all resistance, and could never, upon the highest provocation, make us feel the effects of their resentment; the necessary consequence, I think, is that we should be bound by the laws of humanity to give gentle usage to these creatures, but should not, properly speaking, lie under any restraint of justice with regard to them, nor could they possess any right or property, exclusive of such arbitrary lords. Our intercourse with them could not be called society, which supposes a degree of equality; but absolute command on the one side, and servile obedience on the other. Whatever we covet, they must instantly resign: Our permission is the only tenure, by which they hold their possessions: our compassion and kindness the only check, by which they curb our lawless will: and as no inconvenience ever results from the exercise of a power, so firmly established in nature, the restraints of justice and property, being totally useless, would never have place in so unequal a confederacy.

This is plainly the situation of men, with regard to animals; and how far these may be said to possess reason, I leave it to others to determine. The great superiority of civilized Europeans above barbarous Indians, tempted us to imagine ourselves on the same footing with regard to them, and made us throw off all restraints of justice, and even of humanity, in our treatment of them. In many nations, the female sex are reduced to like slavery, and are rendered incapable of all property, in opposition to their lordly masters. But though the males, when united, have in all countries bodily force sufficient to maintain this severe tyranny, yet such are the insinuation, address, and charms of their fair companions, that women are commonly able to break the confederacy, and share with the other sex in all the rights and privileges of society.

Were the human species so framed by nature as that each individual possessed within himself every faculty, requisite both for his own preservation and for the propagation of his kind: were all society and intercourse cut off between man and man, by the primary intention of the supreme Creator: it seems evident, that so solitary a being would be as much incapable of justice, as of social discourse and conversation. Where mutual regards and forbearance serve to no manner of purpose, they would never direct the conduct of any reasonable man. The headlong course of the passions would be checked by no reflection on future consequences. And as each man is here supposed to love himself alone, and to depend only on himself and his own activity for safety and happiness, he would, on every occasion, to the utmost of his power, challenge the preference above every other being, to none of which he is bound by any ties, either of nature or of interest.

But suppose the conjunction of the sexes to be established in nature, a family immediately arises; and particular rules being found requisite for its subsistence, these are immediately embraced; though without comprehending the rest of mankind within their prescriptions. Suppose that several families unite together into one society, which is totally disjoined from all others, the rules, which preserve peace and order, enlarge themselves to the utmost extent of that society; but becoming then entirely useless, lose their force when carried one step farther. But again suppose, that several distinct societies maintain a kind of intercourse for mutual convenience and advantage, the boundaries of justice still grow larger, in proportion to the largeness of men's views, and the force of their mutual connexions. History, experience, reason sufficiently instruct us in this natural progress of human sentiments, and in the gradual enlargement of our regards to justice, in proportion as we become acquainted with the extensive utility of that virtue.

David Hume, *Enquiry Concerning the Principles of Morals* [1751] ed L.A. Selby-Brigge (Oxford: Clarendon Press, 1902) pp. 189-92.

8. Differences do Not Justify Inequality

Humphry Primatt   c.1742

I presume there is no Man of feeling, that has any idea of Justice, but would confess upon the principles of reason and common sense, that if he were to be put to unnecessary and unmerited pain by another man, his tormentor would do him an act of injustice; and from a sense of the injustice in his *own* case, now that He is the sufferer, he must naturally infer, that if he were to put another man of feeling to the same unnecessary and unmerited pain which He now suffers, the injustice in himself to the other would be exactly the same as the injustice in his tormentor to Him. Therefore the man of feeling and justice will not put another man to unmerited pain, because he will not do that to another, which he is unwilling should be done to himself. Nor will he take any advantage of his own superiority of strength, or of the accidents of fortune, to abuse them to the oppression of his inferior; because he knows that in the article of feeling all men are equal; and that the differences of strength or station are as much the gifts and appointments of God, as the differences of understanding, colour, or stature. Superiority of rank or station may give ability to communicate happiness, and seems so intended; but it can give no right to inflict unnecessary or unmerited pain. A wise man would impeach his own wisdom, and be unworthy of the blessing of a good understanding, if he were to infer from thence that he had a right to despise or make game of a fool, or put him to any degree of pain. The folly of the fool ought rather to excite his compassion, and demands the wise man's care and attention to one that cannot take care of himself.

It has pleased God the Father of all men, to cover some men with white skins, and others with black skins; but as there is neither merit nor demerit in complexion, the white man, notwithstanding the barbarity of custom and prejudice, can have no right, by virtue of his colour, to enslave and tyrannize over a black man; nor has a fair man any right to despise, abuse, and insult a brown man. Nor do I believe that a tall man, by virtue of his stature, has any legal right to trample a dwarf under his foot. For, whether a man is wise or foolish, white or black, fair or brown, tall or short, and I might add, rich or poor, for it is no more a man's choice to be poor, than it is to be a fool, or a dwarf, or black, or tawny – such he is by God's appointment; and, abstractedly considered, is neither a subject for pride, nor an object of contempt. Now, if amongst men, the differences of their powers of the mind, and of their complexion, stature, and accidents of fortune, do not give any one man a right to abuse or insult any other man on account of these differences; for the same reason, a man can have no natural right to abuse and torment a beast, merely because a beast has not the mental powers of a man. For, such as the man is, he is but as God made him; and the very same is true of the beast. Neither of them can lay claim to any intrinsic Merit, for being such as they are; for, before they were created, it was impossible that either of them could deserve; and at their creation, their shapes, perfections, or defects were invariably fixed, and their bounds set which they cannot pass. And being such, neither more nor less than God made them, there is no more demerit in a beast being a beast, than there is merit in a man being a man; that is, there is neither merit nor demerit in either of them.

A Brute is an animal no less sensible of pain than a Man. He has similar nerves and organs of sensation; and his cries and groans, in case of violent impressions upon his body, though he cannot utter his complaints by speech, or human voice, are as strong indications to us of his sensibility of pain, as the cries and groans of a human being, whose language we do not understand. Now, as pain is what we are all averse to, our own sensibility of pain should teach us to commiserate it in others, to alleviate it if possible, but never wantonly or unmeritedly to inflict it. As the differences amongst men in the above particulars are no bars to their feelings, so neither does the difference of the shape of a brute from that of a man exempt the brute from feeling; at least, we have no ground to suppose it. But shape or figure is as much the appointment of God, as complexion or stature. And if the difference of complexion or stature does not convey to one man a right to despise and abuse another man, the difference of shape between a man and a brute, cannot give to a man any right to abuse and torment a brute. For he that made man and man to differ in complexion or stature, made man and brute to differ in shape or figure. And in this case likewise there is neither merit nor demerit; every creature, whether man or brute, bearing that shape which the supreme Wisdom judged most expedient to answer the end for which the creature was ordained.

Humphry Primatt, *A Dissertation on the Duty of Mercy and the Sin of Cruelty to Brute Animals* [1776] (Edinburgh: T. Constable, 1834) pp. 15–21.

9. Duties to Animals are Indirect

Immanuel Kant   1724–1804

Baumgarten speaks of duties towards beings which are beneath us and beings which are above us. But so far as animals are concerned, we have no direct duties. Animals are not self-conscious and are there merely as a means to an end. That end is man. We can ask, 'Why do animals exist?' But to ask, 'Why does man exist?' is a meaningless question. Our duties towards animals are merely indirect duties towards humanity. Animal nature has analogies to human nature, and by doing our duties to animals in respect of manifestations which correspond to manifestations of human nature, we indirectly do our duty towards humanity. Thus, if a dog has served his master long and faithfully, his service, on the analogy of human service, deserves reward, and when the dog has grown too old to serve, his master ought to keep him until he dies. Such action helps to support us in our duties towards human beings, where they are bounden duties. If then any acts of animals are analogous to human acts and spring from the same principles, we have duties towards the animals because thus we cultivate the corresponding duties towards human beings. If a man shoots his dog because the animal is no longer capable of service, he does not fail in his duty to the dog, for the dog cannot judge, but his act is inhuman and damages in himself that humanity which it is his duty to show towards mankind. If he is not to stifle his human feelings, he must practise kindness towards animals, for he who is cruel to animals becomes hard also in his dealings with men. We can judge the heart of a man by his treatment of animals. Hogarth depicts this in his engravings. He shows how cruelty grows and develops. He shows the child's cruelty to animals, pinching the tail of a dog or a cat; he then depicts the grown man in his cart running over a child; and lastly, the culmination of cruelty in murder. He thus brings home to us in a terrible fashion the rewards of cruelty, and this should be an impressive lesson to children. The more we come in contact with animals and observe their behaviour, the more we love them, for we see how great is their care for their young. It is then difficult for us to be cruel in thought even to a wolf. Leibnitz used a tiny worm for purposes of observation, and then carefully replaced it with its leaf on the tree so that it should not come to harm through any act of his. He would have been sorry – a natural feeling for a humane man – to destroy such a creature for no reason. Tender feelings towards dumb animals develop humane feelings towards mankind. In England butchers and doctors do not sit on a jury because they are accustomed to the sight of death and hardened. Vivisectionists, who use living animals for their experiments, certainly act cruelly, although their aim is praise-worthy, and they can justify their cruelty, since animals must be regarded as man's instruments; but any such cruelty for sport cannot be justified. A master who turns out his ass or his dog because the animal can no longer earn its keep manifests a small mind. The Greeks' ideas in this respect were high-minded, as can be seen from the fable of the ass and the bell of ingratitude. Our duties towards animals, then, are indirect duties towards mankind.

Our duties towards immaterial beings are purely negative. Any course of conduct which involves dealings with spirits is wrong. Conduct of this kind makes men visionaries and fanatics, renders them superstitious, and is not in keeping with the dignity of mankind; for human dignity cannot subsist without a healthy use of reason, which is impossible for those who have commerce with spirits. Spirits may exist or they may not; all that is said of them may be true; but we know them not and can have no intercourse with them. This applies to good and to evil spirits alike. Our Ideas of good and evil are coordinate, and as we refer all evil to hell so we refer all good to heaven. If we personify the perfection of evil, we have the Idea of the devil. If we believe that evil spirits can have an influence upon us, can appear and haunt us at night, we become a prey to phantoms and incapable of using our powers in a reasonable way. Our duties towards such beings must, therefore, be negative.

Immanuel Kant, *Lectures on Ethics – Duties Towards Animals and other Spirits* [1780–1] tr. Louis Infield (New York: Harper and Row, 1963) pp. 239–41.

10. Animals are Not Constitutional Persons

James Madison 1751–1836

It is not contended that the number of people in each State ought not to be the standard for regulating the proportion of those who are to represent the people of each State. The establishment of the same rule for the apportionment of taxes will probably be as little contested; though the rule itself, in this case, is by no means founded on the same principle. In the former case, the rule is understood to refer to the personal rights of the people, with which it has a natural and universal connection. In the latter, it has reference to the proportion of wealth of which it is in no case a precise measure, and in ordinary cases a very unfit one. But notwithstanding the imperfection of the rule as applied to the relative wealth and contributions of the States, it is evidently the least exceptionable among the practicable rules, and had too recently obtained the general sanction of America not to have found a ready preference with the convention.

All this is admitted, it will perhaps be said; but does it follow, from an admission of numbers for the measure of representation, or of slaves combined with free citizens as a ratio of taxation, that slaves ought to be included in the numerical rule of representation? Slaves are considered as property, not as persons. They ought therefore to be comprehended in estimates of taxation which are founded on property, and to be excluded from representation which is regulated by a census of persons. This is the objection, as I understand it, stated in its full force. I shall be equally candid in stating the reasoning which may be offered on the opposite side.

'We subscribe to the doctrine' might one of our Southern brethren observe, 'that representation relates more immediately to persons, and taxation more immediately to property, and we join in the application of this distinction to the case of our slaves. But we must deny the fact that slaves are considered merely as property, and in no respect whatever as persons. The true state of the case is that they partake of both these qualities: being considered by our laws, in some respects, as persons, and in other respects as property. In being compelled to labour, not for himself, but for a master; in being vendible by one master to another master; and in being subject at all times to be restrained in his liberty and chastised in his body, by the capricious will of another – the slave may appear to be degraded from the human rank, and classed with those irrational animals which fall under the legal denomination of property. In being protected, on the other hand, in his life and in his limbs, against the violence of all others, even the master of his labour and his liberty; and in being punishable himself for all violence committed against others – the slave is no less evidently regarded by the law as a member of the society, not as a part of the irrational creation; as a moral person, not as a mere article of property. The federal Constitution, therefore, decides with great propriety on the case of our slaves, when it views them in the mixed character of persons and of property. This is in fact their true character. It is the character bestowed on them by the laws under which they live; and it will not be denied that these are the proper criterion; because it is only under the pretext that the laws have transformed the Negroes into subjects of property that a place is disputed them in the computation of numbers; and it is admitted that if the laws were to restore the rights which have been taken away, the Negroes could no longer be refused an equal share of representation with the other inhabitants ...'

Such is the reasoning which an advocate for the southern interests might employ on this subject; and although it may appear to be a little strained in some points, yet on the whole, I must confess that it fully reconciles me to the scale of representation which the convention have established ...

James Madison, *The Federalist Papers* [1787] (New York: New American Library, 1961) pp. 336–7, 340.

11. The Inalienable Rights of Animals

Herman Daggett   1766–1832

The design of my appearing in public, at this time, is to say a few things in favour of a certain class of beings, whose rights have seldom been advocated, either from the pulpit, from the stage, or from the press. I mean the inferior animals.

The cruelty, and injustice, with which this class of beings has been treated, by their boasted superiors of the human race, is too notorious to need a particular recital. In general, their welfare and happiness has been looked upon as a matter of very little importance, in the system; and in our treatment of them, hardly to be regarded. And one species, in particular, has, by almost universal consent, been totally excluded from any place in the benevolent regards of mankind; so that now, 'whosoever killeth them thinketh that he doth God service.' Yea, and many are so absurd as to suppose, that this is a fulfilment of that antient prophecy, 'That the seed of the woman should bruise the serpent's head'.

As every sinful indulgence, and every act of injustice, arises from the blind and criminal selfishness of the human heart; to this must we look, as the cause of that unfeeling disposition, together with all those acts of injustice and cruelty, which are spent upon the inferior animals. It is the nature of selfishness, to exclude all beings but ourselves, and those whom we consider as being related to ourselves, from any friendly, benevolent attention. If we are exercised with any pain, or are the subjects of any misfortune; or if this be the case with any of those, who belong to our family, or the circle of our friends, we immediately become affected by it: and always in proportion to the nearness of the relation. Whereas, if any calamity befall those, who are no way related to us, but who belong to a different class, or circle in society, our feelings are not wont to be interested. This will account, at once, for that disposition and conduct in men, which we are now censuring. For the lower order of sensible beings, are considered as moving in a very different sphere, and belonging to a community of a far different nature from that of ours; so far different, that the feelings of benevolence, are, commonly, not at all interested in their favour.

A well known circumstance, which attends some of these animals, contributes, not a little, to confirm us in the truth of this observation. For those of them which are tamed, and domesticated by us, immediately become the objects of our kind regards, and our sensibility is deeply wounded, when they are abused. But where there is no such relation, by which they are distinguished from the common herd, to use a phrase denoting cruelty, they are treated like brutes. Without the least regard to justice, we commonly treat them in that manner, which we suppose, will make them conduce the most to our own advantage; and subject them, in all things, to what happens to be our pleasure. Though sometimes, it must be acknowledged, that our malevolence towards them, is of a disinterested nature, and they are tormented only for the sake of the unnatural pleasure, which is taken in doing it.

Now, in order to determine, in what light, these animals ought to be considered, and how they ought to be treated, let us carefully attend to a few things, of known and acknowledged truth, with regard to the objects of our benevolence. And here, I think, it is past dispute, that all beings, capable of happiness belong to the number. Let their circumstances or characters, dispositions or abilities, color or shape, be what they may; if they are sensible beings, and capable of happiness, they ought to be the objects of our benevolent regards. If the moral character of any being has become hateful, and inconsistent with truth and justice, we cannot, 'tis true, as such, have any complacency in it: but, we observe, that the Being itself, may, nevertheless, be as proper an object of our benevolence, as any being whatever: and we ought to wish, and actually endeavor, to promote the welfare, and real happiness of such a being, as much as we possibly can, consistently with the rights and claims of other beings. This is the nature of true benevolence. True benevolence is universal, and uniform. The good man, like his merciful Creator, wishes to promote the highest happiness of that system to which his influence extends: and feels devoted to parties in society, no farther than the present state of things, and his limited capacities render it necessary. We may, and ought to have a true regard for all beings, according to their real worth, and to wish them well, according to their capacity for enjoyment; although, in this life, we are necessarily limited in the execution of such benevolent wishes. The case is such with us, at present, that we cannot do good to all beings alike, to whom, nevertheless, we may wish well, with equal sincerity, and with equal ardour. But we observe, that whenever an opportunity of securing, or increasing the happiness of any being, offers itself, the benevolent man, acting as such, always improves it.

These observations, it is hoped, will help us to determine, in what light, we ought to consider the inferior animals. That they are sensible beings, and capable of happiness, none can doubt: That their sensibility of corporeal pleasure and pain, is less than ours, none can prove. And that there is any kind of reason, why they should not be regarded with proportionable tenderness, we cannot conceive.

But lest this mode of reasoning should be thought too nice, let us call into view a rule of judging, instituted by a divine Philanthropist, and oracle of wisdom, in the days of Julius (Tiberius) Caesar. 'That we do to others as we would have them do unto us'; i.e. in a change of circumstances. This is a maxim which approves itself to the reason and conscience of every man. Whatever obscurity may involve other rules of judging, this is always clear, and unexceptionable. And it must extend to all sensible beings, with whom we have any dealings, and in whose situation we are capable of imagining ourselves to be. Supposing therefore (as some have supposed) that the doctrine of transmigration is true, and that, after this life, we shall pass into the forms of some of the inferior animals, and move in their sphere; how should we wish to be considered, and treated, by those above us? Here, there is left not the least room to doubt, what our feelings would be. Let this rule, therefore, be faithfully applied, in every case, and cruelty to animals would no longer be indulged.

God has appointed to all his creatures, a certain sphere to move in, and has granted them certain privileges, which may be called their own. If we judge impartially, we shall acknowledge that there are the rights of a beast, as well as the rights of a man. And because man is considered as the Lord of this lower creation, he is not thereby licensed to infringe on the rights of those below him, any more than a King, or Magistrate, is licensed to infringe on the rights of his subjects. If the Governor of the universe has given us liberty to prepare animal food; or, if the rights of these creatures, in certain instances interfere with the rights of others, or with the rights of men, so as thereby to become forfeited; we may, in such cases, take away their lives, or deprive them of their privileges, without the imputation of blame. And I know of nothing in nature, in reason, or in revelation, which obliges us to suppose, that the unalienated rights of a beast, are not as sacred, and inviolable, as those of a man: or that the person, who wantonly commits an outrage upon the life, happiness, or security of a bird, is not as really amenable, at the tribunal of eternal justice, as he, who wantonly destroys the rights and privileges, or injuriously takes away the life of one of his fellow creatures of the human race. Here, perhaps, some of my auditory will feel shocked; and will recur, in their minds, to that horror, and desperation, which arises in the breasts of murderers: Whereas, there is no such consciousness of guilt, when one of the inferior animals only has been the subject of human cruelty. But this difference, I would observe, is owing to education, and to certain contracted habits of thinking and acting. Only let a person be taught, from his earliest years, that it is criminal to torment, and unnecessarily to destroy, these innocent animals, and he will feel a guilty conscience, in consequence of any injury, which he shall do them, in this way, no less really, than if the injury were offered to human beings. The force of education, and of wrong habits, in setting aside natural principles, is amazing, and almost incredible. Witness the feelings of those, who are employed in forcing away the Natives, from the coasts of Africa. Witness the cruelties, and the deaths, which are inflicted upon them, in the West Indies, and in the Southern States; and witness the indifference, with which, in some countries, they kill their children, when they become too numerous, and their parents, when they become too old. The question, therefore, is not what can be done, without remorse of conscience, but what ought to be done, according to the rules of justice and dictates of benevolence.

Herman Daggett, *The Rights of Animals: An Oration* [1791] (New York: American Society for the Prevention of Cruelty to Animals, 1926) pp. 1–8.

12. All Nature Suffers

William Godwin   1756–1836

Let us not amuse ourselves with a pompous and delusive survey of the whole, but let us examine parts severally and individually. All nature swarms with life. This may in one view afford an idea of an extensive theatre of pleasure. But unfortunately every animal preys upon his fellow. Every animal however minute, has a curious and subtile structure, rendering him susceptible, as it should seem, of piercing anguish. We cannot move our foot without becoming the means of destruction. The wounds inflicted are of a hundred kinds. These petty animals are capable of palpitating for days in the agonies of death. It may be said with little licence of phraseology that all nature suffers. There is no day nor hour, in which in some regions of the many-peopled globe, thousands of men, and millions of animals, are not tortured to the utmost extent that organized life will afford. Let us turn our attention to our own species. Let us survey the poor; oppressed, hungry, naked, denied all the gratifications of life and all that nourishes the mind. They either are tormented with the injustice or chilled into lethargy. Let us view man writhing under the pangs of disease, or the fiercer tortures that are stored up for him by his brethren. Who is there that will look on and say 'All this is well; there is no evil in the world?' Let us recollect the pains of the mind; the loss of friends, the rankling tooth of ingratitude, the unrelenting rage of tyranny, the slow progress of justice, the brave and honest consigned to the fate of guilt. Let us plunge into the depth of dungeons. Let us observe youth languishing in hopeless despair, and talents and virtue shrouded in eternal oblivion. The evil does not consist merely in the pain endured. It is the injustice that inflicts it that gives it its sharpest sting. Malignity, an unfeeling disposition, vengeance and cruelty, are inmates of every climate. As these are felt by the sufferer with peculiar acuteness, so they propagate themselves. Severity begets severity, and hatred engenders hate. The whole history of the human species, taken in one point of view, appears a vast abortion. Man seems adapted for wisdom and fortitude and benevolence. But he has always, through a vast majority of countries, been the victim of ignorance and superstition. Contemplate the physiognomy of the species. Observe the traces of stupidity, of low cunning, of rooted insolence, of withered hope, and narrow selfishness, where the characters of wisdom, independence, and disinterestedness, might have been inscribed. Recollect the horrors of war, that last invention of deliberate profligacy for the misery of man. Think of the variety of wounds, the multiplication of anguish, the desolation of countries, towns destroyed, harvests flaming, inhabitants perishing by thousands of hunger and cold.

A sound philosophy will teach us to contemplate this scene without madness. Instructed in its lessons, we shall remember that though there is much of evil, there is also much of good in the world, much pleasure as well as much pain. We shall not even pronounce that some small portion of this evil is not relatively not an evil. Above all, we shall be cheered with the thought of brighter prospects and happier times. But the optimist must be particularly rash, who takes upon him to affirm of all this mass of evil without exception, that it is relatively not evil, and that nothing could have happened otherwise than it has happened, without the total being worse than it is.

There is reason to think that the creed of optimism, or an opinion bearing some relation to that creed, has done much harm in the world.

William Godwin, *Enquiry Concerning Political Justice and Its Influence on Modern Morals and Happiness* [1798] (London: J. Watson, 1842) pp. 216–18.

13. Limits to the Rights over Animals

Artur Schopenhauer   1788–1860

If, however, as a rare exception, we meet a man who possesses a considerable income, but uses very little of it for himself and gives all the rest to the poor, while he denies himself many pleasures and comforts, and we seek to explain the action of this man, we shall find, apart altogether from the dogmas through which he tries to make his action intelligible to his reason, that the simplest general expression and the essential character of his conduct is that he makes less distinction than is usually made between himself and others ...

... He sees that the distinction between himself and others, which to the bad man is so great a gulf, only belongs to a fleeting and illusive phenomenon. He recognises directly and without reasoning that the in-itself of his own manifestation is also that of others, the will to live, which constitutes the inner nature of everything and lives in all; indeed, that this applies also to the brutes and the whole of nature, and therefore he will not cause suffering even to a brute.

(The right of man over the life and powers of the brutes rests on the fact that, because with the growing clearness of consciousness suffering increases in like measure; the pain which the brute suffers through death or work is not so great as man would suffer by merely denying himself the flesh, or the powers of the brutes. Therefore man may carry the assertion of his existence to the extent of denying the existence of the brute, and the will to live as a whole endures less suffering in this way than if the opposite course were adopted. This at once determines the extent of the use man may make of the powers of the brutes without wrong; a limit, however, which is often transgressed, especially in the case of beasts of burden and dogs used in the chase; to

which the activity of societies for the prevention of cruelty to anim...
is principally devoted. In my opinion, that right does not extend to
vivisection, particularly of the higher animals. On the other hand, the
insect does not suffer so much through its death as a man suffers from
its sting. The Hindus do not understand this.)

Artur Schopenhauer, *The World as Will and Idea* [1819] tr. R.B. Haldane and John
Kemp, 6th edn (London: Kegan Paul, Trench, Trubner, 1909) vol. I, pp. 480–
1; also translated as *The World as Will and Representation*, tr. E.F.J. Payne
(New York: Dover Publications, 1969).

14. Duty to Minimize Suffering

Jeremy Bentham   1748–1832

What other agents then are there, which, at the same time that they are
under the influence of man's direction, are susceptible of happiness?
They are of two sorts: (1) other human beings who are styled persons,
(2) other animals, which on account of their interests having been
neglected by the insensibility of the ancient jurists, stand degraded into
the class of things.

(Under the Gentoo and Mahometan religions, the interests of the rest
of the animal creation seem to have met with some attention. Why have
they not, universally, with as much as those of human creatures,
allowance made for the difference in point of sensibility? Because the
laws that are have been the work of mutual fear; a sentiment which the
less rational animals have not had the same means as man has of turning
to account. Why ought they not? No reason can be given. If the being
eaten were all, there is very good reason why we should be suffered to
eat such of them as we like to eat: we are the better for it, and they are
never the worse. They have none of those long protracted anticipations
of future misery which we have. The death they suffer in our hands
commonly is, and always may be, a speedier, and by that means a less
painful one, than that which would await them in the inevitable course
of nature. If the being killed were all, there is very good reason why we
should be suffered to kill such as molest us; we should be the worse for
their living, and they are never the worse for being dead. But is there
any reason why we should be suffered to torment them? Not any that I
can see. Are there any why we should not be suffered to torment them?
Yes, several. The day has been, I grieve to say in many places it is not yet
past, in which the greater part of the species, under the denomination of

slaves, have been treated by the law exactly upon the same footing, as, in England for example, the inferior races of animals are still. The day may come, when the rest of the animal creation may acquire those rights which never could have been withholden from them but by the hand of tyranny. The French have already discovered that the blackness of the skin is no reason why a human being should be abandoned without redress to the caprice of a tormentor. It may come one day to be recognized, that the number of the legs, the villosity of the skin, or the termination of the *os sacrum*, are reasons equally insufficient for abandoning a sensitive being to the same fate? What else is it that should trace the insuperable line? Is it the faculty of reason, or, perhaps, the faculty of discourse? But a full-grown horse or dog, is beyond comparison a more rational, as well as a more conversable animal, than an infant of a day, or a week, or even a month, old. But suppose the case were otherwise, what would it avail? The question is not, Can they reason? nor, Can they talk? but, Can they suffer?)

Jeremy Bentham, 'An Introduction to the Principles of Morals and Legislation' [1789] in *A Fragment on Government and An Introduction to the Principles of Morals and Legislation*, ed. Wilfred Harrison, 1823 edn (Oxford: Blackwell, 1948) pp. 411–12.

*   *   *

Sir, I never have seen, nor ever can see, any objection to the putting of dogs and other inferior animals to pain, in the way of medical experiment, when that experiment has a determinate object, beneficial to mankind, accompanied with a fair prospect of the accomplishment of it. But I have a decided and insuperable objection to the putting of them to pain without any such view. To my apprehension, every act by which, without prospect of preponderant good, pain is knowingly and willingly produced in any being whatsoever, is an act of cruelty: and, like other bad habits, the more the correspondent habit is indulged in, the stronger it grows, and the more frequently productive of bad fruits. I am unable to comprehend how it should be, that to him, to whom it is a matter of amusement to see a dog or a horse suffer, it should not be a matter of like amusement to see a man suffer; and seeing, as I do, how much more morality, as well as intelligence, an adult quadruped of those and many other species has in him, than any biped has for months after he has been brought into existence: nor does it appear to me, how it should be, that a person to whom the production of pain, either in the one or the other instance, is a source of amusement, would scruple to give himself that amusement when he could do so under an assurance of impunity.

To one who is in this way of thinking, you will judge, Sir, whether it be possible to believe that the desire and endeavour to lessen the sum of pain on the part of the species inferior to man, and subject to his dominion, can afford any tolerably grounded presumption of an indifference to human suffering, in the instance of any part of the human species. Judge then, Sir, again, of the surprise and affliction with which, being, as I am, one of the sincerest admirers and most zealous friends of the *Morning Chronicle*, I have for such a length of time been beholding the endeavours so repeatedly and zealously employed in it, to oppose and frustrate, if it be possible, the exertions making in Parliament to repress antisocial propensities, by imposing restraints on the wanton and useless manifestation of them.

Of these ungracious endeavours, the morality and the logic seem to me pretty equally in unison. Thus persevering in the exertions which the Parliamentary men in question have been, *ergo*, they are insincere. In sympathy towards the animals inferior to man, thus they have been abundant, *ergo*, in sympathy, good will, and good deeds, as towards men, they are deficient. With concern I say it, the exertions made in the *Morning Chronicle* to encourage and promote barbarity, have equalled, at least, in ardour and perseveringness, those made in Parliament for the repression of it. By nothing but by fallacies could an argument such as this have been supported. Accordingly, what a tissue of them is that which I have been witnessing. Such a tissue of fallacies, all of them so trite and so transparent; fallacies forming so marked a contrast with the close and genuine reasoning which I have been accustomed to witness with admiration and delight. All this, too, from so powerful and successful a champion of the cause of the people, with the laurels won by the discomfiture of the would-be conqueror of Naboth's vineyard still fresh upon his head. Were it not for that inconsistency which ever has been, and for a long time will continue to be, so unhappily abundant even in the best specimens of the human species, that such opposite exhibitions should have been made in so short a time, by the same individual, would have been altogether inconceivable.

In the ardent wish to see a stop put to a warfare, in my own view of it, so much more dangerous to the reputation of the *Morning Chronicle*, than to that of the public men whom it has taken for its objects – I remain, Sir, your sincere and sorrowing friend, J.B.

Jeremy Bentham, Letter to the Editor, *The Morning Chronicle*, 4 March 1825.

15. Duties to Animals are Direct

John Stuart Mill   1806–73

Dr Whewell's remark, that the approval of our fellow-creatures, presupposing moral ideas, cannot be the foundation of morality, has no application against Bentham, nor against the principle of utility. It may, however, be pertinently remarked, that the moral ideas which this approval presupposes, are no other than those of utility and hurtfulness. There is no great stretch of hypothesis in supposing that in proportion as mankind are aware of the tendencies of actions to produce happiness or misery, they will like and commend the first, abhor and reprobate the second. How these feelings of natural complacency and natural dread and aversion directed towards actions, come to assume the peculiar character of what we term *moral* feelings, is not a question of ethics but of metaphysics, and very fit to be discussed in its proper place. Bentham did not concern himself with it. He left it to other thinkers. It sufficed him that the perceived influence of actions on human happiness is cause enough, both in reason and in fact, for strong feelings of favour to some actions and of hatred towards others. From the sympathetic reaction of these feelings in the imagination and self-consciousness of the agent, naturally arise the more complex feelings of self-approbation and self-reproach, or, to avoid all disputed questions, we will merely say of satisfaction and dissatisfaction with ourselves. All this must be admitted, whatever else may be denied. Whether the greatest happiness is the principle of morals or not, people do desire their own happiness, and do consequently like the conduct in other people which they think promotes it, and dislike that which visibly endangers it. This is absolutely all that Bentham postulates. Grant this, and you have his popular sanction, and its reaction on the agent's own mind, two influences tending, in proportion to mankind's enlightenment, to keep the conduct of each in the line which promotes the general happiness. Bentham thinks that there is no other true morality than this, and that the so-called moral sentiments, whatever their origin or composition, should be trained to act in this direction only. And Dr Whewell's attempt to find anything illogical or incoherent in this theory, only proves that he does not yet understand it.

Dr Whewell puts the last hand to his supposed refutation of Bentham's principle, by what he thinks a crushing *reductio ad absurdum*. The reader might make a hundred guesses before discovering what this is. We have not yet got over our astonishment, not at Bentham, but at Dr Whewell. See, he says, to what consequences your greatest-happiness principle leads! Bentham says that it is as much a moral duty to regard the pleasures and pains of other animals as those of human beings. We cannot resist quoting the admirable passage which Dr Whewell cites from Bentham, with the most *naïf* persuasion that everybody will regard it as reaching the last pitch of paradoxical absurdity.

Under the Gentoo and Mahometan religions the interests of the rest of the animal kingdom seem to have met with some attention. Why have they not, universally, with as much as those of human creatures, allowance made for the difference in point of sensibility? Because the laws that are, have been the work of mutual fear; a sentiment which the less rational animals have not had the same means as man has of turning to account. Why ought they not? No reason can be given. The day may come when the rest of the animal creation may acquire those rights which never could have been withholden from them but by the hand of tyranny. It may come one day to be recognised that the number of the legs, the villosity of the skin, or the termination of the *os sacrum*, are reasons insufficient for abandoning a sensitive being to the caprice of a tormentor. What else is it that should trace the insuperable line? Is it the faculty of reason, or perhaps the faculty of discourse? But a full-grown horse or dog is beyond comparison a more rational, as well as a more conversable animal, than an infant of a day, a week, or even a month old. But suppose the case were otherwise, what would it avail? The question is not, can they reason? nor, can they speak? but, can they suffer?

This noble anticipation, in 1780, of the better morality of which a first dawn has been seen in the laws enacted nearly fifty years afterwards against cruelty to animals, is in Dr Whewell's eyes the finishing proof that the morality of happiness is absurd!

The pleasures of animals are elements of a very different order from the pleasures of man. We are bound to endeavour to augment the pleasures of men, not only because they are pleasures, but because they are human pleasures. We are bound to men by the universal tie of humanity, of human brotherhood. We have no such tie to animals.

This then is Dr Whewell's noble and disinterested ideal of virtue. Duties, according to him, are only duties to ourselves and our like.

We are to be humane to them, because we are human, not because we and they alike feel animal pleasures ... The morality which depends upon the increase of pleasure alone, would make it our duty to increase the pleasure of pigs or of geese rather than that of men, if we were sure that the pleasures we could give them were greater than the pleasures of men ... It is not only not an obvious, but to most persons not a tolerable doctrine, that we may sacrifice the happiness of men provided we can in that way produce an overplus of pleasure to cats, dogs, and hogs.

It is 'to most persons' in the Slave States of America not a tolerable doctrine that we may sacrifice any portion of the happiness of white men for the sake of a greater amount of happiness to black men. It would have been intolerable five centuries ago 'to most persons' among the feudal nobility, to hear it asserted that the greatest pleasure or pain of a hundred serfs ought not to give way to the smallest of a nobleman. According to the standard of Dr Whewell, the slavemasters and the nobles were right. They too felt themselves 'bound' by a 'tie of brotherhood' to the white men and to the nobility, and felt no such tie to the negroes and serfs. And if a feeling on moral subjects is right because it is natural, their feeling was justifiable. Nothing is more natural to human beings, nor, up to a certain point in cultivation, more universal, than to estimate the pleasures and pains of others as deserving of regard exactly in proportion to their likeness to ourselves. These superstitions of selfishness had the characteristics by which Dr Whewell recognises his moral rules; and his opinion on the rights of animals shows that in this case at least he is consistent. We are perfectly willing to stake the whole question on this one issue. Granted that any practice causes more pain to animals than it gives pleasure to man; is that practice moral or immoral? And if, exactly in proportion as human beings raise their heads out of the slough of selfishness, they do not with one voice answer 'immoral', let the morality of the principle of utility be for ever condemned.

John Stuart Mill, 'Three Essays on Religion' [1874] in J.M. Robson (ed) *John Stuart Mill: Essays on Ethics, Religion and Society* (London: Routledge and Kegan Paul, 1969) pp. 184–7.

16. The Principle of Animal Rights

Henry S. Salt   1851–1939

Have the lower animals 'rights?' Undoubtedly – if men have. That is the point I wish to make evident.

But have men rights? Let it be stated at the outset that I have no intention of discussing the abstract theory of natural rights, which, at the present time, is looked upon with suspicion and disfavour by many social reformers, since it has not unfrequently been made to cover the most extravagant and contradictory assertions. But though its phraseology is confessedly vague and perilous, there is nevertheless a solid truth underlying it – a truth which has always been clearly apprehended by the moral faculty, however difficult it may be to establish it on an unassailable logical basis. If men have not 'rights' – well, they have an unmistakable intimation of something very similar; a sense of justice which marks the boundary-line where acquiescence ceases and resistance begins; a demand for freedom to live their own life, subject to the necessity of respecting the equal freedom of other people.

Such is the doctrine of rights as formulated by Herbert Spencer. 'Every man', he says, 'is free to do that which he wills, provided he infringes not the equal liberty of any other man. And again, 'Whoever admits that each man must have a certain restricted freedom, asserts that it is *right* he should have this restricted freedom ... And hence the several particular freedoms deducible may fitly be called, as they commonly are called, his *rights*.'

The fitness of this nomenclature is disputed, but the existence of some real principle of the kind can hardly be called in question; so that the controversy concerning 'rights' is little else than an academic battle over words, which leads to no practical conclusion. I shall assume, therefore, that men are possessed of 'rights' in the sense of Herbert Spencer's definition; and if any of my readers object to this qualified use of the term, I can only say that I shall be perfectly willing to change the word as soon as a more appropriate one is forthcoming. The immediate question that claims our attention is this – if men have rights, have animals their rights also?

From the earliest times there have been thinkers who, directly or indirectly, answered this question with an affirmative. The Buddhist and Pythagorean canons, dominated perhaps by the creed of reincarnation, included the maxim 'not to kill or injure any innocent animal.' The humanitarian philosophers of the Roman empire, among whom Seneca and Plutarch and Porphyry were the most conspicuous, took still higher ground in preaching humanity on the broadest principle of universal benevolence. 'Since justice is due to rational beings', wrote Porphyry, 'how is it possible to evade the admission that we are bound also to act justly towards the races below us?'

It is a lamentable fact that during the churchdom of the middle ages, from the fourth century to the sixteenth, from the time of Porphyry to the time of Montaigne, little or no attention was paid to the question of the rights and wrongs of the lower races. Then, with the Reformation and the revival of learning, came a revival also of humanitarian feeling, as may be seen in many passages of Erasmus and More, Shakespeare and Bacon; but it was not until the eighteenth century, the age of enlightenment and 'sensibility', of which Voltaire and Rousseau were the spokesmen, that the rights of animals obtained more deliberate recognition. From the great Revolution of 1789 dates the period when the world-wide spirit of humanitarianism, which had hitherto been felt by but one man in a million – the thesis of the philosopher or the vision of the poet – began to disclose itself, gradually and dimly at first, as an essential feature of democracy.

A great and far-reaching effect was produced in England at this time by the publication of such revolutionary works as Paine's *Rights of Man*, and Mary Wollstonecraft's *Vindication of the Rights of Women*; and looking back now, after the lapse of a hundred years, we can see that a still wider extension of the theory of rights was thenceforth inevitable. In fact, such a claim was anticipated – if only in bitter jest – by a contemporary writer, who furnishes us with a notable instance of how the mockery of one generation may become the reality of the next. There was published anonymously in 1792 a little volume entitled *A Vindication of the Rights of Brutes*, a *reductio ad absurdum* of Mary Wollstonecraft's essay, written, as the author informs us, 'to evince by demonstrative arguments the perfect equality of what is called the irrational species to the human.' The further opinion is expressed that 'after those wonderful productions of Mr Paine and Mrs Wollstonecraft, such a theory as the present seems to be necessary.' It *was* necessary; and a very short term of years sufficed to bring it into effect; indeed, the theory had already been put forward by several English pioneers of nineteenth-century humanitarianism.

To Jeremy Bentham, in particular, belongs the high honour of first asserting the rights of animals with authority and persistence. 'The legislator', he wrote, 'ought to interdict everything which may serve to lead to cruelty ... Why should the law refuse its protection to any sensitive being? The time will come when humanity will extend its mantle over everything which breathes. We have begun by attending to the condition of slaves; we shall finish by softening that of all the animals which assist our labours or supply our wants.'

So, too, wrote one of Bentham's contemporaries: 'The grand source of the unmerited and superfluous misery of beasts exists in a defect in the constitution of all communities. No human government, I believe, has ever recognized the *jus animalium*, which ought surely to form a part of the jurisprudence of every system founded on the principles of justice and humanity.' A large number of later moralists have followed on the same lines, with the result that the rights of animals have already, to a certain limited extent, been established both in private usage and by legal enactment.

It is interesting to note the exact commencement of this new principle in law ... From 1822 onward, the principle of that *jus animalium* for which Bentham had pleaded, was recognized, however partially and tentatively at first, by English law, and the animals included in the Act ceased to be the mere property of their owners; moreover the Act has been several times supplemented and extended during the past half century. It is scarcely possible, in the face of this legislation, to maintain that 'rights' are a privilege with which none but human beings can be invested; for if *some* animals are already included within the pale of protection, why should not more and more be so included in the future?

For the present, however, what is most urgently needed is some comprehensive and intelligible principle, which shall indicate, in a more consistent manner, the true lines of man's moral relation towards the lower animals. And here, it must be admitted, our position is still far from satisfactory; for though certain very important concessions have been made, as we have seen, to the demand for the *jus animalium*, they have been made for the most part in a grudging, unwilling spirit, and rather in the interests of property than of principle; while even the leading advocates of animals' rights seem to have shrunk from basing their claim on the only argument which can ultimately be held to be a really sufficient one – the assertion that animals, as well as men, though, of course, to a far less extent than men, are possessed of a distinctive individuality, and, therefore, are in justice entitled to live their lives with a due measure of that 'restricted freedom' to which Herbert Spencer alludes. It is of little use to claim 'rights' for animals in a vague general way, if with the same breath we explicitly show our determination to subordinate those rights to anything and everything that can be construed into a human 'want'; nor will it ever be possible to obtain full justice for the lower races so long as we continue to regard them as beings of a wholly different order, and to ignore the significance of their numberless points of kinship with mankind ...

As far as any excuses can be alleged, in explanation of the insensibility or inhumanity of the western nations in their treatment of animals, these excuses may be mostly traced back to one or the other of two theoretical contentions, wholly different in origin, yet alike in this – that both postulate an absolute difference of nature between men and the lower kinds.

The first is the so-called 'religious' notion, which awards immortality to man, but to man alone, thereby furnishing (especially in Catholic countries) a quibbling justification for acts of cruelty to animals, on the plea that they 'have no souls' ...

The second and not less fruitful source of modern inhumanity is to be found in the 'Cartesian' doctrine – the theory of Descartes and his followers – that the lower animals are devoid of consciousness and feeling; a theory which carried the 'religious' notion a step further, and deprived the animals not only of their claim to a life hereafter, but of anything that could, without mockery, be called a life in the present, since mere 'animated machines', as they were thus affirmed to be, could in no real sense be said to *live* at all! ...

Yet no human being is justified in regarding any animal whatsoever as a meaningless automaton, to be worked, or tortured, or eaten, as the case may be, for the mere object of satisfying the wants or whims of mankind. Together with the destinies and duties that are laid on them and fulfilled by them, animals have also the right to be treated with gentleness and consideration, and the man who does not so treat them, however great his learning or influence may be, is, in that respect, an ignorant and foolish man, devoid of the highest and noblest culture of which the human mind is capable ...

So anomalous is the attitude of man towards the lower animals, that it is no marvel if many humane thinkers have wellnigh despaired over this question. 'The whole subject of the brute creation', wrote Dr Arnold, 'is to me one of such painful mystery, that I dare not approach it;' and this (to put the most charitable interpretation on their silence) appears to be the position of the majority of moralists and teachers at the present time. Yet there is urgent need of some key to the solution of the problem; and in no other way can this key be found than by the full inclusion of the lower races within the pale of human sympathy. All the promptings of our best and surest instincts point us in this direction. 'It is abundantly evident', says Lecky, 'both from history and from present experience, that the instinctive shock, or natural feelings of disgust, caused by the sight of the sufferings of men, is not generically different from that which is caused by the sight of the suffering of animals.'

If this be so – and the admission is a momentous one – can it be seriously contended that the same humanitarian tendency which has already emancipated the slave, will not ultimately benefit the lower races also? Here, again, the historian of *European Morals* has a significant remark: 'At one time', he says, 'the benevolent affections embrace merely the family, soon the circle expanding includes first a class, then a nation, then a coalition of nations, then all humanity; and finally its influence is felt in the dealings of man with the animal world. In each of these cases a standard is formed, different from that of the preceding stage, but in each case the same tendency is recognized as virtue.'

But, it may be argued, vague sympathy with the lower animals is one thing, and a definite recognition of their 'rights' is another; what reason is there to suppose that we shall advance from the former phase to the latter? Just this; that every great liberating movement has proceeded exactly on these lines. Oppression and cruelty are invariably founded on a lack of imaginative sympathy; the tyrant or tormentor can have no true sense of kinship with the victim of his injustice. When once the sense of affinity is awakened, the knell of tyranny is sounded, and the ultimate concession of 'rights' is simply a matter of time. The present condition of the more highly organized domestic animals is in many ways very analogous to that of the negro slaves of a hundred years ago; look back, and you will find in their case precisely the same exclusion from the common pale of humanity; the same hypocritical fallacies, to justify that exclusion; and, as a consequence, the same deliberate stubborn denial of their social 'rights'. Look back – for it is well to do so – and then look forward, and the moral can hardly be mistaken.

We find so great a thinker and writer as Aristotle seriously pondering whether a slave may be considered as in any sense a man. In emphasizing the point that friendship is founded on propinquity, he expresses himself as follows: 'Neither can men have friendships with horses, cattle, or slaves, considered merely as such; for a slave is merely a living instrument, and an instrument a living slave. Yet, considered as a man, a slave may be an object of friendship, for certain rights seem to belong to all those capable of participating in law and engagement. A slave, then, considered as a man, may be treated justly or unjustly.' 'Slaves', says Bentham, 'have been treated by the law exactly upon the same footing as in England, for example, the inferior races of animals are still. The day *may* come when the rest of the animal creation may acquire those rights which could never have been withholden from them but by the hand of tyranny.'

Let us unreservedly admit the immense difficulties that stand in the way of this animal enfranchisement. Our relation towards the animals is complicated and embittered by innumerable habits handed down through centuries of mistrust and brutality; we cannot, in all cases, suddenly relax these habits, or do full justice even where we see that justice will have to be done. A perfect ethic of humaneness is therefore impracticable, if not unthinkable; and we can attempt to do no more than to indicate in a general way the main principle of animals' rights, noting at the same time the most flagrant particular violations of those rights, and the lines on which the only valid reform can hereafter be effected. But, on the other hand, it may be remembered, for the comfort and encouragement of humanitarian workers, that these obstacles are, after all, only such as are inevitable in each branch of social improvement; for at every stage of every great reformation it has been repeatedly argued, by indifferent or hostile observers, that further progress is impossible; indeed, when the opponents of a great cause begin to demonstrate its 'impossibility', experience teaches us that that cause is already on the high road to fulfilment ...

Our main principle is now clear. If 'rights' exist at all – and both feeling and usage indubitably prove that they do exist – they cannot be consistently awarded to men and denied to animals, since the same sense of justice and compassion apply in both cases. 'Pain is pain', says an honest old writer, whether it be inflicted on man or on beast; and the creature that suffers it, whether man or beast, being sensible of the misery of it while it lasts, suffers evil; and the sufferance of evil, unmeritedly, unprovokedly, where no offence has been given, and no good can possibly be answered by it, but merely to exhibit power or gratify malice, is Cruelty and Injustice in him that occasions it.'

I commend this outspoken utterance to the attention of those ingenious moralists who quibble about the 'discipline' of the suffering, and deprecate immediate attempts to redress what, it is alleged, may be a necessary instrument for the attainment of human welfare. It is, perhaps, a mere coincidence, but it has been observed that those who are most forward to disallow the rights of others, and to argue that suffering and subjection are the natural lot of all living things, are usually themselves exempt from the operation of this beneficent law, and that the beauty of self-sacrifice is most loudly belauded by those who profit most largely at the expense of their fellow creatures.

But 'nature is one with rapine,' say some, and this utopian theory of 'rights', if too widely extended, must come in conflict with that iron rule of internecine competition, by which the universe is regulated. But is the universe so regulated? We note that this very objection, which was confidently relied on a few years back by many opponents of the emancipation of the working classes, is not heard of in that connection now! Our learned economists and men of science, who set themselves to play the defenders of the social *status quo*, have seen their own weapons of 'natural selection', 'survival of the fittest', and what not, snatched from their hands and turned against them, and are therefore beginning to explain to us, in a scientific manner, what we untutored humanitarians had previously felt to be true, viz. that competition is not by any means the sole governing law among the human race. We are not greatly dismayed, then, to find the same old bugbear trotted out as an argument against animals' rights – indeed, we see already unmistakable signs of a similar complete reversal of the scientific judgment. (See Prince Kropotkin's articles on *Mutual Aid among Animals*, *Nineteenth Century*, 1890, where the conclusion is arrived at that 'sociability is as much a law of nature as mutual struggle.')

The charge of 'sentimentalism' is frequently brought against those who plead for animals' rights. Now 'sentimentalism', if any meaning at all can be attached to the word, must signify an inequality, an ill balance of sentiment, an inconsistency which leads men into attacking one abuse, while they ignore or condone another where a reform is equally desirable. That this weakness is often observable among 'philanthropists' on the one hand, and 'friends of animals' on the other, and most of all among those acute 'men of the world', whose regard is only for themselves, I am not concerned to deny; what I wish to point out is, that the only real safeguard against sentimentality is to take up a consistent position towards the rights of men and of the lower animals alike, and to cultivate a broad sense of universal justice (not 'mercy') for all living things. Herein, and herein alone, is to be sought the true sanity of temperament.

It is an entire mistake to suppose that the rights of animals are in any way antagonistic to the rights of men. Let us not be betrayed for a moment into the specious fallacy that we must study human rights first, and leave the animal question to solve itself hereafter; for it is only by a wide and disinterested study of *both* subjects that a solution of either is possible. 'For he who loves all animated nature', says Porphyry, 'will not hate any one tribe of innocent beings, and by how much greater his love for the whole, by so much the more will he cultivate justice towards a part of them, and that part to which he is most allied.' To omit all worthier reasons, it is too late in the day to suggest the indefinite postponement of a consideration of animals' rights, for from a moral point of view, and even from a legislative point of view, we are daily confronted with this momentous problem, and the so-called 'practical' people who affect to ignore it are simply shutting their eyes to facts which they find it disagreeable to confront.

Once more then, animals have rights, and these rights consist in the 'restricted freedom' to live a natural life – a life, that is, which permits of the individual development – subject to the limitations imposed by the permanent needs and interests of the community. There is nothing quixotic or visionary in this assertion; it is perfectly compatible with a readiness to look the sternest laws of existence fully and honestly in the face. If we must kill, whether it be man or animal, let us kill and have done with it; if we must inflict pain, let us do what is inevitable, without hypocrisy, or evasion, or cant. But (here is the cardinal point) let us first be assured that it *is* necessary; let us not wantonly trade on the needless miseries of other beings, and then attempt to lull our consciences by a series of shuffling excuses which cannot endure a moment's candid investigation. As Leigh Hunt well says:

> That there is pain and evil, is no rule
> That I should make it greater, like a fool.

Henry S. Salt, *Animals' Rights; Considered in Relation to Social Progress* [1892]
    (Clarks Summit, Pa. International Society for Animal Rights, 1987) pp. 1–29.

17. Pity for Animals

Friedrich Nietzsche   1844–1900

The deeper minds of all ages have had pity for animals, because they suffer from life and have not the power to turn the sting of the suffering against themselves, and understand their being metaphysically. The sight of blind suffering is the spring of the deepest emotion. And in many quarters of the earth men have supposed that the souls of the guilty have entered into beasts, and that the blind suffering which at first sight calls for such pity has a clear meaning and purpose to the divine justice – of punishment and atonement: and a heavy punishment it is, to be condemned to live in hunger and need, in the shape of a beast, and to reach no consciousness of one's self in this life. I can think of no harder lot than the wild beast's; he is driven to the forest by the fierce pang of hunger, that seldom leaves him at peace; and peace is itself a torment, the surfeit after horrid food, won, maybe, by a deadly fight with other animals. To cling to life, blindly and madly, with no other aim, to be ignorant of the reason, or even the fact, of one's punishment, nay, to thirst after it as if it were a pleasure, with all the perverted desire of a fool – this is what it means to be an animal. If universal nature leads up to man, it is to show us that he is necessary to redeem her from the curse of the beast's life, and that in him existence can find a mirror of itself wherein life appears, no longer blind, but in its real metaphysical significance. But we should consider where the beast ends and the man begins – the man, the one concern of Nature. As long as any one desires life as a pleasure in itself, he has not raised his eyes above the horizon of the beast; he only desires more consciously what the beast seeks by a blind impulse. It is so with us all, for the greater part of our lives. We do not shake off the beast, but are beasts ourselves, suffering we know not what.

But there are moments when we do know; and then the clouds break, and we see how, with the rest of nature, we are straining towards the man, as to something that stands high above us. We look round and behind us, and fear the sudden rush of light; the beasts are transfigured, and ourselves with them. The enormous migrations of mankind in the wildernesses of the world, the cities they found and the wars they wage, their ceaseless gatherings and dispersions and fusions, the doctrines they blindly follow, their mutual frauds and deceits, the cry of distress, the shriek of victory – are all a continuation of the beast in us: as if the education of man has been intentionally set back, and his promise of self-consciousness frustrated; as if, in fact, after yearning for man so long, and at last reaching him by her labour, Nature should now recoil from him and wish to return to a state of unconscious instinct. Ah! she has need of knowledge, and shrinks before the very knowledge she needs: the flame flickers unsteadily and fears its own brightness, and takes hold of a thousand things before the one thing for which knowledge is necessary. There are moments when we all know that our most elaborate arrangements are only designed to give us refuge from our real task in life: we wish to hide our heads somewhere, as if our Argus-eyed conscience could not find us out; we are quick to send our hearts on state service, or money-making, or social duties, or scientific work, in order to possess them no longer ourselves; we are more willing and instinctive slaves of the hard day's work than mere living requires, because it seems to us more necessary not to be in a position to think. The hurry is universal, because every one is fleeing before himself; its concealment is just as universal, as we wish to seem contented and hide our wretchedness from the keener eyes; and so there is a common need for a new carillon of words to hang in the temple of life, and peal for its noisy festival. We all know the curious way in which unpleasant memories suddenly throng on us, and how we do our best by loud talk and violent gestures to put them out of our minds; but the gestures and the talk of our ordinary life make one think we are all in this condition, frightened of any memory or any inward gaze. What is it that is always troubling us? what is the gnat that will not let us sleep? There are spirits all about us, each moment of life has something to say to us, but we will not listen to the spirit-voices. When we are quiet and alone, we fear that something will be whispered in our ears, and so we hate the quiet, and dull our senses in society.

We understand this sometimes, as I say, and stand amazed at the whirl and the rush and the anxiety and all the dream that we call our life; we seem to fear the awakening, and our dreams too become vivid and restless, as the awakening draws near. But we feel as well that we are too weak to endure long those intimate moments, and that we are not the men to whom universal nature looks as her redeemers. It is something to be able to raise our heads but for a moment and see the stream in which we are sunk so deep. We cannot gain even this transitory moment of awakening by our own strength; we must be lifted up – and who are they that will uplift us?

The sincere men who have cast out the beast, the philosophers, artists and saints. Nature – *quae nunquam facit saltum* – has made her one leap in creating them; a leap of joy, as she feels herself for the first time at her goal, where she begins to see that she must learn not to have goals above her, and that she has played the game of transition too long. The knowledge transfigures her, and there rests on her face the gentle weariness of evening that men call 'beauty'. Her words after this transfiguration are as a great light shed over existence: and the highest wish that mortals can reach is to listen continually to her voice with ears that hear. If a man think of all that Schopenhauer, for example, must have heard in his life, he may well say to himself – The deaf ears, the feeble understanding and shrunken heart, everything that I call mine, how I despise them! Not to be able to fly but only to flutter one's wings! To look above one's self and have no power to rise! To know the road that leads to the wide vision of the philosopher, and to reel back after a few steps! Were there but one day when the great wish might be fulfilled, how gladly would we pay for it with the rest of life! To rise as high as any thinker yet into the pure icy air of the mountain, where there are no mists and veils, and the inner constitution of things is shown in a stark and piercing clarity! Even by thinking of this the soul becomes infinitely alone; but were its wish fulfilled, did its glance once fall straight as a ray of light on the things below, were shame and anxiety and desire gone for ever – one could find no words for its state then, for the mystic and tranquil emotion with which, like the soul of Schopenhauer, it would look down on the monstrous hieroglyphics of existence and the petrified doctrines of 'becoming'; not as the brooding night, but as the red and glowing day that streams over the earth. And what a destiny it is only to know enough of the fixity and happiness of the philosopher to feel the complete unfixity and unhappiness of the false philosopher, 'who without hope lives in desire': to know one's self to be the fruit of a tree that is too much in the shade ever to ripen, and to see a world of sunshine in front, where one may not go!'

There were sorrow enough here, if ever, to make such a man envious and spiteful: but he will turn aside, that he may not destroy his soul by a vain aspiration; and will discover a new circle of duties.

I can now give an answer to the question whether it be possible to approach the great ideal of Schopenhauer's man 'by any ordinary activity of our own'. In the first place, the new duties are certainly not those of a hermit; they imply rather a vast community, held together not by external forms but by a fundamental idea, namely that of *culture*; though only so far as it can put a single task before each of us – to bring the philosopher, the artist and the saint, within and without us, to the light, and to strive thereby for the completion of Nature. For Nature needs the artist, as she needs the philosopher, for a metaphysical end, the explanation of herself, whereby she may have a clear and sharp picture of what she only saw dimly in the troubled period of transition – and so may reach self-consciousness. Goethe, in an arrogant yet profound phrase, showed how all Nature's attempts only have value in so far as the artist interprets her stammering words, meets her half-way, and speaks aloud what she really means. 'I have often said, and will often repeat,' he exclaims in one place, 'the *causa finalis* of natural and human activity is dramatic poetry. Otherwise the stuff is of no use at all.'

Finally, Nature needs the saint. In him the ego has melted away, and the suffering of his life is, practically, no longer felt as individual, but as the spring of the deepest sympathy and intimacy with all living creatures: he sees the wonderful transformation scene that the comedy of 'becoming' never reaches, the attainment, at length, of the high state of man after which all nature is striving, that she may be delivered from herself. Without doubt, we all stand in close relation to him, as well as to the philosopher and the artist: there are moments, sparks from the clear fire of love, in whose light we understand the word 'I' no longer; there is something beyond our being that comes, for those moments, to the hither side of it: and this is why we long in our hearts for a bridge from here to there. In our ordinary state we can do nothing towards the production of the new redeemer, and so we hate ourselves in this state with a hatred that is the root of the pessimism which Schopenhauer had to teach again to our age, though it is as old as the aspiration after culture. – Its root, not its flower; the foundation, not the summit; the beginning of the road, not the end: for we have to learn at some time to hate something else, more universal than our own personality with its wretched limitation, its change and its unrest – and this will be when we shall learn to love something else than we can love now. When we are ourselves received into that high order of philosophers, artists and saints, in this life or a reincarnation of it, a new object for our love and hate will also rise before us. As it is, we have our task and our circle of duties, our hates and our loves. For we know that culture requires us to make ready for the coming of the Schopenhauer man – and this is the 'use' we are to make of him – we must know what obstacles there are and strike them from our path – in fact, wage unceasing war against everything that hindered our fulfilment, and prevented us from becoming Schopenhauer's men ourselves.

Friedrich Wilhelm Nietzsche, 'Schopenhauer as Educator' [1874] in Adrian Collins (tr) *Thoughts Out of Season* (Edinburgh: T.N. Foulis, 1909) Part II, pp. 149–55.

18. Duties to Life

Albert Schweitzer   1875–1965

With Descartes, philosophy starts from the dogma: 'I think therefore I exist.' With this paltry, arbitrarily chosen beginning it is landed irretrievably on the road to the abstract. It never finds the right approach to ethics, and remains entangled in a dead world- and life-view. True philosophy must start from the most immediate and comprehensive fact of consciousness, which says: 'I am life which wills to live, in the midst of life which wills to live.' This is not an ingenious dogmatic formula. Day by day, hour by hour, I live and move in it. At every moment of reflection it stands fresh before me. There bursts forth from it again and again, as from roots that can never dry up, a living world- and life-view, which can deal with all the facts of Being. A mysticism of ethical union with Being grows out of it.

As in my own will-to-live there is a longing for wider life and for the mysterious exaltation of the will-to-live which we call pleasure, with dread of annihilation and of the mysterious depreciation of the will-to-live which we call pain; so is it also in the will-to-live all around me, whether it can express itself before me, or remains dumb.

Ethics consist, therefore, in my experiencing the compulsion to show to all will-to-live the same reverence as I do to my own. There we have given us that basic principle of the moral which is a necessity of thought. It is good to maintain and to encourage life; it is bad to destroy life or to obstruct it.

As a matter of fact, everything which in the ordinary ethical valuation of the relations of men to each other ranks as good can be brought under the description of material and spiritual maintenance or promotion of human life, and of effort to bring it to its highest value. Conversely, everything which ranks as bad in human relations is in the last analysis material or spiritual destruction or obstruction of human life, and negligence in the endeavour to bring it to its highest value. Separate individual categories of good and evil which lie far apart and have apparently no connection at all with one another fit together like the pieces of a jig-saw puzzle, as soon as they are comprehended and deepened in this the most universal definition of good and evil.

The basic principle of the moral which is a necessity of thought means, however, not only an ordering and deepening, but also a widening of the current views of good and evil. A man is truly ethical only when he obeys the compulsion to help all life which he is able to assist, and shrinks from injuring anything that lives. He does not ask how far this or that life deserves one's sympathy as being valuable, nor, beyond that, whether and to what degree it is capable of feeling. Life as such is sacred to him. He tears no leaf from a tree, plucks no flower, and takes care to crush no insect. If in summer he is working by lamplight, he prefers to keep the window shut and breathe a stuffy atmosphere rather than see one insect after another fall with singed wings upon his table.

If he walks on the road after a shower and sees an earthworm which has strayed on to it he bethinks himself that it must get dried up in the sun, if it does not return soon enough to ground into which it can burrow, so he lifts it from the deadly stone surface, and puts it on the grass. If he comes across an insect which has fallen into a puddle, he stops a moment in order to hold out a leaf or a stalk on which it can save itself.

He is not afraid of being laughed at as sentimental. It is the fate of every truth to be a subject for laughter until it is generally recognised. Once it was considered folly to assume that men of colour were really men and ought to be treated as such, but the folly has become an accepted truth. To-day it is thought to be going too far to declare that constant regard for everything that lives, down to the lowest manifestations of life, is a demand made by rational ethics. The time is coming, however, when people will be astonished that mankind needed so long a time to learn to regard thoughtless injury to life as incompatible with ethics.

Ethics are responsibility without limit towards all that lives.

Albert Schweitzer, *Civilisation and Ethics* [1923] (London: Unwin Books, 1961) pp. 213–15.

19. Outside the Scope of the Theory of Justice

John Rawls

I now turn to the basis of equality, the features of human beings in virtue of which they are to be treated in accordance with the principles of justice. Our conduct toward animals is not regulated by these principles, or so it is generally believed. On what grounds then do we distinguish between mankind and other living things and regard the constraints of justice as holding only in our relations to human persons? We must examine what determines the range of application of conceptions of justice.

To clarify our question, we may distinguish three levels where the concept of equality applies. The first is to the administration of institutions as public systems of rules. In this case equality is essentially justice as regularity. It implies the impartial application and consistent interpretation of rules according to such precepts as to treat similar cases similarly (as defined by statutes and precedents) and the like. Equality at this level is the least controversial element in the common sense idea of justice. The second and much more difficult application of equality is to the substantive structure of institutions. Here the meaning of equality is specified by the principles of justice which require that equal basic rights be assigned to all persons. Presumably this excludes animals; they have some protection certainly but their status is not that of human beings. But this outcome is still unexplained. We have yet to consider what sorts of beings are owed the guarantees of justice. This brings us to the third level at which the question of equality arises.

The natural answer seems to be that it is precisely the moral persons who are entitled to equal justice. Moral persons are distinguished by two features: first they are capable of having (and are assumed to have) a conception of their good (as expressed by a rational plan of life); and second they are capable of having (and are assumed to acquire) a sense of justice, a normally effective desire to apply and to act upon the principles of justice, at least to a certain minimum degree. We use the characterization of the persons in the original position to single out the kind of beings to whom the principles chosen apply. After all, the parties are thought of as adopting these criteria to regulate their common institutions and their conduct toward one another; and the description of their nature enters into the reasoning by which these principles are selected. Thus equal justice is owed to those who have the capacity to take part in and to act in accordance with the public understanding of the initial situation. One should observe that moral personality is here defined as a potentiality that is ordinarily realized in due course. It is this potentiality which brings the claims of justice into play. I shall return to this point below.

We see, then, that the capacity for moral personality is a sufficient condition for being entitled to equal justice. Nothing beyond the essential minimum is required. Whether moral personality is also a necessary condition I shall leave aside. I assume that the capacity for a sense of justice is possessed by the overwhelming majority of mankind, and therefore this question does not raise a serious practical problem. That moral personality suffices to make one a subject of claims is the essential thing. We cannot go far wrong in supposing that the sufficient condition is always satisfied ...

Last of all, we should recall here the limits of a theory of justice. Not only are many aspects of morality left aside, but no account is given of right conduct in regard to animals and the rest of nature. A conception of justice is but one part of a moral view. While I have not maintained that the capacity for a sense of justice is necessary in order to be owed the duties of justice, it does seem that we are not required to give strict justice anyway to creatures lacking this capacity. But it does not follow that there are no requirements at all in regard to them, nor in our relations with the natural order. Certainly it is wrong to be cruel to animals and the destruction of a whole species can be a great evil. The capacity for feelings of pleasure and pain and for the forms of life of which animals are capable clearly imposes duties of compassion and humanity in their case. I shall not attempt to explain these considered beliefs. They are outside the scope of the theory of justice, and it does not seem possible to extend the contract doctrine so as to include them in a natural way. A correct conception of our relations to animals and to nature would seem to depend upon a theory of the natural order and our place in it. One of the tasks of metaphysics is to work out a view of the world which is suited for this purpose; it should identify and systematize the truths decisive for these questions. How far justice as fairness will have to be revised to fit into this larger theory it is impossible to say. But it seems reasonable to hope that if it is sound as an account of justice among persons, it cannot be too far wrong when these broader relationships are taken into consideration.

John Rawls, *A Theory of Justice* (Oxford University Press, 1972) pp. 504–12.

20. The Rights of Animals

Brigid Brophy

Were it announced tomorrow that anyone who fancied it might, without risk of reprisals or recriminations, stand at a fourth-storey window, dangle out of it a length of string with a meal (labelled 'Free') on the end, wait till a chance passer-by took a bite and then, having entangled his cheek or gullet on a hook hidden in the food, haul him up to the fourth floor and there batter him to death with a knobkerry, I do not think there would be many takers.

Most sane adults would, I imagine, sicken at the mere thought. Yet sane adults do the equivalent to fish every day: not in panic, sexual jealousy, ideological frenzy or even greed – many of our freshwater fish are virtually inedible, and not one of them constitutes a threat to the life, love or ideology of a human on the bank – but for amusement. Civilization is not outraged at their behaviour. On the contrary: that a person's hobby is fishing is often read as a guarantee of his sterling and innocent character.

The relationship of *homo sapiens* to the other animals is one of unremitting exploitation. We employ their work; we eat and wear them. We exploit them to serve our superstitions: whereas we used to sacrifice them to our gods and tear out their entrails in order to foresee the future, we now sacrifice them to Science and experiment on their entrails in the hope – or on the mere off-chance – that we might thereby see a little more clearly into the present. When we can think of no pretext for causing their death and no profit to turn it to, we often cause it none the less, wantonly, the only gain being a brief pleasure for ourselves, which is usually only marginally bigger than the pleasure we could have had without killing anything; we could quite well enjoy our marksmanship or cross-country galloping without requiring a real dead wild animal to show for it at the end.

It is rare for us to leave wild animals alive; when we do, we often do not leave them wild. Some we put on display in a prison just large enough for them to survive, but not in any full sense to live in. Others we trundle about the country in their prisons, pausing every now and then to put them on public exhibition performing, like clockwork, 'tricks' we have 'trained' into them. However, animals are not clockwork but instinctual beings. Circus 'tricks' are spectacular or risible as the case may be precisely *because* they violate the animals' instinctual nature – which is precisely why they ought to violate both our moral and our aesthetic sense.

But where animals are concerned humanity seems to have switched off its morals and aesthetics – indeed, its very imagination. Goodness knows, those facilities function erratically enough in our dealings with one another. But at least we recognize their faultiness. We spend an increasing number of our cooler moments trying to forestall the moral and aesthetic breakdowns which are liable, in a crisis, to precipitate us into atrocities against each other. We have bitter demarcation disputes about where the rights of one man end and those of the next man begin, but most men now acknowledge that there are such things as the rights of the next man. Only in relation to the next animal can civilized humans persuade themselves that they have absolute and arbitrary rights – that they may do anything whatever that they can get away with.

The reader will have guessed in some detail by now what sort of person he confronts in me: a sentimentalist; probably a killjoy; a person with no grasp on economic realities; a twee anthropomorphist, who attributes human feelings (and no doubt human names and clothes as well) to animals, and yet actually prefers animals to humans and would sooner succour a stray cat than an orphan child; a latter-day version of those folklore English spinsters who, in the nineteenth century, excited the ridicule of the natives by walking around Florence requesting them not to ill-treat their donkeys; and *par excellence*, of course, a crank.

Well. To take the last item first: if by 'crank' you mean 'abnormal', yes. My views are shared by only a smallish (but probably not so small as you think) part of the citizenry – as yet. Still, that proves nothing either way about the validity of our views. It is abnormal to be a lunatic convinced you are Napoleon, but equally (indeed, numerically considered, probably even more) abnormal to be a genius. The test of a view is its rationality, not the number of people who endorse it. It would have been cranky indeed in the ancient world to raise the question of the rights of slaves – so cranky that scarcely a voice went on record as doing so. To us it seems incredible that the Greek philosophers should have scanned so deep into right and wrong and yet never *noticed* the immorality of slavery. Perhaps three thousand years from now it will seem equally incredible that we do not notice the immorality of our oppression of animals.

Slavery was the ancient world's patch of moral and aesthetic insensitivity. Indeed, it was not until the eighteenth and nineteenth centuries of our own era that the human conscience was effectively and universally switched on in that respect. Even then, we went on with economic and social exploitations which stopped short of slavery only in constitutional status, and people were found to justify them. But by then the exploiters had at least been forced on to the defensive and felt obliged to produce the feeble arguments that had never even been called for in the ancient world. Perhaps it is a sign that our conscience is about to be switched on in relation to animals that some animal-exploiters are now seeking to justify themselves. When factory-farmers tell us that animals kept in 'intensive' (i.e. concentration) camps are being kindly spared the inclemency of a winter outdoors, and that calves do not mind being tethered for life on slate because they have never known anything else, an echo should start in our historical consciousness: do you remember how the childlike blackamoors were kindly spared the harsh responsibilities of freedom, how the skivvy didn't feel the hardship of scrubbing all day because she was used to it, how the poor didn't mind their slums because they had never known anything else?

The first of the factory-farmers' arguments is, of course, an argument for ordinary farms to make better provision for animals in winter, not for ordinary farms to be replaced by torture chambers. As for the one about the animals' never having known anything else, I still shan't believe it to be valid but I shall accept that the factory-farmers genuinely believe it themselves when they follow out its logic by using their profits to finance the repatriation of every circus and zoo animal that was caught in the wild, on the grounds that those *have* known something else.

Undismayed by being a crank, I will make you a free gift of another stick to beat me with, by informing you that I am a vegetarian. Now, surely, you have me. Not only am I a more extreme crank, a member of an even smaller minority, than you had realized; surely I *must,* now, be a killjoy. Yet which, in fact, kills more joy: the killjoy who would deprive you of your joy in eating steak, which is just one of the joys open to you, or the kill-animal who puts an end to all the animal's joys along with its life?

Beware, however (if we may now take up the first item in your Identikit portrait of me), how you call me a sentimentalist in this matter. I may be less of one than you are. I won't kill an animal in order to eat it, but I am no respecter of dead bodies as such. If our chemists discovered (as I'm sure they quickly would were there a demand) how to give tenderness and hygiene to the body of an animal which had died of old age, I would willingly eat it; and in principle that goes for human animals, too. In practice I suspect I should choke on a rissole which I knew might contain bits of Great-Aunt Emily (whether through love or repulsion I am not quite sure), and I admit I might have to leave rational cannibalism to future generations brought up without my irrational prejudice (which is equally irrational whether prompted by love or by repulsion). But you were accusing me, weren't you, of sentimentality and ignorance of economic realities. Have you thought how much of the world's potential food supply *you* unrealistically let go to waste because of your sentimental compunction about eating your fellow-citizens after they have lived out their natural lives?

If we are going to rear and kill animals for our food, I think we have a moral obligation to spare them pain and terror in both processes, simply because they are sentient. I can't *prove* they are sentient; but then I have no proof *you* are. Even though you are articulate, whereas an animal can only scream or struggle, I have no assurance that your 'It hurts' expresses anything like the intolerable sensations I experience in pain. I know, however, that when I visit my dentist and say 'It hurts', I am grateful that he gives me the benefit of the doubt.

I don't myself believe that, even when we fulfil our minimum obligation not to cause pain, we have the right to kill animals. I know I would have no right to kill you, however painlessly, just because I like your flavour, and I am not in a position to judge that your life is worth more to you than the animal's to it. If anything, you probably value yours less; unlike the animal, you are capable of acting on an impulse to suicide. Christian tradition would permit me to kill the animal but not you, on the grounds that you have, and it hasn't, an immortal soul. I am not a Christian and do not avail myself of this licence; but if I were, I should in elementary justice see the soul theory as all the more reason to let the animal live out the one mortal life it has.

The only genuine moral problem is where there is a direct clash between an animal's life and a human one. Our diet proposes no such clash, meat not being essential to a human life; I have sustained a very healthy one for ten years without. And in fact such clashes are much rarer in reality than in exam papers, where we are always being asked to rescue either our grandmother or a Rubens from a blazing house. Human fantasy often fabricates a dilemma (yours did when you suggested I love animals in preference to people – there is no psycho-logical law which prevents me from loving both) as an excuse for inertia. It is a principle of 'divide and do nothing'. In reality, unless you truly send a cheque to a relief organization for humans, your preference for humans over animals does not justify you in resisting my hint that you should send one to the Wood Green Animal Shelters (601 Lordship Lane, London N22 5LG) and to Zoo Check, which was founded by Virginia McKenna and William Travers with the motto 'Keeping Wildlife in the Wild' (Cherry Tree Cottage, Coldharbour, Dorking, Surrey RH5 6HA).

The most seemingly genuine clash is on the subject of vivisection. To hold vivisection to be never justified is a hard belief. But so is its opposite. I believe it is never justified because I can see nothing (except our being able to get away with it) which lets us pick on animals that would not equally let us pick on idiot humans (who would be more useful) or, for the matter of that, on a few humans of any sort whom we might sacrifice for the good of the many. If we do permit vivisection, here if anywhere we are under the most stringent minimum obligations. The very least we must make sure of is that no experiment is ever duplicated, or careless, or done for mere teaching's sake or as a substitute for thinking. Knowing how often, in every other sphere, pseudo-work proliferates in order to fill time and jobs, and how often activity substitutes for thought, and then reading the official statistics about vivisection, do you truly believe we *do* make sure? (The National Anti-Vivisection Society is at 51 Harley Street, London W1.)

Our whole relation to animals is tinted by a fantasy – and a fallacy – about our toughness. We feel obliged to demonstrate we can take it; in fact, it is the animals who take it. So shy are we of seeming sentimental that we often disguise our humane impulses under 'realistic' arguments:

foxhunting is snobbish; factory-farmed food doesn't taste so nice. But foxhunting would still be an atrocity if it were done by authenticated, pedigreed proletarians, and so would factory-farming, even if a way were found of making its corpses tasty. So, incidentally, would slavery, even it were proved a hundred times more economically realistic than freedom.

The saddest and silliest of the superstitions to which we sacrifice animals is our belief that by killing them we ourselves somehow live more fully. We might live more fully by entering imaginatively into their lives. But shedding their blood makes us no more full-blooded. It is a mere myth, often connected with our myth about the *savoir vivre* and sexiness of the sunny south (which is how you managed to transform me into a frustrated British virgin in Florence). There is no law of nature which makes *savoir vivre* incompatible with 'live and let live'. The bullfighter who torments a bull to death and then castrates it of an ear has neither proved nor increased his own virility; he has merely demonstrated that he is a butcher with balletic tendencies.

Superstition and dread of sentimentality weight all our questions against the animals. We *don't* scrutinize vivisection rigorously – we somehow think it would be soft of us to do so, which we apparently think a worse thing to be than cruel. When, in February 1965, the House of Lords voted against a Bill banning animal acts from circuses, it was pointed out that the animal-trainers would lose their jobs. (Come to think of it, many human-trainers must have lost theirs when it was decided to ban gladiator acts from circuses.) No one pointed out how many unemployed acrobats and jugglers would *get* jobs to replace the animals. (I'm not, you see by the way, the sort of killjoy who wants to abolish the circus as such.) Similarly with the anthropomorphism argument, which works in both directions but is always wielded in one only. In the same House of Lords debate, Lady Summerskill, who had taken the humane side, was mocked by a noble lord on the grounds that were *she* shut up in a cage she would indeed suffer from mortification and the loss of her freedom, but an animal, not being human, wouldn't. Why did no one point out that a human, in such circumstances, dreadful as they are, would have every consolation of the human intellect and imagination, from reading books to analysing his circumstances and writing to the Home Secretary about them, whereas the animal suffers the raw terror of not comprehending what is being done to it?

In point of fact, I am the very opposite of an anthropomorphist. I don't hold animals superior or even equal to humans. The whole case for behaving decently to animals rests on the fact that we are the superior species. We are the species uniquely capable of imagination, rationality and moral choice – and that is precisely why we are under the obligation to recognize and respect the rights of animals.

Brigid Brophy, 'The Rights of Animals', *Reads* (London: Sphere, 1989) pp. 123–34.

21. All Animals are Equal

Peter Singer

In recent years a number of oppressed groups have campaigned vigorously for equality. The classic instance is the Black Liberation movement, which demands an end to the prejudice and discrimination that has made blacks second-class citizens. The immediate appeal of the black liberation movement and its initial, if limited, success made it a model for other oppressed groups to follow. We became familiar with liberation movements for Spanish-Americans, gay people, and a variety of other minorities. When a majority group – women – began their campaign, some thought we had come to the end of the road. Discrimination on the basis of sex, it has been said, is the last universally accepted form of discrimination, practised without secrecy or pretence even in those liberal circles that have long prided themselves on their freedom from prejudice against racial minorities.

One should always be wary of talking of 'the last remaining form of discrimination.' If we have learnt anything from the liberation movements, we should have learnt how difficult it is to be aware of latent prejudice in our attitudes to particular groups until this prejudice is forcefully pointed out.

A liberation movement demands an expansion of our moral horizons and an extension or reinterpretation of the basic moral principle of equality. Practices that were previously regarded as natural and inevitable come to be seen as the result of an unjustifiable prejudice. Who can say with confidence that all his or her attitudes and practices are beyond criticism? If we wish to avoid being numbered amongst the oppressors, we must be prepared to re-think even our most fundamental attitudes. We need to consider them from the point of view of those most disadvantaged by our attitudes, and the practices that follow from these attitudes. If we can make this unaccustomed mental switch we may discover a pattern in our attitudes and practices that consistently operates so as to benefit one group – usually the one to which we ourselves belong – at the expense of the other. In this way we may come to see that there is a case for a new liberation movement. My aim is to advocate that we make this mental switch in respect of our attitudes and practices towards a very large group of beings: members of species other than our own – or, as we popularly though misleadingly call them, animals. In other words, I am urging that we extend to other species the basic principle of equality that most of us recognize should be extended to all members of our own species ...

If a being suffers, there can be no moral justification for refusing to take that suffering into consideration. No matter what the nature of the being, the principle of equality requires that its suffering be counted equally with the like suffering – in so far as rough comparisons can be made – of any other being. If a being is not capable of suffering, or of experiencing enjoyment or happiness, there is nothing to be taken into account. This is why the limit of sentience (using the term as a convenient, if not strictly accurate, shorthand for the capacity to suffer or experience enjoyment or happiness) is the only defensible boundary of concern for the interests of others. To mark this boundary by some characteristic like intelligence or rationality would be to mark it in an arbitrary way. Why not choose some other characteristic, like skin colour?

The racist violates the principle of equality by giving greater weight to the interests of members of his own race, when there is a clash between their interests and the interests of those of another race. Similarly the speciesist allows the interests of his own species to override the greater interests of members of other species. The pattern is the same in each case. Most human beings are speciesists. I shall now very briefly describe some of the practices that show this.

For the great majority of human beings, especially in urban, industrialized societies, the most direct form of contact with members of other species is at meal-times: we eat them. In doing so we treat them purely as means to our ends. We regard their life and well-being as subordinate to our taste for a particular kind of dish. I say 'taste' deliberately – this is purely a matter of pleasing our palate. There can be no defence of eating flesh in terms of satisfying nutritional needs, since it has been established beyond doubt that we could satisfy our need for protein and other essential nutrients far more efficiently with a diet that replaced animal flesh by soy beans, or products derived from soy beans, and other high-protein vegetable product.

It is not merely the act of killing that indicates what we are ready to do to other species in order to gratify our tastes. The suffering we inflict on the animals while they are alive is perhaps an even clearer indication of our speciesism than the fact that we are prepared to kill them. In order to have meat on the table at a price that people can afford, our society tolerates methods of meat production that confine sentient animals in cramped, unsuitable conditions for the entire durations of their lives. Animals are treated like machines that convert fodder into flesh, and any innovation that results in a higher 'conversion ratio' is liable to be adopted. As one authority on the subject has said, 'cruelty is acknowledged only when profitability ceases' ...

Since, as I have said, none of these practices cater for anything more than our pleasures of taste, our practice of rearing and killing other animals in order to eat them is a clear instance of the sacrifice of the most important interests of other beings in order to satisfy trivial interests of our own. To avoid speciesism we must stop this practice, and each of us has a moral obligation to cease supporting the practice. Our custom is all the support that the meat-industry needs. The decision to cease giving it that support may be difficult, but it is no more difficult than it would have been for a white Southerner to go against the traditions of his society and free his slaves: if we do not change our dietary habits, how can we censure those slaveholders who would not change their own way of living?

The same form of discrimination may be observed in the widespread practice of experimenting on other species in order to see if certain substances are safe for human beings, or to test some psychological theory about the effect of severe punishment on learning, or to try out various new compounds just in case something turns up ...

It is significant that the problem of equality, in moral and political philosophy, is invariably formulated in terms of human equality. The effect of this is that the question of the equality of other animals does not confront the philosopher, or student, as an issue itself – and this is already an indication of the failure of philosophy to challenge accepted beliefs. Still, philosophers have found it difficult to discuss the issue of human equality without raising, in a paragraph or two, the question of the status of animals. The reason for this, which should be apparent from what I have said already, is that if humans are to be regarded as equals to one another, we need some sense of 'equal' that does not require any actual, descriptive equality of capacities, talents or other qualities. If equality is to be related to any actual characteristics of humans, these characteristics must be some lowest common denominator, pitched so low that no human lacks them – but then the philosopher comes up against the catch that any such set of characteristics which covers *all* humans will not be possessed *only by humans*. In other words, it turns out that in the only sense in which we can truly say, as an assertion of fact, that all humans are equal, at least some members of other species are also equal – equal, that is, to each other and to humans. If, on the other hand, we regard the statement 'All humans are equal' in some non-factual way, perhaps as a prescription, then, as I have already argued, it is even more difficult to exclude non-humans from the sphere of equality.

This result is not what the egalitarian philosopher originally intended to assert. Instead of accepting the radical outcome to which their own reasonings naturally point, however, most philosophers try to reconcile their beliefs in human equality and animal inequality by arguments that can only be described as devious.

As a first example, I take William Frankena's well-known article *The Concept of Social Justice.* Frankena opposes the idea of basing justice on merit, because he sees that this could lead to highly inegalitarian results. Instead he proposes the principle that

> ... all men are to be treated as equals, not because they are equal, in any respect, but simply because they are human. They are human because they have emotions and desires, and are able to think, and hence are capable of enjoying a good life in a sense in which other animals are not.[1]

But what is this capacity to enjoy the good life which all humans have, but no other animals? Other animals have emotions and desires, and appear to be capable of enjoying a good life. We may doubt that they can think – although the behaviour of some apes, dolphins and even dogs suggests that some of them can – but what is the relevance of thinking? Frankena goes on to admit that by 'the good life' he means 'not so much the morally good life as the happy or satisfactory life,' so thought would appear to be unnecessary for enjoying the good life; in fact to emphasize the need for thought would make difficulties for the egalitarian since only some people are capable of leading intellectually satisfying lives, or morally good lives. This makes it difficult to see what Frankena's principle of equality has to do with simply being *human.* Surely every sentient being is capable of leading a life that is happier or less miserable than some alternative life, and hence has a claim to be taken into account. In this respect the distinction between humans and nonhumans is not a sharp division, but rather a continuum along which we move gradually, and with overlaps between the species, from simple capacities for enjoyment and satisfaction, or pain and suffering, to more complex ones.

Faced with a situation in which they see a need for some basis for the moral gulf that is commonly thought to separate humans and animals, but can find no concrete difference that will do the job without undermining the equality of humans, philosophers tend to waffle. They resort to high-sounding phrases like 'the intrinsic dignity of the human individual';[2] They talk of the 'intrinsic worth of all men' as if men (humans?) had some worth that other beings did not[3] or they say that humans, and only humans, are 'ends in themselves', while 'everything other than a person can only have value for a person.'[4]

This idea of a distinctive human dignity and worth has a long history; it can be traced back directly to the Renaissance humanists, for instance to Pico della Mirandola's *Oration on the Dignity of Man.* Pico and other humanists based their estimate of human dignity on the idea that man possessed the central, pivotal position in the 'Great Chain of Being' that led from the lowliest forms of matter to God himself; this view of the universe, in turn, goes back to both classical and Judaeo-Christian doctrines. Contemporary philosophers have cast off these metaphysical and religious shackles and freely invoke the dignity of mankind without needing to justify the idea at all. Why should we not attribute 'intrinsic dignity' or 'intrinsic worth' to ourselves? Fellow humans are unlikely to reject the accolades we so generously bestow on them, and those to whom we deny the honour are unable to object. Indeed, when one thinks only of humans, it can be very liberal, very progressive, to talk of the dignity of all human beings. In so doing, we implicitly condemn slavery, racism, and other violations of human rights. We admit that we ourselves are in some fundamental sense on a par with the poorest, most ignorant members of our own species. It is only when we think of humans as no more than a small sub-group of all the beings that inhabit our planet that we may realize that in elevating our own species we are at the same time lowering the relative status of all other species.

The truth is that the appeal to the intrinsic dignity of human beings appears to solve the egalitarian's problems only as long as it goes unchallenged. Once we ask *why* it should be that all humans – including infants, mental defectives, psychopaths, Hitler, Stalin and the rest – have some kind of dignity or worth that no elephant, pig, or chimpanzee can ever achieve, we see that this question is as difficult to answer as our original request for some relevant fact that justifies the inequality of humans and other animals. In fact, these two questions are really one: talk of intrinsic dignity or moral worth only takes the problem back one step, because any satisfactory defence of the claim that all and only humans have intrinsic dignity would need to refer to some relevant capacities or characteristics that all and only humans possess. Philosophers frequently introduce ideas of dignity, respect and worth at the point at which other reasons appear to be lacking, but this is hardly good enough. Fine phrases are the last resource of those who have run out of arguments.

In case there are those who still think it may be possible to find some relevant characteristic that distinguishes all humans from all members of other species, I shall refer again, before I conclude, to the existence of some humans who quite clearly are below the level of awareness, self-consciousness, intelligence, and sentience, of many nonhumans. I am thinking of humans with severe and irreparable brain damage, and also of infant humans. To avoid the complication of the relevance of a being's potential, however, I shall henceforth concentrate on permanently retarded humans.

Philosophers who set out to find a characteristic that will distinguish humans from other animals rarely take the course of abandoning these groups of humans by lumping them in with the other animals. It is easy to see why they do not. To take this line without re-thinking our attitudes to other animals would entail that we have the right to perform painful experiments on retarded humans for trivial reasons; similarly it would follow that we had the right to rear and kill these humans for food. To most philosophers these consequences are as unacceptable as the view that we should stop treating nonhumans in this way.

Peter Singer, 'All Animals are Equal' in *Philosophical Exchange*, vol. 1. no. 5, 1974; reprinted in Tom Regan and Peter Singer (eds) *Animal Rights and Human Obligations* (Englewood Cliffs, NJ: Prentice-Hall, 1976) pp. 148–62.

1. In R. Brandt (ed) *Social Justice* (Englewood Cliffs, NJ: Prentice-Hall, 1962) p. 19.
2. Frankena, op. cit., p. 23.
3. H.A. Bedau, 'Egalitarianism and the Idea of Equality' in *Nomos IX: Equality*, ed. J.R. Pennock and J.W. Chapman (New York, 1967).
4. G. Vlastos, 'Justice and Equality' in Brandt, *Social Justice*, p. 48.

22. Constraints and Animals

Robert Nozick

We can illuminate the status and implications of moral side constraints by considering living beings for whom such stringent side constraints (or any at all) usually are not considered appropriate: namely, nonhuman animals. Are there any limits to what we may do to animals? Have animals the moral status of mere objects? Do some purposes fail to entitle us to impose great costs on animals? What entitles us to use them at all?

Animals count for something. Some higher animals, at least, ought to be given some weight in people's deliberations about what to do. It is difficult to *prove* this. (It is also difficult to prove that people count for something!) We first shall adduce particular examples, and then arguments. If you felt like snapping your fingers, perhaps to the beat of some music, and you knew that by some strange causal connection your snapping your fingers would cause 10,000 contented, unowned cows to die after great pain and suffering, or even painlessly and instantaneously, would it be perfectly all right to snap your fingers? Is there some reason why it would be morally wrong to do so?

Some say people should not do so because such acts brutalize them and make them more likely to take the lives of persons, solely for pleasure. These acts that are morally unobjectionable in themselves, they say, have an undesirable moral spillover. (Things then would be different if there were no possibility of such spillover – for example, for the person who knows himself to be the last person on earth.) But why *should* there be such a spillover? If it is, in itself, perfectly all right to do anything at all to animals for any reason whatsoever, then provided a person realizes the clear line between animals and persons and keeps it in mind as he acts, why should killing animals tend to brutalize him and make him more likely to harm or kill persons? Do butchers commit more murders? (Than other persons who have knives around?) If I enjoy hitting a baseball squarely with a bat, does this significantly increase the danger of my doing the same to someone's head? Am I not capable of understanding that people differ from baseballs, and doesn't this understanding stop the spillover? Why should things be different in the case of animals? To be sure, it is an empirical question whether spillover does take place or not; but there *is* a puzzle as to why it should, at least among readers of this essay, sophisticated people who are capable of drawing distinctions and differentially acting upon them.

If some animals count for something, which animals count, how much do they count, and how can this be determined? Suppose (as I believe the evidence supports) that eating animals is not necessary for health and is not less expensive than alternate equally healthy diets available to people in the United States. The gain, then, from the eating of animals is pleasures of the palate, gustatory delights, varied tastes. I would not claim that these are not truly pleasant, delightful, and interesting. The question is: do they, or rather does the marginal addition in them gained by eating animals rather than only nonanimals, outweigh the moral weight to be given to animals' lives and pain? Given that animals are to count for *something*, is the extra gain obtained by eating them rather than nonanimal products greater than the moral cost? How might these questions be decided?

We might try looking at comparable cases, extending whatever judgments we make on those cases to the one before us. For example, we might look at the case of hunting, where I assume that it's not all right to hunt and kill animals merely for the fun of it. Is hunting a special case, because its object and what provides the fun is the chasing and maiming and death of animals? Suppose then that I enjoy swinging a baseball bat. It happens that in front of the only place to swing it stands a cow. Swinging the bat unfortunately would involve smashing the cow's head. But I wouldn't get fun from doing *that*; the pleasure comes from exercising my muscles, swinging well, and so on. It's unfortunate that as a side effect (not a means) of my doing this, the animal's skull gets smashed. To be sure, I could forego swinging the bat, and instead bend down and touch my toes or do some other exercise. But this wouldn't be as enjoyable as swinging the bat; I won't get as much fun, pleasure, or delight out of it. So the question is: would it be all right for me to swing the bat in order to get the *extra* pleasure of swinging it as compared to the best available alternative activity that does not involve harming the animal? Suppose that it is not merely a question of foregoing today's special pleasures of bat swinging; suppose that each day the same situation arises with a different animal. Is there some principle that would allow killing and eating animals for the additional pleasure this brings, yet would not allow swinging the bat for the extra pleasure it brings? What could that principle be like? (Is this a better parallel to eating meat? The animal is killed to get a bone out of which to make the best sort of bat to use; bats made out of other material don't give quite the same pleasure. Is it all right to kill the animal to obtain the extra pleasure that using a bat made out of its bone would bring? Would it be morally more permissible if you could hire someone to do the killing for you?)

Such examples and questions might help someone to see what sort of line he wishes to draw, what sort of position he wishes to take. They face, however, the usual limitations of consistency arguments; they do not say, once a conflict is shown, which view to change. After failing to devise a principle to distinguish swinging the bat from killing and eating an animal, you might decide that it's really all right, after all, to swing the bat. Furthermore, such appeal to similar cases does not greatly help us to assign precise moral weight to different sorts of animals ...

My purpose here in presenting these examples is to pursue the notion of moral side constraints, not the issue of eating animals. Though I should say that in my view the extra benefits Americans today can gain from eating animals do *not* justify doing it. So we shouldn't. One ubiquitous argument, not unconnected with side constraints, deserves mention: because people eat animals, they raise more than otherwise would exist without this practice. To exist for a while is better than never to exist at all. So (the argument concludes) the animals are better off because we have the practice of eating them. Though this is not our object, fortunately it turns out that we really, all along, benefit them! (If tastes changed and people no longer found it enjoyable to eat animals, should those concerned with the welfare of animals steel themselves to an unpleasant task and continue eating them?) I trust I shall not be misunderstood as saying that animals are to be given the same moral weight as people if I note that the parallel argument about people would not look very convincing. We can imagine that population problems lead every couple or group to limit their children to some number fixed in advance. A given couple, having reached the number, proposes to have an additional child and dispose of it at the age of three (or twenty-three) by sacrificing it or using it for some gastronomic purpose. In justification, they note that the child will not exist at all if this is not allowed; and surely it is better for it to exist for some number of years. However, once a person exists, not everything compatible with his overall existence being a net plus can be done, even by those who created him. An existing person has claims, even against those whose purpose in creating him was to violate those claims. It would be worthwhile to pursue moral objections to a system that permits parents to do anything whose permissibility is necessary for their choosing to have the child, that also leaves the child better off than if it hadn't been born. (Some will think the only objections arise from difficulties in accurately administering the permission.) Once they exist, animals too may have claims to certain treatment. These claims may well carry less weight than those of people. But the fact that some animals were brought into existence only because someone wanted to do something that would violate one of these claims does not show that the claim doesn't exist at all.

Consider the following (too minimal) position about the treatment of animals. So that we can easily refer to it, let us label this position 'utilitarianism for animals, Kantianism for people.' It says: (1) maximize the total happiness of all living beings; (2) place stringent side constraints on what one may do to human beings. Human beings may not be used or sacrificed for the benefit of others; animals may be used or sacrificed for the benefit of other people or animals *only if* those benefits are greater than the loss inflicted. (This inexact statement of the utilitarian position is close enough for our purposes, and it can be handled more easily in discussion.) One may proceed only if the total utilitarian benefit is greater than the utilitarian loss inflicted on the animals. This utilitarian view counts animals as much as normal utilitarianism does persons. Following Orwell, we might summarize this view as: all animals are equal but some are more equal than others. (None may be sacrificed except for a greater total benefit; but persons may not be sacrificed at all, or only under far more stringent conditions, and never for the benefit of non-human animals. I mean (1) above merely to exclude sacrifices which do not meet the utilitarian standard, not to mandate a utilitarian goal. We shall call this position negative utilitarianism.)

We can now direct arguments for animals counting for something to holders of different views. To the 'Kantian' moral philosopher who imposes stringent side constraints on what may be done to a person, we can say:

> You hold utilitarianism inadequate because it allows an individual to be sacrificed to and for another, and so forth, thereby neglecting the stringent limitations on how one legitimately may behave toward persons. But *could* there be anything morally intermediate between persons and stones, something without such stringent limitations on its treatment, yet not to be treated merely as an object? One would expect that by subtracting or diminishing some features of persons, we would get this intermediate sort of being. (Or perhaps beings of intermediate moral status are gotten by subtracting some of our characteristics and adding others very different from ours.)
>
> Plausibly, animals are the intermediate beings, and utilitarianism is the intermediate position. We may come at the question from a slightly different angle. Utilitarianism assumes both that happiness is all that matters morally and that all beings are interchangeable. This conjunction does not hold true of persons. But isn't (negative) utilitarianism true of whatever beings the conjunction does hold for, and doesn't it hold for animals?

To the utilitarian we may say:

> If only the experiences of pleasure, pain, happiness, and so on (and the capacity for these experiences) are morally relevant, then animals must be counted in moral calculations to the extent they *do* have these capacities and experiences. Form a matrix where the rows

represent alternative policies or actions, the columns represent different individual organisms, and each entry represents the utility (net pleasure, happiness) the policy will lead to for the organism. The utilitarian theory evaluates each policy by the sum of the entries in its row and directs us to perform an action or adopt a policy whose sum is maximal. Each column is weighted equally and counted once, be it that of a person or a non-human animal. Though the structure of the view treats them equally, animals might be less important in the decisions because of facts about them. If animals have less capacity for pleasure, pain, happiness than humans do, the matrix entries in animals' columns will be lower generally than those in people's columns. In this case, they will be less important factors in the ultimate decisions to be made.

A utilitarian would find it difficult to deny animals this kind of equal consideration. On what grounds could he consistently distinguish persons' happiness from that of animals, to count only the former? Even if experiences don't get entered in the utility matrix unless they are above a certain threshold, surely *some* animal experiences are greater than some people's experiences that the utilitarian wishes to count. (Compare an animal's being burned alive unanaesthetized with a person's mild annoyance.) Bentham, we may note, does count animals' happiness equally in just the way we have explained.

Under 'utilitarianism for animals, Kantianism for people', animals will be used for the gain of other animals and persons, but persons will never be used (harmed, sacrificed) against their will, for the gain of animals. Nothing may be inflicted upon persons for the sake of animals. (Including penalties for violating laws against cruelty to animals?) Is this an acceptable consequence? Can't one save 10,000 animals from excruciating suffering by inflicting some slight discomfort on a person who did not cause the animals' suffering? One may feel the side constraint is not absolute when it is *people* who can be saved from excruciating suffering. So perhaps the side constraint also relaxes, though not as much, when animals' suffering is at stake. The thorough-going utilitarian (for animals *and* for people, combined in one group) goes further and holds that, *ceteris paribus*, we may inflict some suffering on a person to avoid a (slightly) greater suffering of an animal. This permissive principle seems to me to be unacceptably strong, even when the purpose is to avoid greater suffering to a person!

Utilitarian theory is embarrassed by the possibility of utility monsters who get enormously greater gains in utility from any sacrifice of others than these others lose. For, unacceptably, the theory seems to require that we all be sacrificed in the monster's maw, in order to increase total utility. Similarly if people are utility devourers with respect to animals, always getting greatly counterbalancing utility from each sacrifice of an animal, we may feel that 'utilitarianism for animals, Kantianism for people', in requiring (or allowing) that almost always animals be sacrificed, makes animals too subordinate to persons.

Since it counts only the happiness and suffering of animals, would the utilitarian view hold it all right to kill animals painlessly? Would it be all right, on the utilitarian view, to kill people painlessly, in the night, provided one didn't first announce it? Utilitarianism is notoriously inept with decisions where the number of persons is at issue. (In this area, it must be conceded, eptness is hard to come by.) Maximizing the total happiness requires continuing to add persons so long as their net utility is positive and is sufficient to counterbalance the loss in utility their presence in the world causes others. Maximizing the average utility allows a person to kill everyone else if that would make him ecstatic, and so happier than average. (Don't say he shouldn't because after his death the average would drop lower than if he didn't kill all the others.) Is it all right to kill someone provided you immediately substitute another (by having a child or, in science-fiction fashion, by creating a full-grown person) who will be as happy as the rest of the life of the person you killed? After all, there would be no net diminution in total utility, or even any change in its profile of distribution. Do we forbid murder only to prevent feelings of worry on the part of potential victims? (And how does a utilitarian explain what it is they're worried about, and would he really base a policy on what he must hold to be an irrational fear?) Clearly, a utilitarian needs to supplement his view to handle such issues; perhaps he will find that the supplementary theory becomes the main one, relegating utilitarian considerations to a corner.

But isn't utilitarianism at least adequate for animals? I think not. But if not only the animals' felt experiences are relevant, what else is? Here a tangle of questions arises. How much does an animal's life have to be respected once it's alive, and how can we decide this? Must one also introduce some notion of a nondegraded existence? Would it be all right to use genetic-engineering techniques to breed natural slaves who would be contented with their lots? Natural animal slaves? Was that the domestication of animals? Even for animals, utilitarianism won't do as the whole story, but the thicket of questions daunts us.

Robert Nozick, *Anarchy, State and Utopia* (Oxford: Blackwell, 1974) pp. 35–42.

23. The Feminist Challenge

Lynda Birke

One of the significant changes accompanying the scientific revolution was ... the categorisation of nature in terms of mechanism; nature was to be understood, for many eighteenth-century writers, in terms of machine analogies. As the scientific revolution progressed, the view of nature as dead inert matter – mere mechanism – become dominant over the view that humans could coexist harmoniously with other forms of life. For animals this meant that, being *part* of nature, they were consigned to the category of machines. What distinguished humanity from the rest of brute creation was the possession of a soul. This dualism did not allow for sentimental feelings towards animals: following Descartes' suggestion that animals were nothing but mechanism, one seventeenth-century woman is reported to have objected most strongly to the prospect of a dog as a pet on the grounds that 'we want only rational creatures here, and belonging to the sect we belong to we refuse to burden ourselves with these machines.'[1]

This view of animals as machines became absorbed into the values of the emerging sciences. During the eighteenth and nineteenth centuries, for example, many physiological experiments were conducted on living animals – long before the days of anaesthesia. The screams and howls of the tortured animals were assimilated to the concept of mechanism: the howls were merely the grinding of machinery. Even with the advent of clinical anaesthesia, little changed in the physiology labs: dogs and cats were still being nailed to boards and eviscerated while still alive. Indeed, some nineteenth-century physiologists, such as the Frenchman François Magendie, seemed positively to revel in the infliction of pain in experiments and demonstrations.

In the face of such obvious cruelty, it is scarcely surprising that opposition to vivisection and other forms of animal cruelty grew during this period. Significantly, this opposition was linked in the minds of many people to other forms of oppression, such as slavery and the oppression of women. Jeremy Bentham, the utilitarian philosopher, wrote in 1780:

Why should the law refuse its protection to any sensitive being? The time will come when humanity will extend its mantle over every-

thing which breathes. We
of slaves; we shall finish by s
assist our labours or supply our wa

Feminism and animal rights became ex
nineteenth-century. In her account of feminism
Olive Banks has described how many feminists invo
paign for moral reform were also involved in anti-vivi
paigns, their interest being:

> in part an expression of their concern for the weak and helpless ...
> Moreover the anti-vivisection movement appealed particularly to
> women who were not only heavily represented in the membership
> but were even prominent in the leadership. Indeed Frances Power
> Cobbe, one of the most active of the anti-vivisectionists, was also an
> enthusiastic feminist who believed in women's suffrage as a means
> of raising the moral level of society. For her, feminism and the anti-
> vivisection movement were part of the same crusade.[3]

They remain part of the same crusade for some contemporary feminists,
who see connections between the ways in which women and animals
are subordinated in their proximity to exploited nature. One feminist
writer suggested that 'Perhaps the sympathy that many women feel
towards animals is recognition of the mutual victimisation of both
women and animals by men,' and went on to observe that membership
of many ecological or anti-vivisection groups is 'made up predom-
inantly of women.'[4] Sympathy, however, may not be enough and it
has also been argued that feminists *must* recognise and be aware of the
suffering of other animals if they are to achieve the overthrow of
patriarchy:

> But if while aiming for this change (the overthrow of patriarchy) we
> do not become aware of the sufferings of non-humans, then I feel we
> will not have understood the concept of liberty. If we struggle to
> free ourselves, without realising that we are also crushing the most
> oppressed and exploited creatures on the planet, we can only fail.[5]

The concern for animal rights is thus seen as a logical extension of the
more general feminist concern for nature or for less privileged human
groups, all of whom are seen to share some features of oppression
within patriarchal society.

llenge (Brighton:

Sexual Oppression:
London: Weidenfeld

nemann, 1974) p. 9.
) pp. 81–2.
d Vegetarianism' in *The*
kland, California: Amazon

of Animals', in *Reclaim the*
ds) (London: Women's Press,

nimal Rights

To

I regard myself as an adv   imal rights – as a part of the animal rights movement. That movem   t, as I conceive it, is committed to a number of goals, including: the total abolition of the use of animals in science; the total dissolution of commercial animal agriculture; the total elimination of commercial and sport hunting and trapping.

There are, I know, people who profess to believe in animal rights but do not avow these goals. Factory farming, they say, is wrong – it violates animals' rights – but traditional animal agriculture is all right. Toxicity tests of cosmetics on animals violates their rights, but important medical research – cancer research, for example – does not. The clubbing of baby seals is abhorrent, but not the harvesting of adult seals. I used to think I understood this reasoning. Not any more. You don't change unjust institutions by tidying them up.

What's wrong – fundamentally wrong – with the way animals are treated isn't the details that vary from case to case. It's the whole system. The forlornness of the veal calf is pathetic, heart wrenching; the pulsing pain of the chimp with electrodes planted deep in her brain is repulsive; the slow, torturous death of the raccoon caught in the leghold trap is agonizing. But what is wrong isn't the pain, isn't the suffering, isn't the deprivation. These compound what's wrong. Sometimes – often – they make it much, much worse. But they are not the fundamental wrong.

The fundamental wrong is the system that allows us to view animals as our resources, here for us – to be eaten, or surgically manipulated, or exploited for sport or money. Once we accept this view of animals

– our resources – the rest is as predictable as it is regrettable. Why worry about their loneliness, their pain, their death? Since animals exist for us, to benefit us in one way or another, what harms them really doesn't matter – or matters only if it starts to bother us, makes us feel a trifle uneasy when we eat our veal escalope, for example. So, yes, let us get veal calves out of solitary confinement, give them more space, a little straw, a few companions. But let us keep our veal escalope.

But a little straw, more space and a few companions won't eliminate – won't even touch – the basic wrong that attaches to our viewing and treating these animals as our resources. A veal calf killed to be eaten after living in close confinement is viewed and treated in this way: but so, too, is another who is raised (as they say) 'more humanely'. To right the wrong of our treatment of farm animals requires more than making rearing methods 'more humane'; it requires the total dissolution of commercial animal agriculture.

How we do this, whether we do it or, as in the case of animals in science, whether and how we abolish their use – these are to a large extent political questions. People must change their beliefs before they change their habits. Enough people, especially those elected to public office, must believe in change – must want it – before we will have laws that protect the rights of animals. This process of change is very complicated, very demanding, very exhausting, calling for the efforts of many hands in education, publicity, political organization and activity, down to the licking of envelopes and stamps. As a trained and practising philosopher, the sort of contribution I can make is limited but, I like to think, important. The currency of philosophy is ideas – their meaning and rational foundation – not the nuts and bolts of the legislative process, say, or the mechanics of community organization. That's what I have been exploring over the past ten years or so in my essays and talks and, most recently, in my book, *The Case for Animal Rights*. I believe the major conclusions I reach in the book are true because they are supported by the weight of the best arguments. I believe the idea of animal rights has reason, not just emotion, on its side.

In the space I have at my disposal here I can only sketch, in the barest outline, some of the main features of the book. Its main themes – and we should not be surprised by this – involve asking and answering deep, fundamental moral questions about what morality is, how it should be understood and what is the best moral theory, all considered. I hope I can convey something of the shape I think this theory takes. The attempt to do this will be (to use a word a friendly critic once used to describe my work) cerebral, perhaps too cerebral. But this is misleading. My feelings about how animals are sometimes treated run just as deep and just as strong as those of my more volatile compatriots. Philosophers do – to use the jargon of the day – have a right side to their brains. If it's the left side we contribute (or mainly should), that's because what talents we have reside there.

How to proceed? We begin by asking how the moral status of animals has been understood by thinkers who deny that animals have rights. Then we test the mettle of their ideas by seeing how well they stand up under the heat of fair criticism. If we start our thinking in this way, we soon find out that some people believe that we have no duties directly to animals, that we owe nothing to them, that we can do nothing that wrongs them. Rather, we can do wrong acts that involve animals, and so we have duties regarding them, though none to them. Such views may be called indirect duty views. By way of illustration: suppose your neighbour kicks your dog. Then your neighbour has done something wrong. But not to your dog. The wrong that has been done is a wrong to you. After all, it is wrong to upset people, and your neighbour's kicking your dog upsets you. So you are the one who is wronged, not your dog. Or again: by kicking your dog your neighbour damages your property. And since it is wrong to damage another person's property, your neighbour has done something wrong – to you, of course, not to your dog. Your neighbour no more wrongs your dog than your car would be wronged if the windshield were smashed. Your neighbour's duties involving your dog are indirect duties to you. More generally, all of our duties regarding animals are indirect duties to one another – to humanity.

How could someone try to justify such a view? Someone might say that your dog doesn't feel anything and so isn't hurt by your neighbour's kick, doesn't care about the pain since none is felt, is as unaware of anything as is your windshield. Someone might say this, but no rational person will, since, among other considerations, such a view will commit anyone who holds it to the position that no human being feels pain either – that human beings also don't care about what happens to them. A second possibility is that though both humans and your dog are hurt when kicked, it is only human pain that matters. But, again, no rational person can believe this. Pain is pain wherever it occurs. If your neighbour's causing you pain is wrong because of the pain that is caused, we cannot rationally ignore or dismiss the moral relevance of the pain that your dog feels.

Philosophers who hold indirect duty views – and some still do – have come to understand that they must avoid the two defects just noted:

that is, both the views that animals don't feel anything as well as the idea that only human pain can be morally relevant. Among such thinkers the sort of view now favoured is one or other form of what is called contractarianism.

Here, very crudely, is the root idea: morality consists of a set of rules that individuals voluntarily agree to abide by, as we do when we sign a contract (hence the name contractarianism). Those who understand and accept the terms of the contract are covered directly; they have rights created and recognized by, and protected in, the contract. And these contractors can also have protection spelled out for others who, though they lack the ability to understand morality and so cannot sign the contract themselves, are loved or cherished by those who can. Thus young children, for example, are unable to sign contracts and lack rights. But they are protected by the contract none the less because of the sentimental interests of others, most notably their parents. So we have, then, duties involving these children, duties regarding them, but no duties to them. Our duties in their case are indirect duties to other human beings, usually their parents.

As for animals, since they cannot understand contracts, they obviously cannot sign; and since they cannot sign, they have no rights. Like children, however, some animals are the objects of the sentimental interest of others. You, for example, love your dog or cat. So those animals that enough people care about (companion animals, whales, baby seals, the American bald eagle), though they lack rights themselves, will be protected because of the sentimental interests of people. I have, then, according to contractarianism, no duty directly to your dog or any other animal, not even the duty not to cause them pain or suffering; my duty not to hurt them is a duty I have to those people who care about what happens to them. As for other animals, where no or little sentimental interest is present – in the case of farm animals, for example, or laboratory rats – what duties we have grow weaker and weaker, perhaps to vanishing point. The pain and death they endure, though real, are not wrong if no one cares about them.

When it comes to the moral status of animals' contractarianism could be a hard view to refute if it were an adequate theoretical approach to the moral status of human beings. It is not adequate in this latter respect, however, which makes the question of its adequacy in the former case, regarding animals, utterly moot. For consider: morality, according to the (crude) contractarian position before us, consists of rules that people agree to abide by. What people? Well, enough to make a difference – enough, that is, collectively to have the power to enforce the rules that are drawn up in the contract. That is very well and good for the signatories but not so good for anyone who is not asked to sign. And there is nothing in contractarianism of the sort we are discussing that guarantees or requires that everyone will have a chance to participate equally in framing the rules of morality. The result is that this approach to ethics could sanction the most blatant forms of social, economic, moral and political injustice, ranging from a repressive caste system to systemic racial or sexual discrimination. Might, according to this theory, does make right. Let those who are the victims of injustice suffer as they will. It matters not so long as no one else – no contractor, or too few of them – cares about it. Such a theory takes one's moral breath away as if, for example, there would be nothing wrong with apartheid in South Africa if few white South Africans were upset by it. A theory with so little to recommend it at the level of the ethics of our treatment of our fellow humans cannot have anything more to recommend it when it comes to the ethics of how we treat our fellow animals.

The version of contractarianism just examined is, as I have noted, a crude variety, and in fairness to those of a contractarian persuasion it must be noted that much more refined, subtle and ingenious varieties are possible. For example, John Rawls in his *A Theory of Justice*, sets forth a version of contractarianism that forces contractors to ignore the accidental features of being a human being – for example, whether one is white or black, male or female, a genius or modest intellect. Only by ignoring such features, Rawls believes, can we ensure that the principles of justice that contractors would agree upon are not based on bias or prejudice. Despite the improvement a view such as Rawls's represents over the cruder forms of contractarianism, it remains deficient: it systematically denies that we have direct duties to those human beings who do not have a sense of justice – young children, for instance, and many mentally retarded humans. And yet it seems reasonably certain that, were we to torture a young child or a retarded elder, we would be doing something that wronged him or her, not something that would be wrong if (and only if) other humans with a sense of justice were upset. And since this is true in the case of these humans, we cannot rationally deny the same in the case of animals.

Indirect duty views, then, including the best among them, fail to command our rational assent. Whatever ethical theory we should accept rationally, therefore, it must at least recognize that we have some duties directly to animals, just as we have some duties directly to each other. The next two theories I'll sketch attempt to meet this requirement.

The first I call the cruelty–kindness view. Simply stated, this says that we have a direct duty to be kind to animals and a direct duty not to be cruel to them. Despite the familiar, reassuring ring of these ideas, I do not believe that this view offers an adequate theory. To make this clearer, consider kindness. A kind person acts from a certain kind of motive – compassion or concern, for example. And that is a virtue. But there is no guarantee that a kind act is a right act. If I am a generous racist, for example, I will be inclined to act kindly towards members of my own race, favouring their interests above those of others. My kindness would be real and, so far as it goes, good. But I trust it is too obvious to require argument that may kind acts may not be above moral reproach – may, in fact, be positively wrong because rooted in injustice. So kindness, notwithstanding its status as a virtue to be encouraged, simply will not carry the weight of a theory of right action.

Cruelty fares no better. People or their acts are cruel if they display either a lack of sympathy for or, worse, the presence of enjoyment in another's suffering. Cruelty in all its guises is a bad thing, a tragic human failing. But just as a person's being motivated by kindness does not guarantee that he or she does what is right, so the absence of cruelty does not ensure that he or she avoids doing what is wrong. Many people who perform abortions, for example, are not cruel, sadistic people. But that fact alone does not settle the terribly difficult question of the morality of abortion. The case is no different when we examine the ethics of our treatment of animals. So yes, let us be for kindness and against cruelty. But let us not suppose that being for the one and against the other answers questions about moral right and wrong.

Some people think that the theory we are looking for is utilitarianism. A utilitarian accepts two moral principles. The first is that of equality: everyone's interests count, and similar interests must be counted as having similar weight or importance. White or black, American or Iranian, human or animal – everyone's pain and frustration matter, and matter just as much as the equivalent pain or frustration of anyone else. The second principle a utilitarian accepts is that of utility: do the act that will bring about the best balance between satisfaction and frustration for everyone affected by the outcome.

As a utilitarian, then, here is how I am to approach the task of deciding what I morally ought to do: I must ask who will be affected if I choose to do one thing rather than another, how much each individual will be affected, and where the best results are most likely to lie – which option, in other words, is most likely to bring about the best results, the best balance between satisfaction and frustration. That opinion, whatever it may be, is the one I ought to choose. That is where my moral duty lies.

The great appeal of utilitarianism rests with its uncompromising egalitarianism: everyone's interests count as much as the like interests of everyone else. The kind of odious discrimination that some forms of contractarianism can justify – discrimination based on race or sex, for example – seems disallowed in principle by utilitarianism, as is speciesism, systematic discrimination based on species membership.

The equality we find in utilitarianism, however, is not the sort an advocate of animal or human rights should have in mind. Utilitarianism has no room for the equal moral rights of different individuals because it has no room for their equal inherent value or worth. What has value for the utilitarian is the satisfaction of an individual's interests, not the individual whose interests they are. A universe in which you satisfy your desire for water, food and warmth is, other things being equal, better than a universe in which these desires are frustrated. And the same is true in the case of an animal with similar desires. But neither you nor the animal have any value in your own right. Only your feelings do.

Here is an analogy to help make the philosophical point clearer: a cup contains different liquids, sometimes sweet, sometimes bitter, sometimes a mix of the two. What has value are the liquids; the sweeter the better, the bitterer the worse. The cup, the container, has no value. It is what goes into it, not what they go into, that has value. For the utilitarian you and I are like the cup: we have no value as individuals and thus no equal value. What has value is what goes into us, what we serve as receptacles for: our feelings of satisfaction have positive value, our feelings of frustration negative value.

Serious problems arise for utilitarianism when we remind ourselves that it enjoins us to bring about the best consequences. What does this mean? It doesn't mean the best consequences for me alone, or for my family or friends, or any other person taken individually. No, what we must do is, roughly, as follows: we must add up (somehow!) the separate satisfactions and frustrations of everyone likely to be affected by our choice, the satisfactions in one column, the frustrations in the other. We must total each column for each of the options before us. That is what it means to say the theory is aggregative. And then we must choose that option which is most likely to bring about the best balance of totalled satisfactions over totalled frustrations. Whatever act would lead to this outcome is the one we ought morally to perform – it is where our moral duty lies. And that act quite clearly, might not be the same one that would bring about the best results for me personally, or for my family or friends, or for a lab animal. The best aggregated consequences for everyone concerned are not necessarily the best for each individual.

That utilitarianism is an aggregative theory – different individuals' satisfactions or frustrations are added, or summed, or totalled – is the key objection to this theory. My Aunt Bea is old, inactive, a cranky, sour person, though not physically ill. She prefers to go on living. She is also rather rich. I could make a fortune if I could get my hands on her money, money she intends to give me in any event, after she dies, but which she refuses to give me now. In order to avoid a huge tax bite, I plan to donate a handsome sum of my profits to a local children's hospital. Many, many children will benefit from my generosity, and much joy will be brought to their parents, relatives and friends. If I don't get the money rather soon, all these ambitions will come to naught. The once in a lifetime opportunity to make a real killing will be gone. Why, then, not kill my Aunt Bea? Oh, of course I might get caught. But I'm no fool and, besides, her doctor can be counted on to cooperate (he has an eye for the same investment and I happen to know a good deal about his shady past). The deed can be done ... professionally, shall we say. There is very little chance of getting caught. And as for my conscience being guilt-ridden, I am a resourceful sort of fellow and will take more than sufficient comfort – as I lie on the beach at Acapulco – in contemplating the joys and health I have brought to so many others.

Suppose Aunt Bea is killed and the rest of the story comes out as told. Would I have done anything wrong? Anything immoral? One would have thought that I had. Not according to utilitarianism. Since what I have done has brought about the best balance between totalled satisfaction and frustration for all those affected by the outcome, my action is not wrong. Indeed, in killing Aunt Bea the physician and I did what duty required.

This same kind of argument can be repeated in all sorts of cases, illustrating, time after time, how the utilitarian's position leads to results that impartial people find morally callous. It *is* wrong to kill my Aunt Bea in the name of bringing about the best results for others. A good end does not justify an evil means. Any adequate moral theory will have to explain why this is so. Utilitarianism fails in this respect and so cannot be the theory we seek.

What to do? Where to begin anew? The place to begin, I think, is with the utilitarian's view of the value of the individual – or, rather, lack of value. In its place, suppose we consider that you and I, for example, do have value as individuals – what we'll call inherent value.

To say we have such value is to say that we are something more than, something different from, mere receptacles. Moreover, to ensure that we do not pave the way for such injustices as slavery or sexual discrimination, we must believe that all who have inherent value have it equally, regardless of their sex, religion, birthplace and so on. Similarly to be discarded as irrelevant are one's talents or skills, intelligence and wealth, personality or pathology, whether one is loved and admired or despised and loathed. The genius and the retarded child, the prince and the pauper, the brain surgeon and the fruit vendor, Mother Teresa and the most unscrupulous used-car salesman – all have inherent value, all possess it equally, and all have an equal right to be treated with respect, to be treated in ways that do not reduce them to the status of things, as if they existed as resources for others. My value as an individual is independent of my usefulness to you. Yours is not dependent on your usefulness to me. For either of us to treat the other in ways that fail to show respect for the other's independent value is to act immorally, to violate the individual's rights.

Some of the rational virtues of this view – what I call the rights view – should be evident. Unlike (crude) contractarianism, for example, the rights view in principle denies the moral tolerability of any and all forms of racial, sexual or social discrimination; and unlike utilitarianism, this view in principle denies that we can justify good results by using evil means that violate an individual's rights – denies, for example, that it could be moral to kill my Aunt Bea to harvest beneficial consequences for others. That would be to sanction the disrespectful treatment of the individual in the name of the social good, something the rights view will not – categorically will not – ever allow.

The rights view, I believe, is rationally the most satisfactory moral theory. It surpasses all other theories in the degree to which it illuminates and explains the foundations of our duties to one another – the domain of human morality. On this score it has the best reasons, the best arguments, on its side. Of course, if it were possible to show that only human beings are included within its scope, then a person like myself, who believes in animal rights, would be obliged to look elsewhere.

But attempts to limit its scope to humans only can be shown to be rationally defective. Animals, it is true, lack many of the abilities humans possess. They can't read, do higher mathematics, build a bookcase or make *baba ghanoush*. Neither can many human beings, however, and yet we don't (and shouldn't) say that they (these humans) therefore have less inherent value, less of a right to be treated with respect, than do others. It is the similarities between those human beings who most clearly, most non-controversially have such value (the people reading this, for example), not our differences, that matter most. And the really crucial, the basic similarity is simply this: we are each of us the experiencing subject of a life, a conscious creature having an individual welfare that has importance to us whatever our usefulness to others. We want and prefer things, believe and feel things, recall and expect things. And all these dimensions of our life, including our pleasure and pain, our enjoyment and suffering, our satisfaction and frustration, our continued existence or our untimely death – all make a difference to the quality of life as lived, as experienced, by us as individuals. As the same is true of those animals that concern us (the ones that are eaten and trapped, for example), they too must be viewed as the experiencing subjects of a life, with inherent value of their own.

Some there are who resist the idea that animals have inherent value. 'Only humans have such value,' they profess. How might this narrow view be defended? Shall we say that only humans have the requisite intelligence, or autonomy, or reason? But there are many, many humans who fail to meet these standards and yet are reasonably viewed as having value above and beyond their usefulness to others. Shall we claim that only humans belong to the right species, the species *Homo sapiens*? But this is blatant speciesism. Will it be said, then, that all – and only – humans have immortal souls? Then our opponents have their work cut out for them. I am myself not ill-disposed to the proposition that there are immortal souls. Personally, I profoundly hope I have one.

But I would not want to rest my position on a controversial ethical issue or the even more controversial question about who or what has an immortal soul. That is to dig one's hole deeper, not to climb out. Rationally, it is better to resolve moral issues without making more controversial assumptions than are needed. The question of who has inherent value is such a question, one that is resolved more rationally without the introduction of the idea of immortal souls than by its use.

Well, perhaps some will say that animals have some inherent value, only less than we have. Once again, however, attempts to defend this view can be shown to lack rational justification. What could be the basis of our having more inherent value than animals? Their lack of reason, or autonomy, or intellect? Only if we are willing to make the same judgement in the case of humans who are similarly deficient. But it is not true that such humans – the retarded child, for example, or the mentally deranged – have less inherent value than you or I. Neither, then, can we rationally sustain the view that animals like them in being the experiencing subjects of a life have less inherent value. *All* who have inherent value have it equally, whether they be human animals or not.

Inherent value, then, belongs equally to those who are the experiencing subjects of a life. Whether it belongs to others – to rocks and rivers, trees and glaciers, for example – we do not know and may never know. But neither do we need to know, if we are to make the case for animal rights. We do not need to know, for example, how many people are eligible to vote in the next presidential election before we can know whether I am. Similarly, we do not need to know how many individuals have inherent value before we can know that some do. When it comes to the case for animal rights, then, what we need to know is whether the animals that, in our culture, are routinely eaten, hunted and used in our laboratories, for example, are like us in being subjects of a life. And we do know this. We do know that many – literally, billions and billions – of these animals are the subjects of a life in the sense explained and so have inherent value if we do. And since, in order to arrive at the best theory of our duties to one another, we must recognize our equal inherent value as individuals, reason – not sentiment, not emotion – reason compels us to recognize the equal inherent value of these animals and, with this, their equal right to be treated with respect.

Tom Regan, *The Struggle for Animal Rights* (Clarks Summit, Pa: International Society for Animal Rights, 1987) pp. 47–61.

Biographical Notes

Aquinas, St Thomas (1225–74) Theologian, philosopher and Father of the Church. His writings still have immense authority for Roman Catholics. His thought has influenced not only theology but also philosophy and political theory. The *Summa Theologica* and *Summa Contra Gentiles* reconciled Aristotle's thought with Platonic Augustinianism, thus enabling the Church to withstand the intellectual effects of the growing appeal of empiricism. His development of Natural Law theory influenced political theory for centuries and still has considerable appeal.

Aristotle (384–322 BC) Greek philosopher and scientist, who studied under Plato but later established his own school of rhetoric. The *Nicomachean Ethics* lays down the basis for moral philosophy, and the *Politics* outlines the political conditions within which human life might flourish.

Augustine, St (354–430) Bishop of Hippo, an important and influential Church Father. In resting much of his thought on a Platonism, he was able to draw Hellenistic and Judaic strands into Christianity. *The City of God* exhibits this intellectual marriage while also vindicating the Christian Church, which was seen by him as a new order rising on the ruins of the old Roman Empire.

Bentham, Jeremy (1748–1832) English utilitarian philosopher. In his *Introduction to the Principles of Morals and Legislation* Bentham argues that actions are right when they promote happiness for the greatest number.

Berkeley, George (1685–1753) Anglican bishop and philosopher. His *Treatise Concerning the Principles of Human Knowledge* denies the existence of objects outside of human experience. Berkeley concluded that reality is composed of nothing but ideas.

Birke, Lynda, Research Fellow at the Open University. Author and editor of books and articles in the area of biology with a special interest in environmental concerns. She recently edited (with J.S.

187

Silvertown) *More than the Parks: Biology and Politics* (Pluto Press).

Brophy, Brigid. Well-known author, playwright and social critic, with an interest in literature, social education and feminism.

Coward, Rosalind. Lecturer at Goldsmiths' College, University of London. She has written extensively on semiology, ideology and feminism. Two major books are *Language and Materialism* (with J. Ellis) and *Patriarchal Precedents*.

Daggett, Herman (1766–1832) Author of the first known American treatise on animal rights. *The Rights of Animals* was delivered as an oration to Providence College, Yale in 1791.

Descartes, René (1596–1650) French philosopher and mathematician, who applied the methods of mathematics to the foundation of philosophy. Cartesianism is regarded as a foundation of modern epistemology. A central argument of the *Discourses* is that it is the certainty of the thinking 'I' which provides the foundation for other forms of knowledge.

Fichte, Johann Gottlieb (1762–1814) German philosopher of the Kantian tradition. Fichte sought to establish the ego as the source of creative action, the basis of each individual's ordering of reality. The world has no independent existence, but serves to afford humans the occasion to realise the ends of their own existence.

Godwin, William (1756–1836) English political thinker. His *Enquiries Concerning Political Justice*, inspired by the French Revolution, was critical of many of the established laws of his time. His condemnation of the use of violence saved him from prosecution.

Hegel, Georg Wilhelm Friedrich (1770–1831) German idealist philosopher whose exposition of the principle of the dialectic came to dominate German philosophy. His *Lecture on the Philosophy of World History* was published posthumously. Hegel argued that reality consisted in the whole rather than in its individual parts.

Herder, Johann Gottfried (1744–1803) German philosopher who explained human history as a consequence of human nature and the effects of the physical environment. Embodying Enlightenment principles, Herder believed in the ultimate development of justice based on reason. His *Ideas for the Philosophy of the History of Mankind* is based on evolutionary theories.

Hobbes, Thomas (1588–1679) English philosopher and political theorist. Hobbes argued that human nature was naturally egoistic and that in the absence of effective political authority, social order and justice would collapse. The outcome would be a condition of universal conflict. *De Cive* is a statement of Hobbes' views on government, and a defence of absolute authority of a sovereign. *De Homine* presents Hobbes' thoughts on human nature. His best known work *Leviathan* combines these two aspects of his work.

Hooker, Richard (1554–1600) English theologian whose *Laws of Ecclesiastical Polity* set forth a basis for church government. This five-volume work gave credence to the foundation of Anglican theology. His Thomistic views on natural law and his statement on the duty of charity had a strong influence on John Locke.

Horkheimer, Max (1895–1973) German philosopher of the Frankfurt School forced to live in America in order to escape Nazi persecution. His major work centres around the theme that the quest for the domination of nature would lead, inevitably, to the suppression of human freedom.

Hume, David (1711–76) Scottish philosopher who developed an empiricist foundation of knowledge. *A Treatise of Human Nature* is an argument against the Cartesian tradition of innate ideas. His empiricist views led him to postulate the 'regularity' theory of causation which has been of lasting influence. In his *Enquiry Concerning the Principles of Morals* Hume rejects rationalist systems for determining the principles of justice and political government, linking morality to social and psychological factors.

Kant, Immanuel (1724–1804) German philosopher. Kant argued, against Hume, that knowledge could not be reduced to mere sense impressions of objects but was also dependent on an a priori ordering of reality. Kant's practical philosophy centres on the view that only unconditioned actions can be morally worthy. Actions based on mere passion cannot be moral.

Kropotkin, Prince Peter (1842–1921) Russian political thinker of the anarchist tradition. Lived and wrote in France but returned to the

Soviet Union after the Revolution. Kropotkin's concept of 'Mutual Aid' was developed in order to counter authoritarian tendencies in socialism. The notion of 'mutual aid' would promote human progress towards the satisfaction of the needs of all without wasted human energy.

Leibniz, Gottfried Wilhelm (1646–1716) German rationalist philosopher and mathematician who argued that the fundamental substance was isolated units, monads, each one reflecting the world from its own point of view. For Leibniz, the operation of the universe, including human action, is based on a pre-established harmony and the actual world is the best of all possible worlds.

Locke, John (1632–1704) English philosopher, sometimes regarded as a major founder of English liberalism. He established a basis for the English empiricist tradition. The ethical arguments underlying his political views are expounded in *An Essay Concerning Human Understanding*. His *Two Treatises of Government* (published anonymously) presents his more practical ideas on the nature and role of government, including arguments against the principle of 'divine right'.

Machiavelli, Niccolò di Bernardo dei (1469–1527) Italian statesman and writer. He argued that political action was governed by the needs of each individual state. The main theme of *The Prince* is that expediency may be resorted to for the establishment and maintenance of authority.

Madison, James (1751–1836) Republican and fourth president of the United States of America whose *Federalist Papers* provided some of the basis from which the Constitution was drafted.

Marx, Karl (1818–83) German philosopher influenced by Aristotle and Hegel. For Marx, human life is determined by material needs. He saw history as having the potential to produce a form of life in which human necessity would be overcome. The *Economic and Philosophical Manuscripts* provide a philosophical basis for his theory of human needs and actions.

Midgley, Mary. Philosopher at the University of Newcastle Upon Tyne. She has written many articles and books in the area of moral philosophy. Major works include *Beast and Man* and *Animals and Why They Matter*.

Mill, John Stuart (1806–73) English empiricist philosopher and political economist. He modified Bentham's utilitarianism and promoted a liberal acceptance of individual thought and action.

Montaigne, Michel Eyquem de (1533–92) French essayist whose critical essays sought to provide a wide understanding of human experience. His writings influenced much of French thought in the following centuries. The essay *Apology for Raymond Sebond* reveals the extent of Montaigne's unrelenting criticism of the social world in which he lived.

Nietzsche, Friedrich Wilhelm (1844–1900) German philosopher influenced by Schopenhauer. His critique of morality, religion and other social mores formed part of an attack on the entire Aristotelian–Thomist, and related, traditions. He valued the pre-Socratic emphasis on the development of culture as the basis for individual existence. *The Joyful Wisdom* encourages the rejection of the mediocre and those values and sentiments that inhibit the 'will-to-power'.

Nozick, Robert American philosopher whose book *Anarchy, State and Utopia* consists of an argument for the rights of the individual and a reduction in state power.

Plato (427–347 BC) Greek philosopher who thought that reality was composed of ideas in which the human and material world participated. The dialogue form of enquiry was intended to reveal to the participants knowledge which was latent but not yet revealed. The *Timaeus* provides an explanation of how the world and life were created and the *Statesman*, an insight into the role of politics.

Pope, Alexander (1688–1744) English poet and social critic. His moral essays criticise and popularise many of the intellectual ideas of his time.

Primatt, Humphry (c.1742) was an eighteenth-century English theologian, whose treatise *A Dissertation on the Duty of Mercy and the Sin of Cruelty to Brute Animals* is one of the most comprehensive discussions of the status of animals ever published.

Pufendorf, Samuel (1632–92) German writer on jurisprudence. His *The Law of Nature and Nations* was influenced by the writings of Hobbes and sought to outline the basic tenets of natural law. He was highly critical of the constitution of the Germanic Empire. He sought to provide a fairer and more philosophically grounded system of law based on the notion of human dignity and a common right to equality and freedom.

Rawls, John. American political philosopher. He follows the tradition of Locke, Rousseau and Kant in arguing for a system of ethics that is based on the notion of the social contract rather than upon utilitarian principles. His *A Theory of Justice* is an argument for a free and just society based on an initial acceptance of equality.

Regan, Tom. Professor of Philosophy at North Carolina State University, and President of the Culture and Animals Foundation. His *The Case for Animal Rights* presents a moral and philosophical case for the humane treatment of animals.

Rousseau, Jean-Jacques (1712–88) French philosopher whose political writings include *A Dissertation on the Origin and Foundation of the Inequality of Mankind* which compares modern society unfavourably with the natural human condition.

Russell, Bertrand (1872–1970) English philosopher, mathematician and passionate social reformer. His *American Essays* were originally published in American newspapers and represent many of his controversial views.

Salt, Henry S. (1851–1939) English humanitarian, who wrote and campaigned on many social issues, including capital punishment, penal reform, women's equality and animal rights. His work *Animals' Rights* had considerable influence on Gandhi and George Bernard Shaw.

Schopenhauer, Artur (1788–1860) German philosopher whose principal thesis as outlined in his major work *The World as Will and Representation* is that the only reality available to the self is that of the will. The world can only take on an appearance through the self's subjective idea of it.

Schweitzer, Albert (1875–1965) Philosopher and missionary who developed a liberal, eschatological interpretation of the principal tenets of Christianity. He devoted his life to serving humanity. His *Civilisation and Ethics* outlines his basic guiding principle of 'the reverence for life'. He was awarded the Nobel Peace Prize in 1952.

Sidgwick, Henry (1838–1900) Moral philosopher influenced by the utilitarianism of J.S. Mill and Kant's concept of the categorical imperative. His *Elements of Politics* suggest a means by which the conflict between individual pleasure and that of others could be resolved.

Singer, Peter. Professor of Philosophy at Monash University, Melbourne, Australia. His article 'All Animals are Equal' outlines his basic position which is further developed in his book *Animal Liberation*.

* * *

Dr Paul A.B. Clarke is a lecturer in political theory in the Department of Government, University of Essex. He is the author of articles and books on political philosophy, political theory, and ethical and political issues surrounding biotechnology, medicine and law. Recent publications include: *The Autonomy of Politics* (London, Gower, 1988), *AIDS: Medicine, Politics, Society* (1988) and (with A. Linzey), *Research on Embryos: Politics, Theology and Law* (1988) and *Theology, The University and The Modern World* (1988).

The Revd Dr Andrew Linzey is Chaplain and Director of Studies at the Centre for the Study of Theology in the University of Essex. He has written or edited nine books specialising in contemporary ethical questions including: *Christianity and the Rights of Animals* (London and New York, SPCK/ Crossroad, 1986), *Research on Embryos: Politics, Theology and Law* (with P.A.B. Clarke) (1988); *Animals and Christianity: A Book of Readings* (with Tom Regan) (London and New York, SPCK/Crossroad, 1988) and *Theology, Law and the Use of Armed Force* (with Françoise Hampson) (1989).

What is phonics?

Phonics helps children learn to read and write by teaching them the letter sounds (known as phonemes), rather than the letter names, e.g. the sound that 'c' makes rather than its alphabetic name. They then learn how to blend the sounds: the process of saying the sounds in a word or 'sounding out' and then blending them together to make the word, for example c – a – t = cat. Once the phonemes and the skill of blending are learnt, children can tackle reading any phonetically decodable word they come across, even ones they don't know, with confidence and success.

However, there are of course many words in the English language that aren't phonetically decodable, e.g. if a child gets stuck on 'the' it doesn't help if they sound it out and blend it. We call these 'tricky words' and they are just taught as words that are so 'tricky' that children have to learn to recognise them by sight.

How do phonic readers work?

Phonic reading books are written especially for children who are beginning to learn phonics at nursery or school, and support any programme being used by providing plenty of practice as children develop the skills of decoding and blending. By targeting specific phonemes and tricky words, increasing in difficulty, they ensure systematic progression with reading.

Because phonic readers are primarily decodable – aside from the target tricky words which need to be learnt, children should be able to read the books with real assurance and accomplishment.

Big Cat phonic readers:
Gorillas

In Big Cat phonic readers the specific phonemes and tricky words being focussed on are highlighted here in these notes, so that you can be clear about what your child's learning and what they need to practise.

While reading at home together, there are all sorts of fun additional games you can play to help your child practise those phonemes and tricky words, which can be a nice way to familiarise yourselves with them before reading, or remind you of them after you've finished. In *Gorillas*, for example:

- the focus phonemes are oo (shoots), al (walk), are (rare), ow (lowlands), ai (tails), a-e (apes), aw (jaw), air (hair), ur (fur). Why not write them down and encourage your child to practise saying the sounds as you point to them in a random order. This is called 'Speed Sounds' and as you get faster and faster with your pointing, it encourages your child to say them as quickly as possible. You can try reversing the roles, so that you have a practice too!

- the tricky words are 'where', 'what', 'they', 'like', 'do', 'are', 'the', 'have', 'their', 'very', 'little', 'she', 'one' and 'down'. You can play 'Hide and Seek' by asking your child to close their eyes and count to 10, while you write each word on a piece of paper, hiding them somewhere in the room you're in or the garden for your child to find. As they find each one, they should try reading and spelling the word out.

Reading together

- Why not start by looking at the front cover of *Gorillas* and talking about what you can see.

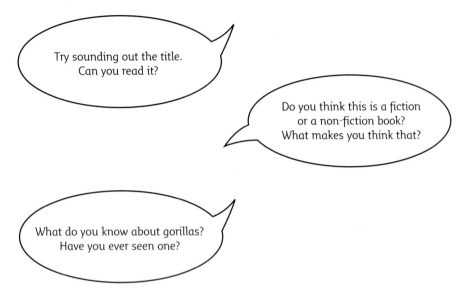

Try sounding out the title.
Can you read it?

Do you think this is a fiction
or a non-fiction book?
What makes you think that?

What do you know about gorillas?
Have you ever seen one?

- Enjoy reading *Gorillas* together, noticing the focus phonemes (oo, al, are, ow, ai, a-e, aw, air, ur) and tricky words (where, what, they, like, do, are, the, have, their, very, little, she, one, down). It's useful to point to each word as your child reads, and encouraging to give them lots of praise as they go.

- If your child gets stuck on a word, and it's phonetically decodable, encourage them to sound it out. You can practise blending by saying the sounds aloud a few times, getting quicker and quicker. If they still can't read it, tell them the word and move on.

Talking about the book

- Look at the pictures on pp18–19 together and discuss what each picture shows about how gorillas live.

- Practise the focus phonemes from *Gorillas* by asking your child to find specific words with, for example, the 'ai' phoneme, or sounding out some of the key words, for example, 'mountains'.

Gorillas

Contents

Written by Teresa Heapy

Collins

Where do gorillas live?

Gorillas are found in Africa.
They mainly live in forests.

Key: ☐ Gorillas

6

Africa

Some gorillas live in the mountains.
Some live in lowlands.

What do they look like?

Gorillas are the biggest apes.
Apes have arms that are
longer than their legs.
Apes do not have tails.

Silverback gorilla

jaw

big chest

silver hair

thick, black fur

up to 1.75 m tall

Gorillas have fingers and thumbs.
They have big brains, too.

thumb

Walking and eating

Gorillas can climb trees, but are mainly found on the ground.

Gorillas can stand on two feet, but they like to walk like this.

10

Gorillas mainly eat bark, shoots and leaves. They spend a lot of their day eating.

Gorillas can eat up to 25 kg of food a day!

11

Infant gorillas

At birth, a gorilla is
very small.
But it gets
bigger quickly.

A mother will carry
a young gorilla.

12

At first, a little gorilla will drink his mother's milk. Then she teaches him to eat leaves and shoots.

13

Living together

Gorillas mainly live together in troops. They make nests. They sleep in the nests at night.

Gorillas are big but they are shy.
One gorilla is the leader.
He protects the troop if he
needs to.

Are gorillas rare?

Gorillas are very rare.
Their homes may be cut down.
Some are hunted for their meat.

This was a
gorilla's home.

Some may get ill and die.
We must take care to protect them.

How gorillas live

Getting creative

- Have some fun with your child by playing a jumping game, where you write the focus phonemes on pieces of paper, spread them close together over the floor, and when you call out a phoneme, for example 'air', your child jumps on it. You can call them faster and faster for added excitement!

- You could work together to design a word search, which contains all the tricky words from *Gorillas*.

- Have a look in an atlas or on the internet to find where the continent of Africa is, and the parts of Africa where gorillas live.

- Talk with your child about other endangered species, and see if your child is interested in doing some research on a particular animal, using books or the internet to find out more information.

Other books at Level 2:

Fiction	Non-fiction
Zog and Zebra — Mal Peet and Elspeth Graham, Sarah Horne	The Sun and the Moon — Paul Shipton
A Day Out — Petr Horáček	The Rainforest at Night — Nic Bishop
The Singing Beetle — Linda Strachan, Oliver Hurst	Gorillas — Teresa Heapy

Collins Big Cat
Reading Lions

Published by Collins
An imprint of HarperCollins*Publishers*
1 London Bridge Street
London
SE1 9GF

Author: Teresa Heapy

British Library Cataloguing in Publication Data
A catalogue record for this publication is available from the British Library.

Designer: Anna Stasinska, anna@annastasinska.demon.co.uk
Parent notes authors: Sue Reed and Liz Webster
Picture researcher: Frances Vargo

Acknowledgements
Front cover: photolibrary.com/Bios/Cyril Ruoso; p1: Alamy/Steve Bloom Images; p2,
top: FLPA/Terry Whittaker; p3: FLPA/Minden Pictures/Thomas Marent; p4: Alamy/
imagebroker/Andreas Rose; p5, top: naturepl.com/Ingo Arndt; p5, bottom: Alamy/
Martin Shields; p6: Alamy/Terry Whittaker; p7: Getty Images/Gallo Images/Daryl
Balfour; p8, top: Getty Images/Joe Raedle; p8, bottom: Alamy/Juniors Bildarchiv;
p9: naturepl.com/Eric Baccega; p10: Dreamstime.com/Pljvv; p11: Alamy/Steve
Bloom Images; p12: Photoshot/Woodfall; p13: Corbis/Andy Rouse; pp14-15: Alamy/
imagebroker/Andreas Rose; back cover: LPA/Jurgen & Christine Sohns

Printed and bound by RR Donnelley APS

www.collins.co.uk/parents